A Clinician's Guide to Normal Cognitive Development in Childhood

A Clinician's Guide to Normal Cognitive Development in Childhood

Edited by
Elisabeth Hollister Sandberg
Becky L. Spritz

Routledge
Taylor & Francis Group
New York   London

Routledge
Taylor & Francis Group
711 Third Avenue
New York, NY 10017

Routledge
Taylor & Francis Group
27 Church Road
Hove, East Sussex BN3 2FA

International Standard Book Number: 978-0-415-99183-4 (Hardback)

Library of Congress Cataloging-in-Publication Data

A clinician's guide to normal cognitive development in childhood / edited by
   Elisabeth Hollister Sandberg, Becky L. Spritz.
        p. cm.
   Includes bibliographical references and index.
   ISBN 978-0-415-99183-4 (hbk. : alk. paper)
      1. Cognition in children. 2. Developmental psychology. 3. Child development.
   I. Sandberg, Elisabeth Hollister. II. Spritz, Becky L. III. Title.

BF723.C5C55 2009
155.4'13--dc22   2009016167

Visit the Taylor & Francis Web site at
http://www.taylorandfrancis.com

and the Routledge Web site at
http://www.routledgementalhealth.com

We dedicate this book to our children:
Aiden, Liliana, Sam, and Alie.
We hope that they will someday forgive us for exposing
their cognitive foibles for all the world to see.

Contents

Contributors

Sarah M. Bankoff
Department of Psychology
Suffolk University
Boston, Massachusetts

Rolando N. Carol
Department of Psychology
Florida International University
Miami, Florida

Nadja Schreiber Compo
Department of Psychology
Florida International University
Miami, Florida

Daniel P. Corts
Department of Psychology
Augustana College
Rock Island, Illinois

Keith A. Crnic
Department of Psychology
Arizona State University
Tempe, Arizona

Art S. Fergusson
Department of Psychology
Suffolk University
Boston, Massachusetts

Gary D. Fireman
Department of Psychology
Suffolk University
Boston, Massachusetts

Sarahbeth Golden
Department of Psychology
Lasell College
Newton, Massachusetts

Sonia M. Greene
Neuropsychology Associates, Inc.
Providence, Rhode Island

Amy Hyman Gregory
Department of Psychology
Florida International University
Miami, Florida

Allison M. Haskill
Department of Communication
    Sciences and Disorders
Augustana College
Rock Island, Illinois

Karen A. Holler
Department of Psychiatry and
    Human Behavior
The Warren Alpert Medical School
    at Brown University
Providence, Rhode Island

Gary Kose
Department of Psychology
Long Island University, Brooklyn
    Campus
Brooklyn, New York

Sarah E. Martin
Department of Psychology
Simmons College
Boston, Massachusetts

Mary Beth McCullough
Department of Psychology
Suffolk University
Boston, Massachusetts

Samantha Samberg O'Connell
Department of Psychology
Suffolk University
Boston, Massachusetts

John A. Reeder
Department of Psychology
Simmons College
Boston, Massachusetts

Elisabeth Hollister Sandberg
Department of Psychology
Suffolk University
Boston, Massachusetts

Shayna L. Skelley
Department of Psychology
Arizona State University
Tempe, Arizona

Becky L. Spritz
Department of Psychology
Roger Williams University
Bristol, Rhode Island

Geoffrey F. W. Turner
Department of Psychology
Simmons College
Boston, Massachusetts

Joseph C. Viola
Center for Professional Psychology
George Washington University
Washington, D.C.

Mandi L. White-Ajmani
Department of Psychology
Suffolk University
Boston, Massachusetts

Introduction

The Case for Children's Cognitive Development
A Clinical-Developmental Perspective

BECKY L. SPRITZ and ELISABETH HOLLISTER SANDBERG

Parents often watch in wonder as their children achieve developmental milestones—first steps, first words, first make-believe games. As scholars of child development, we (the editors) are particularly drawn to watching children—*really* watching them—as they struggle to understand and master the world. We are struck by how often even we, supposed experts, are bewildered by even our own children's interactions with the world:

EXAMPLE: COGNITION IN ACTION

During the summers, my (BLS) children and I frequent the Rhode Island beaches, one of which has a carousel that my children love to ride. Last summer my youngest, Alison (who was not quite four), became especially passionate about her carousel horses, giving each horse that she rode a different name. One evening, as we were driving home, we reminisced about our experiences that day, leading to the following conversation:

Me:	What a great day! Alison, what was your favorite part?
Alison:	Riding the carousel!
Me:	Oh! So, you really liked riding "Pink Pony" (*the name of today's carousel horse*)?

Suddenly, Alison bursts into tears and rapidly becomes inconsolable. I attempt to assess the situation, particularly with respect to whether it is necessary to find the nearest emergency room.

Me:	Honey, what's wrong?! What is it? Should I stop the car?

Alison:	(*between sobs*) I can't tell you. I'm umbarrassed (Sic).
Me:	(*having now confirmed that no one is bleeding*) Alison! Of course you can. Talk to me! What is wrong?! Are you hurt?
Alison:	(*still whimpering*) I wanted to say her name. You said it first.
Me:	(*confused*) What name?
Alison:	My horse's name. You said it. I wanted to remember it first.
Me:	(*as confusion becomes disbelief ... and irritation*) So, you're hysterical because I said "Pink Pony's" name first?
Alison:	Yes. You remembered it before me. But it was my horse.

The hysterical sobbing continues for another 15 minutes. Her brother begins whining about it being too loud in the car. I become increasingly exasperated, leading to a final, desperate attempt for peace:

Me:	Alison, you know I would never hurt your feelings on purpose, don't you?
Alison:	(*without pause*) No!

Like many other parents, my immediate reaction was, "Why me? What is wrong with this child? Why didn't I leave the beach an hour ago and let her take a nap in the car on the way home? (Or why didn't I just leave her on the beach?)" With a little distance from the conflict, I realized that Alison's reaction strikingly revealed where she was with respect to her cognitive development. Children's cognitive development is multifaceted and encompasses a broad array of skills, including language, memory, reasoning, perspective taking, theory of mind, and executive functioning. Consider the various cognitive domains that were active during Alison's participation in our not atypical parent-child exchange (see Table 1.1).

Failing to consider the full range of children's cognitive skills can lead to misperceptions and assumptions. Alison's well-developed vocabulary and ability to communicate about internal states mask her limited, but developmentally appropriate, skills in perspective taking and theory of mind. One is tempted to label Alison, who is somewhat notorious for her independence, as "argumentative" or "oppositional" rather than viewing her functioning as developmentally appropriate across the multiple domains of her cognitive architecture.

The cognitive errors (or what look like errors from an adult perspective) that children make—that we should *expect* them to make—explain a lot about

Table 1.1 Examples of Cognitive Domains Active in Typical Parent-Child Exchanges

Language	• Understanding and responding to questions • Providing a narrative about the day's events • Being able to communicate about her internal states (thoughts and feelings)
Perspective taking	• Reflecting upon how the situation might look from another's point of view • Recognizing that someone else's thoughts, feelings, and beliefs might differ from hers
Memory	• Remembering the day's activities • Sorting out the memories from that particular day from all of her other memories of trips to the beach
Reasoning	• Drawing conclusions about the reasons why things happen • Understanding the difference between right and wrong and making judgments about another's moral behavior

their interactions with and interpretations of the world. In the example above, Alison's failure to recognize that my memory of Pink Pony is different from her own reflects a developmentally appropriate error in *theory of mind* (see Chapter 5). Her erroneous conclusion regarding my intent to hurt her feelings demonstrates age-expected flaws in *reasoning* (it was erroneous, I assure you!—see Chapter 10). At times, such errors are easy to identify, but more often than not they remain undetected, even to well-trained, experienced professionals. Why?

Views of children's cognitive functioning are often restricted to measures of intelligence (ability, IQ) and academic achievement. While a discussion of the pros and cons of intelligence and achievement testing is outside of the scope of this volume, it can be argued that these cognitive measures provide narrow indicators of *what a child knows,* but limited information about *how a child thinks,* especially across the broad array of domains of children's cognitive development. Yet knowing how a child thinks, and *how a child is supposed to think based upon his or her age,* obviously provides a much more comprehensive picture. It is with this in mind that our book provides an overview of various domains of normal cognitive development, as per the current state of the developmental research. We focus specifically on the ages of 2–12, a period characterized by rapid change in many areas of children's cognitive development that are highly relevant to educators and practitioners working with children.

One of the central themes of this book is that what might appear superficially to be aberrations in children's behavior or adjustment are often reflections of completely normal variations in children's cognitive development. As professionals, we are trained to interpret and understand children's behavior through particular disciplinary lenses; for many clinicians, this lens necessarily focuses on identifying abnormal or clinically "relevant" behavior. But some completely developmentally appropriate things children do are just plain weird, making it easy for professionals to mistakenly pathologize children's behavior and responses. Failure to consider a child's cognitive level might also lead to therapeutic or interventional efforts that are either too simplistic or too challenging for a child's thinking. This book is intended to illustrate the vast undulations of the normal cognitive landscape, and how to interpret the sometimes strange behavior of typically developing children. Every clinician needs to learn, and to regularly be reminded of, the unique peculiarities of developing cognitive processes in order to avoid pathologizing what might be normal developmental phenomena. Within each subdomain of cognitive development there is a wide continuum between the anchors of atypical and optimal development, much of which is not "atypical" in any sense. To the nonexpert, the perspective-taking skills of the 4-year-old, the memory source attributions errors of the 8-year-old, or the causal reasoning errors of the 10-year-old might seem like problems when they are, in fact, quite normal.

Let Your Approaches Be Informed

During the course of childhood, literally all children will at some time face a difficult interpersonal situation (i.e., conflicts with peers, a parent-child disagreement, their parents' divorce) or a stressful experience (i.e., an upcoming musical performance, a challenging test, the death of a loved one). It is of course, not unusual at these times for children to display changes in their emotional or behavioral functioning (Schroeder & Gordon, 2002). As clinicians and educators, we are trained to be sensitive to the contextual and situational forces that impinge on a child's world, and often analyze children's behavior very carefully for indicators of disrupted adjustment.

EXAMPLE

Five-year-old Jack's parents are getting a divorce. This has resulted in multiple major life transitions for Jack in the past three months, including his parents' separation, his parents moving into different residences, and finally the selling of the family home. Several weeks after the closing on the old house, Jack reflected on his experiences during a play therapy session:

Jack:	I really miss my old house. I wish I still lived there.
Therapist:	I'm sure you do! It must be hard now that your mom and dad live apart.

What should we make of Jack's longing for his old home? It is easy for the clinician who knows about Jack's recent family disruption to attribute his musings about his old house to his parents' separation and divorce without even asking Jack, "*Why* do you miss your old house?" Given Jack's age, we may assume that he lacks the cognitive sophistication—the language, the perspective taking, the understanding of internal states, the reasoning—to reflect upon and answer such a question. Yet to fully consider all potential explanations for Jack's response, it is essential that we do not underestimate his capacity to participate in the therapeutic process as a talking, thinking, reasoning, and remembering social partner. Fortunately, in this case, Jack was assertive enough to broaden his therapist's perspective.

EXAMPLE

Jack: I really miss my old house. I wish I still lived there.

Therapist: I'm sure you do! It must be hard now that your mom and dad live apart.

Jack: No, no, no. That's not what I am thinking at all.

Therapist: No? OK, tell me what it is that you miss about your old house.

Jack: I miss the tire swing in the backyard!

Of course, individual variability exists, and although Jack was able to clearly articulate his reasoning to his therapist, other five-year-olds may have much greater difficulty communicating their thoughts, feelings, and beliefs. Unless we provide children with the opportunity to demonstrate their cognitive capacity, however, we will never know what they may be capable of doing. This is similar to what Vygotsky (1930/1978) referred to as the "zone of proximal development"—the range of tasks just above a child's established developmental level. When we target our communications and interventions at "the zone," we get a better view of what the child is capable of and maximize children's opportunities for growth. In practice, this requires an understanding of what is *typical* for children at a particular age, what is *possible* for children at a particular age, as well as what is *typical and possible for a particular child*. It is by knowing the broad range of what children are capable of that we can serve them to the best of our professional capacity.

Still, some of you may also be wondering: Shouldn't we doubt Jack's response? Isn't it more likely that Jack misses his *family unit* than the *tire swing*? Might not he be lying in an effort to mask his true feelings regarding his parents' divorce? While it is certainly possible that Jack is engaging in deception (see Chapter 6), if we rely on sound practices for talking to children (see Chapters

4 and 9) and have no other reasons to doubt his sincerity (see Chapter 11), we should trust his response. The fact that Jack misses his tire swing in no way negates the possibility that he *might* be having difficulty adjusting to his various life transitions, but from the perspective of a five-year-old, the situation may *look* different and *feel* different than we expect. It is precisely in this way that an understanding of children's cognitive development enhances, but does not detract from, educational and clinical practice.

To most effectively serve children in educational and therapeutic settings, professionals need a firm grasp of children's cognitive development. Many of these ideas are not new; they were introduced by developmental psychopathologists more than 20 years ago (Cicchetti, 1984; Shirk, 1988), but all too often are still not put into practice.

EXAMPLE

A colleague (and friend) of one of the editors (BLS) is a school-based mental health consultant. Recently, she was asked to observe a five-year-old boy in a pre-K setting to provide guidance and feedback to the teachers on how to better manage the child's moderately oppositional behavior. On the day of the scheduled visit, she observed "center time," where children were given the opportunity to choose a particular play area (e.g., block area, table toys, dramatic play, etc.). The center had recently received a donation of large, cardboard building blocks, making the block area highly desirable.

Four children were chosen by the teacher to play in the coveted block area. The target child was not among them, and he immediately began to have a tantrum. While the child kicked and screamed, the teacher sweetly explained, "We can only have four children in the block area at one time…. Once a child leaves, you may enter the area…. Many of the centers are now full, but there is an opening in the dramatic play area." As this was occurring, my colleague watched as several other children rotated through the blocks.

Following his interaction with his teacher, the child walked over to dramatic play, which was adjacent to the blocks. He stood, disengaged, watching the children play with the blocks. Occasionally, a block would spill across the classroom dividers and the child would grudgingly hand it back.

After approximately 15 minutes the teacher announced, "Center time is almost over; plan your time accordingly." Another 15 minutes later (during which there was no rotation of children through the centers), free play ended. Not surprisingly, the tantrum resumed.

Several unpleasant aspects of this situation may have been alleviated by a more careful consideration of the cognitive capabilities of both the target child and the class in general. As discussed in Chapter 10, the teacher's extensive efforts to reason with the target child may have been inappropriate given the child's age and cognitive level. A greater awareness of developmental limitations in children's memory (Chapter 7) and planning skills (Chapter 12) could also guide the teacher toward more effective classroom management (e.g., providing visual reminders of the classroom expectations, setting a time limit for children within each center).

Let Development Be Your Guide

Clinical professionals who work with children are usually well trained with respect to developmental norms in more "public" domains of development, such as children's social relationships or children's emotion regulation. Thus, most recognize that the preschool age child who plays alongside her peer is not socially anxious, but rather is engaging in developmentally appropriate parallel play, whereas the same would not be said of a nine-year-old engaging in the same behavior. Similarly, most professionals working with children are well aware that frequent tantrums are the norm before age 6, but not beyond. By contrast, practitioners typically receive much less training about developmental changes in cognitive domains such as language, memory, reasoning, and theory of mind. This may leave many with a somewhat limited understanding of how children are *supposed* to talk, remember, reason, and understand at different ages. The temptation, even for the editors, is to interpret all behavior that deviates from adult norms as "abnormal." We must remember that children are not mini-adults, and that our evaluations of their behavior must allow for deviation that is developmentally predictable and quite common.

While an estimated 80% of all of children's problems fall within the range of typical developmental adjustments, approximately 20% of clinical referrals are for more serious emotional, behavioral, or developmental problems (Nottleman & Jensen, 1995). Many, if not all, of such problems are linked with some aspect of children's cognitive development. Some childhood disorders, such as attention-deficit hyperactivity disorder, appear to be linked to particular problems in children's cognitive functioning (see Chapter 12). Other disorders, such as depression and anxiety, are not (as of yet) linked with specific, isolated cognitive processes, but their symptomotologies vary in relation to development across several cognitive domains, such as language (Chapter 2), perspective taking (Chapter 5), and reasoning (Chapter 10). A common example is childhood depression, which manifests itself differently in a four-year-old, eight-year-old, and twelve-year-old, in large part due to changes in children's development (Cole, Luby, & Sullivan, 2008; Sroufe & Rutter, 1984).

This developmental variability in clinical symptomotology is well documented across a variety of mental health disorders, and is finally being reflected in traditional clinical classification systems, such as the *Diagnostic and statistical manual of mental disorders* (DSM) (American Psychiatric Association, 2004). Further improvements are still needed, however, and a good working understanding of developmental norms—not just what a particular child thinks, but what children of different ages think—is essential to identifying when a child's behavior is *not* normal (Schroeder & Gordon, 2002).

EXAMPLE

Chris has been referred to an outpatient clinic for an evaluation for academic difficulties and questions of depression. Chris lives with his maternal grandparents, who were granted custody after the death of Chris's mother two years before. During the course of the initial clinical interview, other questions arose.

Interviewer:	What are some of the things you like to do for fun, Chris?
Chris:	I like to draw. I have lots of colored pencils. They're my friends.
Interviewer:	You get pretty involved in your drawings, huh?
Chris:	Yes…. Can I tell you a secret? My pencils are magical. They talk to me. And dance and sing.
Interviewer:	Help me understand, Chris. Do they really dance and sing or do you just imagine that they dance and sing?
Chris:	(*with much hesitation*) I know that they are not supposed to dance and sing, but they really do. I haven't told anyone this because I am scared people will think I am crazy!

The clinical interpretation of this exchange depends on Chris's age. If Chris is 4, his disclosure is not particularly disturbing. But what if he is 8? Let's consider one of the cognitive processes related to Chris's disclosure: the appearance-reality distinction. As discussed in Chapter 5, the appearance-reality distinction emerges in early childhood, coinciding with the development of children's theory of mind. This cognitive skill underlies children's ability to identify the difference between what is pretense ("I'm a superhero!") and what is real ("I like to pretend that I'm a superhero, but I'm not really a superhero, so I can't really fly"). Prior to the development of the appearance-reality distinction, children actually have difficulty distinguishing between the real world and their pretend world. Indeed, one of the editors (EHS) was reminded of this when, for nearly a month, her three-year-old daughter insisted on sleeping in a laundry basket because she was a cat! However, while little children can get away with befriending singing pencils (and sleeping in laundry baskets), by age 8 children should have a firm grasp of the appearance-reality distinction. Chris's concerns of what others might think about his beliefs further suggest that he has achieved this cognitive milestone, and therefore point to other potential clinical concerns. Thus, in this case, Chris's cognitive functioning may be used as a point of reference to identify atypical development.

For most clinical issues, of course, a thorough assessment and diagnosis requires the weighting of multiple, overlapping symptoms reported by multiple informants (children's self-reports, parents, teachers), within the confines of an established clinical taxonomy that does not easily translate into cognitive developmental "speak" (Achenbach, 2000). Practical advice is therefore still duly needed, particularly in the way of guidance for applying knowledge of children's cognitive development to day-to-day interactions and interventions with children.

What You Will Find in the Following Chapters

The process of constructing this book has made us acutely aware of the fact that no subtopic within cognitive development is an island in and unto itself. Each cognitive domain you can name is intertwined with and implicitly connected to all of the others. Nonetheless, we have carved our content into rough sections:

Communicating With Children

Part I of the book describes the development of language skills between the ages of 2 and 12, beginning with Haskill and Corts's entertaining and thorough review of the fundamentals of language in Chapter 2. As illustrated by the authors, interactions with children are rich with examples of language development and are useful tools for identifying both normal language development and instances in which language delays are in question.

From a developmental psychopathology perspective, identifying and treating children and families *at risk* for problems is as critical as focusing on children with diagnosable conditions (Rutter & Garmezy, 1983). However, knowing when to make a referral can be difficult, and ultimately requires a good understanding of developmental norms.

EXAMPLE

The mother of three-year-old Molly is extremely worried about what she calls her daughter's "language loss," an event that happened to coincide with a fall down the stairs. Molly, she says, used to be able to talk properly and now does not always do so. During a detailed intake, the mother reports that Molly has begun making mistakes like saying, "I holded the bunny" and "I runned all the way up the driveway." This is actually a developmental milestone, not a cause for alarm—and being able to explain this enables you to provide Molly's mother with some peace of mind.

Carol has two sets of twin boys (ages nine years and three years). Around a year ago, Carol's pediatrician referred the "babies" for early intervention services due to concerns about language delays. Carol admitted that the boys spoke very few words and that most people other than herself and her husband could not understand their speech. Soon afterwards, I (BLS) paid the family a visit. During the course of the morning (a several-hour period), I watched an older twin who is particularly nurturing cater to the babies' every gesture. One baby would point down, and his older brother would get him down from his highchair. The other baby would point for his cup, and his older brother would retrieve his cup from the counter. Indeed, the babies were *not* talking, and after spending time with the family, it was clear why—with their big brother around, they had no need! As a result, however, the babies were falling significantly behind in their language development, and interventions did seem to be warranted.

The other chapters in Part I, Skelley and Crnic's coverage of children's communication about internal states (Chapter 3) and Golden's discussion of language with respect to clinical interviewing (Chapter 4), take us beyond basic language acquisition and consider the practical implications for working with children.

EXAMPLE

You are meeting with Kate, age 5, who has been referred for a cognitive assessment prior to her transition to kindergarten next fall. You have met with Kate on two previous occasions. At this, your third meeting, Kate mentions that she will be "graduating" from her preschool. You see this as a perfect opportunity to find out more about Kate's thoughts and feelings about her current school situation:

Therapist:	How are you feeling about graduating from preschool, Kate?
Kate:	I don't know.
Therapist:	Are you happy, or sad, or mad, or something else?

Kate:	It's good.
Therapist:	What's good about it?
Kate:	Nothing. I'm sad.
Therapist:	So, you're actually feeling sad about leaving your school?
Kate:	No, I'm happy about that. I'm sad about other things. Can I draw a picture now?

Does Kate comprehend what the therapist is saying? How do the therapist's questions influence her responses? Has Kate developed the specific language to explain what she is feeling? These are some of the challenges to communicating with young children highlighted within this section.

Understanding Others' Perspectives

Part II covers the development of children's ability to distinguish between their own minds and those of others. As Fireman and Kose beautifully articulate in Chapter 5, between the ages of 3 and 7 children make enormous gains in understanding that the perspectives of other people can differ from their own. At the younger end of this age range, children do not necessarily appreciate that their personal likes, dislikes, beliefs, fears, and dreams are not shared by all.

EXAMPLE

I (EHS) woke Liliana, age 4, up one morning and she told me that she had a dream (one of her first dream reports.) I asked her what it was about.

Liliana:	I dreamed there was a thunderstorm and I was really afraid and you couldn't hear me but Aiden found me and rescued me! (Aiden is her older brother.)

I made some sympathetic fuss over the dream and told her she was lucky to have such a kind brother. I suggested she tell him about the dream. She trotted off to his room; I went down to the kitchen. Over breakfast, only 10 minutes later, I suggested that she tell her father about her dream.

Liliana:	I dreamed there was a thunderstorm.
Mom:	And...?
Liliana:	Mom couldn't hear me.

Silence.

Mom:	And what happened then?
Liliana:	That was all.
Mom:	What about the part when Aiden saved you?
Liliana:	No, he said he wasn't there!

Gradually, however, children learn that appearance and reality are not always perfectly coincident, and they learn about the concept of false belief—that one can believe something that is in fact not true. False beliefs and their mischievous (and sometimes malicious) counterpart, deception, are considered by Spritz, Fergusson, and Bankoff in Chapter 6.

EXAMPLE

Sam is in kindergarten. One day, a fellow kindergarten mother mentioned to me (BLS) that she was helping out with a craft in the classroom that day. As Sam and I walked home from school, I asked him about his day.

Mom:	What did you do today at school, Sam?
Sam:	Nothing.
Mom:	Nothing at all? Mrs. Einstein mentioned that she was coming in to help with a craft today.
Sam:	I didn't do one.
Mom:	Really? What happened?

At this point, Sam stops walking and covers his face with his hands.

Sam:	I did do one, but I'm not supposed to tell you! Oops! Now I told you!

Finally, I realize that the "craft" must be a surprise gift for the parents. I quickly attempt to alleviate Sam's guilt.

Mom:	That's ok, honey, I won't ask you any more questions about it.
Sam:	Phew! Thanks! You are REALLY going to love it! Wait! Did I say that out loud?

Poor Sam! As adults, we effortlessly shift perspectives, maintain social interactions, and remain focused on our own beliefs and desires. As discussed in the chapters in Part II, this is not so for children.

Children's Memory

In Part III, Reeder, Turner, and Martin (Chapter 7) eloquently review development in the different domains of memory (e.g., memory capacity, procedural memories, autobiographical memory), focusing primarily on development between the ages of 4 and 10. As outlined by these authors, an understanding of the basic structures and functions of children's memory is important for knowing what to expect from children and for helping parents to develop reasonable expectations within the context of family interactions.

EXAMPLE

The family is at the dinner table. Alie (age 4) and Sam (age 6) are taking turns telling jokes. It is Sam's turn, but Alie has a joke that she *really* wants to share. I (BLS) explain that she needs to wait until Sam tells his joke, and then she can have her turn. Sam begins:

Sam:	Why did the banana go to the doctor?
Alie:	I don't know, why?
Sam:	Take a guess.
Alie:	Because he needed a shot?
Sam:	Guess again.
Alie:	Because he had a cold?
Sam:	Nope. Try again.

This continues for several more rounds, until finally:

Alie:	Sam, I don't know!
Sam:	Because he wasn't *peeling* good!

I groan, look to Alie, and offer, "OK, Alie, now it is your turn." She stares at me silently for a long time. Finally,

Alie:	Mommy! I waited so long that I lost my joke!"

Within the other chapters in Part III, special focus is given to the nature of memories and their reliability. As highlighted in Sandberg and Spritz's chapter on remembering (Chapter 8), memories are formed visually, behaviorally, and verbally. Multiple sources of information are often combined, without direct awareness, in the creation of a single memory. Gaps in memories are filled in with information from more general scripts and from input from outside sources. The memories of young children are particularly plastic, and thus subject to considerable influence and unconscious revision. Thus, in Chapter 9, Gregory, Carol, and Compo provide sound guidelines for talking with children about past events.

EXAMPLE

Recently, Patti's nephew (Jake, age 8) began displaying academic and behavioral problems at school. Jake's mother (Patti's sister) was convinced that Jake was having problems with the older boys on the school bus. Although Jake initially denied any issues on the bus, his mother continued to ask him about his bus rides: Were the older boys teasing him? Did they take his belongings? Had they harassed him in any way? Approximately a month later, I saw Jake at a birthday party:

BLS:	Hi Jake! How is school going?
Jake:	Fine, except the older boys tease me on the bus.
BLS:	Oh no! When did this start?
Jake:	It's always been that way. Ever since I started riding the bus.
BLS:	That's too bad! What kind of things do the boys do?
Jake:	I don't exactly remember. But my mom does.

Sorting out what's happening with Jake requires knowledge of both children's basic memory and more complicated, related issues such as remembering and suggestibility. While one might expect considerable overlap across these chapters, the authors' assorted backgrounds and training lead to strikingly different perspectives on children's memory in relation to clinical and educational practice.

Developing Reason and Executive Control

Part IV builds upon the more basic level cognitive processes of the previous parts. Asking a child to consider an idea, choose between options, or make any sort of judgment calls upon advanced cognitive skills such as reasoning and executive functioning. In Chapter 10, Sandberg and McCullough provide a general reasoning primer, with clear, specific examples of the unique reasoning processes evidenced by children between the ages of 2 and 10. This chapter is especially important for anyone who needs to engage a child in an active collaboration about information, ideas, or problems.

Expanding upon this further, White-Ajmani and O'Connell provide an extremely accessible approach to theory and research on children's moral reasoning. The authors discuss moral reasoning as a practical tool for professionals working with young children, thereby demonstrating that in some cases the whole (Chapter 11) is indeed greater than the sum of its parts (basic reasoning/Chapter 10 + false beliefs and deception/Chapter 6).

EXAMPLE

One morning four-year-old Alison found a penny on the bathroom floor. For the next several hours, she carried it with her everywhere, and even asked for special permission to bring it to the lunch table (which she was granted, and which I (BLS) later regretted). Almost immediately after settling in for lunch, Alison announces, "Look! I found a penny! Finders keepers! Losers weepers!" Horrified by her primitive ethos, I ventured into a lengthy monologue about what it means to be a good winner. Alison waited patiently until I was through, paused thoughtfully, and then responded, "OK, OK! How about, Finders keepers, Losers go find something else?!"

The chapter by Holler and Greene (Chapter 12) provides a capstone to the more basic level cognitive processes both within and across sections of the book. Children's executive functioning refers to a diverse set of cognitive processes that include but are not limited to planning, attention, working memory, and inhibitory control (Sabbagh, Moses, & Shiverick, 2006). By reviewing the development of children's executive functioning from early childhood through adolescence, Holler and Greene demonstrate the relevance of these more complex cognitive processes for understanding the variability in children's cognitive profiles.

EXAMPLE

Zachary, age 10, is falling behind in the fifth grade curriculum. He was an outstanding student in early elementary school and was universally acknowledged as being extremely bright. His homework grades and test performance have slipped considerably. He did not pass the state's standardized scholastic achievement exam. His performance is so inconsistent with his earlier academic performance that the school recommends an evaluation. Socially, both at home and at school, everything is status quo.

Results from the educational assessment performed by the school are extremely variable. Zach tests at the 99th percentile for some skills—his scores for letter-word identification, oral spelling, and vocabulary are all eight or more years *above* grade level. He scores at the 80th percentile for applied math problems and quantitative concepts. Passage comprehension, writing samples, and calculation are radically lower, but consistent with grade level.

What is one to make of Zach's highly variable academic profile? And the fact that his previously stellar performance as a student has deteriorated in spite of having at least grade-level mastery in all areas? Closer examination of the testing report reveals some answers:

"Zachary had a quick approach to tasks."

"He did not always attend to all of the details in the directions or in pictures, lowering his scores."

"He did not spend any time thinking about his answers, which also, most probably, hindered his performance."

He took one look at the two-digit division and said, "I'm not going to do this."

Zachary has deficits in the domain of executive function. In spite of an excellent intellect, he is having difficulty navigating the curricular challenges of fifth grade. This is not because he struggles with the concepts, but because he cannot organize and control his cognitive domains to successfully tackle longer, multipart tasks. With these issues in mind, Holler and Greene (Chapter 12) provide a wealth of specific recommendations for working with children with difficulties related to executive functioning.

The Parts That Are Missing

Throughout this book we have endeavored to map out general, normative developmental trajectories across various cognitive domains. The broad strokes, though, are achieved at the expense of consideration of individual and group differences. Children certainly do develop at different rates—no two ten-year-olds are the same! There is also considerable long-standing controversy regarding group differences in many cognitive areas (theory of mind, reasoning, etc.) as a function of gender, race, ethnicity, and culture, with even less known about group differences related to religion and socioeconomic status. Thus, while we recognize that group differences produce variation in cognitive development, we also believe that there are fundamental developmental processes that permeate and intersect with social and environmental factors. It is an overall understanding of these fundamental cognitive developmental processes that we hope to impart in this text. We think it is essential, in spite of the price, to be able to say, "This child is four-years-old. As such...."

As you can see from the description of our topical sections, there are many aspects of cognitive development that we haven't covered within this volume. Some—children's understanding of time, for example—are extremely germane to working with children in educational and clinical settings. Somewhere through this process, however, we surrendered to the realization that cataloging all aspects of cognitive development is a Sisyphean undertaking! It is therefore our hope that the few domains we have chosen to highlight will provide you with good, working insights, and perhaps inspire you to reconsider some of those other "quirks" you've been noticing (e.g., Why can't two children ever be convinced that a can of soda can be shared equally between them?).

References

Achenbach, T. M. (2000). Assessment of psychopathology. In A. J. Sameroff, M. Lewis, & S. M. Miller (Eds.), *Handbook of developmental psychopathology* (2nd ed.). New York: Kluwer Academic/Plenum Press.

American Psychiatric Association. (2004). *Diagnostic and statistical manual of mental disorders IV-TR*. Washington, DC: Author.

Cicchetti, D. (1984). The emergence of developmental psychopathology. *Child Development, 55,* 1–7.

Cole, P. M., Luby, J., & Sullivan, M. W. (2008). Emotions and the development of childhood depression: Bridging the gap. *Child Development Perspectives, 2,* 121–208.

Nottleman, E. D., & Jensen, P. S. (1995). Comorbidity of disorders in children and adolescents: Developmental perspectives. In T. H. Ollendick & R. J. Prinz (Eds.), *Advances in clinical child psychology* (Vol. 17, pp. 109–151). New York: Plenum Press.

Rutter, M., & Garmezy, N. (1983). Developmental psychopathology. In P. H. Mussen & E. M. Hetherington (Eds.), *Handbook of child psychology: Socialization, personality, and social development* (Vol. 4, pp. 775–911). New York: Wiley.

Sabbagh, M. A., Moses, L. J., & Shiverick, S. (2006). Executive functioning and preschoolers' understanding of false-beliefs, false photographs, and false signs. *Child Development, 77,* 1034–1049.

Schroeder, C. S., & Gordon, B. N. (2002). *Assessment and treatment of childhood problems* (2nd ed.). New York: The Guilford Press.

Shirk, S. R. (Ed.). (1988). *Cognitive development and child psychotherapy*. New York: Plenum Press.

Sroufe, A., & Rutter, M. (1984). The domain of developmental psychopathology. *Child Development, 55,* 17–29.

Vygotsky, L. S. (1978). *Mind in society: The development of higher mental processes*. Cambridge, MA: Harvard University Press. (Original work published 1930)

I
Communicating With Children

Spoken language is the medium through which the vast majority of our communication with children occurs. The empirical and theoretical developmental literature is rife with musings and revelations about symbolic representations, innate grammar, Motherese, pronoun acquisition, and hundreds of other technicalities. Scholars can study the minutiae of developmental psycholinguistics for a lifetime and never completely understand how it all works; yet anyone can have a conversation with a child.

In this book we are skating across the sea of language development to ask: From a purely practical perspective, what do you need to know about children's language to move beyond basic mutual comprehension into a place where meaningful therapeutic or educational interchange can be achieved? Some of the insights our contributing authors bring to this question include:

- Vocabulary is just the tip of the iceberg. Appreciate the offset between receptive language skills and expressive language skills. Children cannot express in words everything that they understand. Haskill and Corts, in Chapter 2, map out the development of language form, content, and use in early and middle childhood.
- Think about the shared domains of understanding. Early language is concretely referential; talking about how you *feel* is extremely complicated. Communicating about one's internal states (Chapter 3) requires bridging between language acquisition and theory of mind. Skelley and Crnic lay out how communicating to others about the self changes developmentally.
- Be cognizant of developing syntactic and pragmatic skills. In Chapter 4, Golden offers insights on how to engage the child as a conversational partner. Using the basics of children's language as a guide, the author provides illustrative examples and practical advice for facilitating verbal exchanges with children.

2
Acquiring Language

ALLISON M. HASKILL and DANIEL P. CORTS

To many, language is just a vocabulary with a few grammatical rules thrown in for good measure. With a little examination, however, it is clear that language is much more than that. As Bloom and Lahey (1978) point out, language is a combination of form, content, and use. Although it is possible for us to think and communicate without language, consider what language adds to human experience. It provides *form* to our thoughts and feelings that helps make thoughts and feelings more distinctive. As a child develops, the *content* of language provides a dense storage medium for memories and helps us organize our knowledge. As development continues, children use language to consider the consequences of their actions, negotiate social situations, and share points of view. Thus, language provides raw materials for cognition, relationships, and social behavior.

But what happens when language does not develop normally? Language delays are correlated with various behavioral, emotional, and academic concerns. Depending on the specific types of language delay and other key factors, these problems may include withdrawal and poor social interactions, lower levels of imaginary and pretend play, and lower tolerance for frustration. Some studies have found links between specific types of language delays and aggression, and not surprisingly, there are also correlations between language impairments and parental stress (Irwin, Carter, & Briggs-Gowan, 2002; McCabe, 2005; van Daal, Verhoeven, & van Balkom, 2007).

Given the centrality of language to human activities, it is no wonder parents celebrate an infant's progression from cooing to first words and beyond. Nor is it surprising that parents often compare their own child's language development to that of the child's schoolmates and friends (Newman & McGregor, 2006). A child who does not speak until well after his peer is often the subject of great concern (*Is our child autistic?*), although child language specialists might point out that the child's response to language is perfectly normal. Meanwhile, a child who is speaking in full sentences long before her peers might be seen as a budding genius. Her parents might fail to separate language ability from other aspects of development and wonder: *Why is this brilliant little girl having so many tantrums?* A clinician may have to remind these parents that, in fact, there is wide variability in the rate of development and, from a statistical point of view, both children are likely to be equally competent language users before they reach adulthood.

This sensitivity that parents (and even educators and health care providers) have toward language development can lead them to present with a number of concerns. Given the comorbidity of language delays, clinicians should take parental concerns seriously, but withhold diagnosis until proper evaluations can be made. Therefore, our goal in this chapter is to provide a review of typical language development sequences across content, form, and use. We will provide norms along with a sense of the variability in the speed at which individual children progress. Finally, when concern does seem to be justified, we provide some suggestions for initial evaluation and what types of specialized consultation may be necessary.

What Is Language?

As we have mentioned already, there is much more to language than just a bunch of words. Any understanding of language would be incomplete without acknowledging five basic facets presented in Table 2.1.

We must add that language, across all five of these areas, is both *productive* and *receptive*. For example, children must learn to both produce combinations of morphemes and receive (perceive and understand) them.

Language competence involves intricate and dynamic combinations of perceptual, motor, and cognitive skills; none of these five fundamental areas work very well on their own. To simplify, we will make a distinction between phonological development and other facets of language because phonology is intricately tied to motor skills and auditory perception. Speech production problems are much easier to detect and do not have the same associations with other psychological and development problems that the other four areas do.

Preschool: The First Five Years

Content

The development of a lexicon is a remarkable feat of learning. Children go from a vocabulary of zero words at birth to about 10,000 words in first grade. Children produce their first words between 8 and 10 months, and in the preschool years acquire multiple words on a daily basis (Bloom, 2000).

During the initial phases of lexical development, there seems to be a bias toward learning concrete nouns such as *mommy* and *milk* rather than prepositions or articles and abstract nouns (Brown, 1973). (You can image how disheartening it would be for parents if their child's first word was *although* instead of *mama* or *dada*.) We must be careful not to underestimate the utility of these nouns, however. A single word such as *milk* can be used as a referential term (there is milk on the table) or as a proto-imperative (*I want more milk!*). And infants can also produce some relatively complex quantification terms

Table 2.1 Facets of Language

Facet/Description	Unit of Study	Examples
Phonology: *basic perceptual characteristics*	Phoneme	• Sounds (e.g., in Russian "shch,"as in borscht
Morphology: *form and structure of words*	Morpheme	• Affixes (e.g., ducks) • Grammatical function words (e.g., the)
Syntax: *rules for ordering words in sentences*	Sentence	• Forming questions (e.g., in English, subjects and verbs are inverted to form questions *You are going. Are you going?*
Semantics *how language conveys meaning*	Word	• Using the word "read" both as a noun and as a verb
Pragmatics: *implicit rules guiding the use of language*	Conversation	• Register (language use appropriate for particular partners and/or speaking contexts) • Vocal tone, body language, use of gestures

amidst their first nouns, such as *all gone* and *more* (Gentner & Ratterman, 1991; Menyuk, Liebergott, & Schultz, 1995).

Form

Syntactic development begins in toddlerhood when children combine their first words. In the preschool years, morphological skills are mastered and sentence structure becomes more sophisticated and diverse. Brown (1973) studied young children's morphological development and observed a developmental sequence for 14 morphemes. These forms, presented in Table 2.2, emerge in a predictable sequence. Importantly, protracted use of these forms may be indicative of language impairment.

Brown (1973) and subsequently other researchers described five stages of morphosyntactic development. Each stage corresponds to an approximate age range as well as mean length of utterance (MLU; a commonly used measure used in language assessment as a general indicator of a child's syntactic development). MLU is calculated by dividing the total number of morphemes in a child's language sample by the number of utterances in the sample. Samples should include at least 50 utterances, but for illustrative purposes, the MLU for the 5-utterance sample below would be 3.8 (19 morphemes/5 utterances):

Table 2.2 Brown's Morphemes

Morpheme	Example	Age Range for Mastery in Months (>90% correct usage in obligatory contexts)
1. Present progressive -*ing* initially (without auxiliary)	*Kitty eating*	19–28
2. Preposition *in*	*Dog in house*	27–30
3. Preposition *on*	*Boy on chair*	27–30
4. Plural *s*	*Ducks*	27–33
5. Irregular past tense	*Swam, came, made*	25–46
6. Possessive '*s*	*Dad's shoe*	26–40
7. Uncontractible copula (*to be* main verb, not phonetically able to be contracted)	*Are you happy?* *I am.*	27–39
8. Articles	*a, an, the*	28–46
9. Regular past -*ed*	*kicked* *lifted*	26–48
10. Third person singular present tense -*s*	*jumps* *runs*	26–46
11. Irregular third person present tense	*has* *says* *does*	28–50
12. Uncontractible auxiliary (*to be* used as a helping verb, not able phonetically to be contracted)	*Are you driving?* *I am.*	29–48
13. Contractile copula (*to be* main verb, able to be contracted)	*She's my mom.* *You're nice.*	29–49
14. Contractible auxiliary (*to be* helping verb, able to be contracted)	*She's babysitting me.* *I'm going home.*	30–50

Adapted from Brown (1973) and Owens (2008).

- I am going home (5 morphemes)
- I want banana (3 morphemes)
- Let me have it (4 morphemes)
- Give me bear toys (5 morphemes)
- It broke (2 morphemes)

As indicated in Table 2.3, many accomplishments in language form occur in the preschool years and affect skills such as questions (i.e., interrogatives), negatives, sentence or clause structure, as well as emergence of individual morphemes.

The development of complex syntax occurs relatively early in preschool language development. Broadly defined, complex syntax might involve utterances of two or more verb phrases or clauses in a single sentence. More specifically, a complex sentence includes one independent and at least one dependent clause (clauses include a verb; an independent clause can stand alone, (e.g., *the girl was smiling*), whereas a dependent clause cannot (e.g., the underlined portion of the following sentence is a dependent clause: *The girl who won the race was smiling*). Children's sentence structure increases dramatically from simple subject-verb-object (SVO) to other, more complex constructions, including compound sentences (two independent clauses joined with a conjunction, most commonly *and* (Scott, 1984)), and complex sentences with embedded clauses, such as *the teddy bear that she lost was yellow* (Justice & Ezell, 2002).

As is the case with vocabulary, comprehension of grammatical structures generally precedes expression, and certain forms are more challenging than others for children to comprehend. Passive sentence structures are one such example. In passive grammatical constructions, the order of presentation of the agent and object are inverted from what is typically expected. Preschool age children have been found to comprehend irreversible sentences such as *the dog barked at the boy* (which would be semantically implausible if interpreted as *the boy barked at the dog*) before they comprehend semantically reversible sentences such as *Sam saw the cat* (which would make sense semantically if reversed to be *the cat saw Sam*). Bever (1970) found that by the end of the preschool years, around age 5, children could demonstrate comprehension of reversible passives. It is noteworthy, however, that production errors still may occur in this age period.

In the preschool years, as morphsyntactic development is at the forefront, a variety of developmental errors are expected, such as the following:

- Subject and verb inversion errors in interrogatives (e.g., a child may say *why you are sad?* instead of accurately inverted *why are you sad?*)
- Morpheme omissions (e.g., *last night I stay at Grandma house*, in which the obligatory past tense -*ed* and possessive 's markers were omitted)
- Overgeneralizations or overextensions (e.g., *Jerry swimmed in the pool* or *Jerry swammed in the pool* or even *Jerry swimmeded in the pool*).

Table 2.3 Major Achievements in Brown's (1973) Stages

Stage	Age Range in Months	MLU	Morphosyntactic Achievements[a]
I	12–26	1.0–2.0	• Single words and early word combinations • Begins to expand noun phrases to include articles (*a, an, the*) and demonstratives (*this, that*) • Interrogatives include single words (*yes?*) with rising intonation • *No, all gone* used for negatives, usually outside of the sentence (*no go home*)
II	27–30	2.0–2.5	• Begins to use most morphemes (though most are not mastered until later stages); masters -*ing* and prepositions *in* and *on* • Modifies nouns in object position of sentence (*Mom has brown hair*) • *Do, can, will* inverted in yes/no interrogatives; *what* and *where* question words emerge; early subject-verb inversion in interrogatives • *No, not,* and *don't* used interchangeably as negative markers
III	31–34	2.5–3.0	• Uses a variety of sentence types, including declaratives (comments), imperatives (commands), negatives, and interrogatives (questions) • Pronouns (*your, yours, he, she, we*) demonstratives *this, that, these, those* • Uses a variety of *to be* verbs; *what* and *where* used with copula (main verb) *to be* forms (*is, am, are, was, were*) in interrogatives • Negative markers used correctly between the subject and predicate (*I don't want grapes*); *won't* emerges as a negative marker
IV	35–40	3.0–3.75	• Use of modal auxiliaries (helping verbs): *may, can, will* • Use of several subjective/nominative and possessive pronouns (*they, us, her, hers, his, them*) • Consistent, accurate subject-verb inversion in variety of *wh-* and other interrogatives; uses *when* and *how* consistently • Negative markers used with auxiliary (helping) verbs (*she is not running, isn't, aren't, doesn't, didn't*)

Table 2.3 Major Achievements in Brown's (1973) Stages (Continued)

Stage	Age Range in Months	MLU	Morphosyntactic Achievements[a]
V	41–46	3.7–4.5	• Use of indirect objects (*she gave him the cookie*) • Uses modals in interrogatives (*should, may*); uses some tag questions (*I want this one, okay?*) • Modals and more copula/auxiliary *to be* verbs used in negatives (*wasn't, wouldn't, couldn't, shouldn't*); negatives used with copula (main) *to be* verbs
Post V	47+	4.5+	• Use of why in interrogatives (beyond rote one word *why?*) • Child may use double negatives (*I don't want no spinach*); use of negative indefinite forms (*no one, nobody*)

Adapted from Brown (1973); Klee (1985); Owens (2008); McCormick (1990); Wells (1985). Because morphology and syntax influence each other so closely, some authors such as Rice and Wexler (2001) have used the term morphosyntax to reflect this relationship.

Use

Like morphosyntactic development, pragmatic development begins very early in life, when children first start to engage in joint attention routines prior to their first birthday. Though pragmatics may not develop to the same degree as language form in the preschool years, several achievements are noteworthy. Preschoolers rely heavily on context cues for language use, as demonstrated by considerable deficits in speaking on the telephone, a highly decontextualized situation devoid of visual cues (Warren & Tate, 1992). Owens (2008) explained that the majority of communicative exchanges in preschoolers serve the purposes of regulating someone else's behavior (e.g., requesting a toy) and providing information (commenting on an object). Pragmatic development may be constrained in preschoolers for a variety of reasons, ranging from limited capacities in social interaction, language comprehension and use, and egocentrism. Thus, it is important that clinicians and parents adjust accordingly their expectations about social use of language. Though the preschool child may have an impressive command of grammar and vocabulary, she may not be an able conversationalist. With autism in the spotlight, clinicians, educators, and parents might rightly be nervous about a preschool child's pragmatic development; however, it is important to keep in mind that pragmatic development in this developmental period is far from sophisticated.

Success in topic maintenance in preschoolers tends to be context specific. Schober-Peterson and Johnson (1989) found that preschoolers were more apt to take conversational turns when they related to familiar scenes, play, ongoing events, or items in the immediate environment. Bloom, Rocissano, and Hood (1976) reported that around the age of four years, children can maintain a topic beyond two turns, and by age 5, Brinton and Fujiki (1984) found that children take an average of only five turns on a topic. This number may pale in comparison to the average of 11 turns that adults take on a single topic, but represents a considerable gain from earlier points in the preschool period. Adults who interact with preschoolers are cautioned not to be alarmed when and if the child dominates the conversation and frequently shifts topics. In fact, Owens (2008) reported that five-year-olds can plausibly cover up to 50 topics in a 15-minute period!

In addition to improvements in topic maintenance and turn-taking skills, likely with some prompting from their parents and following increased opportunities for social interactions, preschoolers also improve their polite use of language. By age 4½, children use and understand with increased accuracy indirect requests such as *would you mind turning off the light?* (Wilkinson, Calculator, & Dollaghan, 1982). Ervin-Tripp and Gordon (1986) found that preschool age children were more likely to use *please* when communicating with older or unfamiliar speakers, alluding to the preschooler's emerging sense of social expectations as well as register (adjusting pragmatics differentially to cater to a variety of partners).

Presupposition skills (i.e., considering a speaking partner's background knowledge) emerge around age 4. Sachs, Anselmi, and McMollam (1990), as cited in Pan and Snow (1999), found that children this age can explain referents for proper nouns (e.g., toys and names of unfamiliar people). Though preschoolers have this ability, they may not always demonstrate it in spontaneous speaking contexts. Similar skills are required to manage communication breakdowns—something expected in all phases of development, including adulthood. When breakdowns in message transmission occur in preschoolers, they may attempt to repair (often through repeating a previous statement), but are less skilled at requesting clarification when they do not understand another's message (Garvey, 1984). Brinton, Fujiki, Loeb, and Winkler (1986) reported that if preschoolers are initially unsuccessful in repairing a broken down conversation, they will eventually give up on clarification attempts. For example:

Preschooler: I want a Rofflerocket for my birthday.
Grandmother: I've never heard of a Rofflerocket.
Preschooler: I want a Rofflerocket.
Grandmother: I wonder where I could get a Rofflerocket?
Preschooler: I'm going to watch TV now.

Conversely, older conversationalists tend to attempt clarification until the breakdown is remedied:

School age child: I want a Rofflerocket for my birthday.
Grandmother: I've never heard of a Rofflerocket.
School age child: It goes up high when you launch it.

Grandmother: So it's a toy that flies?
School age child: Yeah, my friend Nate got one for his birthday. It's fun!

Narrative (i.e., storytelling) skills encompass myriad language skills, but commonly are addressed under the category of language use because they inherently require the use of several pragmatic elements, including register, language cohesion and precision, organization, and topicality (McCabe & Bliss, 2003).

Narratives are used ubiquitously in homes, preschools, and schools and may range in complexity from gossiping with one's peers to explaining the day's events in a phone conversation with an uncle to preparing a formal explanatory demonstration. Primitive narration begins at age 2. Four-year-olds most typically generate "leap frog" narratives (Peterson & McCabe, 1983) that are characterized by a series of nonsequential events in which connective terms (e.g., *then* or *so*) are omitted. For example:

- The doctor gave me a shot.
- Mary lost her tooth.
- Mom gave me candy.
- We had spaghetti last night.

Some preschoolers also may produce chronological narratives, in which a series of events are presented with the use of connective terms such as *and* or *then*. Kemper and Edwards (1986) pointed out that although preschoolers may present a basic timeline in their narratives, they may not include causal relationships. Few preschoolers are able to construct a "true" narrative, complete with adult-quality complicating events and resolutions. This means that children may not be expected to generate adult-like narratives, complete with connected events, logical cohesion, or full story grammar, until mid-elementary school age. These topics are further discussed in Chapter 4.

Elementary School Age: Five to Eleven Years

Metalinguistics

The school age child's metalinguistic ability (one's ability to think about language) increases dramatically, allowing for higher-level developments in content, form, and use. Specific evidence of increased metalinguistic ability in the school years includes transitioning from oral language only to written language, understanding of nonliteral references, and identifying and repairing grammatical or pragmatic errors.

Content

The most noticeable growth in vocabulary happens during the preschool years. Although the rate of acquisition slows during the school years, there are other changes in lexical development related to the complexity of new words and the manner in which they are learned. For example, many of a child's first 100 words have a perceptual-semantic link—a one-year-old *sees* a cup of milk and *names* it with a single word—and only a few words refer to things that cannot be directly perceived. In the school years, there is a shift toward learning more abstract nouns, such as *addition* or *champion* (Smith, Turner, Brown, & Henry, 2006), but even some very basic verbs, such as *to pour*, are not mastered until midway through elementary school (Gropen, Pinker, Hollander, & Goldberg, 1991).

One explanation for the increasing sophistication is the increasing ability to produce morphologically complex words. On the other hand, there are over 100 suffixes and prefixes in English, and children are only able to combine a limited number. Therefore, children have more difficulty than adolescents when they encounter a complex noun. For example, a ten-year-old ought to know what a muscle is, but he may have more difficulty than a thirteen-year-old when reading the word *muscular* (Nippold & Sun, 2008). But, there seems to be a great deal of individual differences in this skill, and many children can achieve some level of morphological analysis with guidance from a teacher (Larsen & Nippold, 2007).

Form

As is the case with content, school age developments in form do not occur at the pace or depth as in the preschool child. Slobin (1978) found that persisting overgeneralization errors may occur on irregular verb forms (e.g., a child may misapply the regular -*ed* suffix on what should be an irregular past tense form, as in *falled* or *felled*). One morpheme class that receives continued refinement in the school years is pronouns, with reflexive forms being mastered during this period (e.g., *herself, himself, themselves*). During this period, children improve their anaphoric reference skills (linguistically connecting two entities), which results in improved ability for matching pronouns and their referents, in both comprehension and production (Tager-Flusberg, 2005). For example, a child who demonstrates anaphoric reference ability may say, *The girl picked out her dress*. Children's derivational morphology systems also continue to develop during the school years (Justice & Ezell, 2002). Some derivational morphemes such as *un-*, *dis-*, and -*ir* change the meaning of the base word (e.g., *interested* versus *disinterested*), whereas other derivational forms change the word class, as is the case of applying an -*ly* suffix to cerate adverbs (e.g., *slow* to *slowly*).

Complex syntax development is continued and perfected in the school years. Scott (1984) reported that up to 30% of school age children's utterances contain embedded complex structures, and that in the school years, relative markers *whose, whom,* and *in which* begin to emerge (Scott, 1988). Complex conjoined sentences increase during the school years as well, with increasingly more complex conjunctions being used. Thus, it is expected that, much like adults, in the school years, an impressive proportion of sentences should include multiple verbs. The following utterances were taken from an eight-year-old's narrative retelling sample. Verb phrases are underlined.

> And the little boy said don't be mean to him or else you go back home.
> And then they went for a boat ride and then they heard a sound.
> The frog kicked the little frog off.
> Then he said aha!
> And then one of the animals told the boy.
> And then they heard a sound.
> The boy started looking for him and they couldn't find him.
> He was home crying where the big frog was sad too.
> He didn't mean to make the little boy cry.
> Then he went home and cried on his bed.

Like preschoolers, school age children have difficulty understanding passive sentences (e.g., *the ball was kicked by the boy*); therefore, it is not surprising that compared to other types of sentences, comparatively few passives are used in the early elementary school years (Hulit & Howard, 2006). Horgan (1978) found that both reversible and nonreversible sentences (see explanation in preschool form section) are produced by children by age 11.

Use

Whereas language *form* undergoes only a fine-tuning in the school years, improvements in social interaction, metalinguistics, and overall language production and comprehension lead to pervasive developments in language *use*. Nippold (1998) reported that relative to preschool counterparts, school age children are able to use language more persuasively. They also are able to maintain a single topic for an extended time period. They insert transitions between topics and increase the frequency of use of relevant and factual comments. Finally, improved perspective-taking skills lead to better presupposition and register skills.

Politeness, initiated in preschool, continues to evolve in the school years. In later elementary years, Mitchell-Kernan and Kernan (1977) found that children recognized the need to be polite in specific situations beyond those observed in preschool language use (e.g., when interrupting others or when making an inconvenient request). As often is the case with the competence-performance continuum, it is important to keep in mind that though children have demonstrated (often in experimental contexts) the ability to use polite language in specific contexts, their consistent performance in the skill area may be inconsistent. When asked to make "nice" and "bossy" requests, recall from the preschool section that Becker (1986) found that preschoolers differentiated the two styles through word choice such as choosing to use words such as "please" and "thank you." Conversely, Becker's older school age participants

Table 2.4 Example Conversations With and Without Adult Support

Age Group	Peer-Peer Conversations	Child-Adult Conversations
Preschoolers	Child (to mother): *I want the shovel!* Mother: *Stephanie, ask Sam if you can borrow his shovel.*	Child: *We went to the zoo today.* Father: *Wow, that sounds like fun.* Child: (*silence*) Father: *Tell me what you saw there.*
School age child	*I saw the best movie last weekend. It started out really scary because it was dark and spooky. There was this guy and he …*	Child: *I saw the best movie!* Teacher: *Really?* Child: *Yeah, it was really scary. There was this guy who …*

differentiated such requests in a more sophisticated manner through the use of passive syntax (e.g., *would you mind…?*).

Continuity between utterances in conversation is aided by school age language form developments that include adjuncts and disjuncts (e.g., *now, though*). Further, Garvey (1984) found that, in the elementary school years, children keep a conversation going by using attentive looks and interjections such as *uh-huh* and *I see*. Importantly, children in this age group require considerably less conversational support from adult speaking partners (Pan & Snow, 1999). Table 2.4 contains examples of how children's conversations may occur with (in the case of preschoolers) and without (in the case of school age children) direct adult support.

Narratives undergo major changes in the school years, likely because of increased exposure to literate language and metalinguisitcs. A greater command of story grammar is noted in narratives generated by school age children. Stein and Glenn (1979) identified core story grammar elements of setting (character, time, place) and episodes (initiating or complicating event, characters' internal response, plan to resolve the problem, attempts made by the characters, consequences, and characters' reactions). Peterson and McCabe (1983) found that by age 8, children generated "classic narratives," similar to those produced by adults, that include a high point and more complete episode development than preschool age peers.

Adolescence

Content, Form, and Use

Language development in adolescents shares many of the same themes as that in childhood. The increase in vocabulary is not as rapid as it was before age 5, but it involves phonologically and morphologically complex words (Nippold & Sun, 2008). Adolescent development is reflected in the curriculum through a paradigmatic emphasis that involves increased scientific and logical thought. Such a shift is possible because of continued cognitive and linguistic developments (Clark, 2004). This leads to increasing metalinguistic awareness being observed as well. Adolescents no longer focus on the canonical definition form; instead, they become aware of the purpose of a definition and supply more synonyms and examples that are situation specific.

In terms of language use, adolescent register tends to indicate group membership (Gee, Allen, & Clinton, 2001). Specific word choice and slang, as well as nonstandard use of fillers such as *like* and *you know*, are typical in this register (Siegel, 2002). Verbal aggression, which is related to social hierarchical structure, also is typical in adolescent language (Sluckin, 1981) and begins to emerge even earlier in the elementary school years. Examples of verbal aggression may include reprimands, insults, tattling, rejection, and criticism (McCabe & Lipscomb, 1988). This phenomenon generally decreases by adulthood.

To Refer or Not to Refer: Red Flags for Language Impairment

Individual differences abound in language acquisition and the range of normal for achieving a variety of linguistic milestones may vary considerably across children. Thus, it can be difficult for clinicians and educators to differentiate which children are language delayed and may be likely to catch up with peers from those children who may have persistent language impairment and would benefit from a referral to a speech language pathologist or other specialist. Child language impairments may be characterized as being (1) primary (i.e., specific language impairment, or SLI); (2) secondary to another condition, such as mental retardation, hearing impairment, or autism; or (3) acquired (e.g., language impairment as a result of traumatic brain injury). As many as 7% of kindergarten-age children fit the SLI profile (Tomblin, Records, & Zhang, 1996), meaning they present with significant language deficits despite otherwise normal development in such areas as nonverbal intelligence, behavior, and hearing acuity (Leonard, 1998). Children with SLI are at risk for long-term problems that may impact both spoken and written language as well as a variety of associated social and academic challenges. For children with developmental or secondary language impairment (children whose language impairment is a symptom of another condition) the severity of the language deficit is generally related to the severity of the primary disorder. For this group of children, the language impairment typically is identified and assessed when the primary diagnosis is made.

Child language specialists have not agreed upon one standard definition of language impairment and criteria used in clinical settings versus educational settings. Diagnosis of language impairment generally includes both quantitative measures (e.g., performance below the 10th percentile in more than one domain of language or 1.25 standard deviations below the age mean on language tests) and qualitative measures (e.g., analysis of language sample transcripts, or social judgment based on recess observations in peer interactions).

Thus, it can be a challenging proposition for clinicians to know when to refer children for in-depth language testing after initially poor performance on verbal sections of intelligence or achievement test batteries. Similarly, clinicians may find it difficult to determine which children to refer from the group that performs strongly on omnibus intelligence measures but who in conversation stand out as having atypical language. Referring to developmental norms such as those presented previously in this chapter may be a good starting point in the referral decision-making process. However, specific indicators of long-lasting, significant language deficits exist in the literature and are displayed, along with examples, in Table 2.5.

Conclusion

Most clinicians who work with children will face questions about language from time to time. Parents and teachers alike are sensitive to language development and, for the most part, are good at distinguishing normal from dysfunctional development (e.g., Newman & McGregor, 2006). After all, competent language users are good at recognizing correct and incorrect uses of their own native language. On the other hand, the same research shows that parents tend to look at the "sparkle" in children's use, and so they may become concerned when their own child's language is developing at a slower pace (Keegstra, Knijff, Post, & Goorhuis-Brouwer, 2007).

Table 2.5 presents some of the more frequent language-related issues clinicians encounter, but it is only a partial list. When other problems arise, readers are encouraged to consult Pence and Justice (2007) or Leonard (1998) for a more comprehensive list. Although there is some research to suggest that problems exist with overreferring children (e.g., Goorhuis-Brouwer & Knijff, 2003; Keegstra et al., 2007), we encourage clinicians to err on the side of caution and make the referral when language impairments are suspected. There are no known ill effects of language assessments, but the benefits of early intervention have been well established, and the failure to intervene may have long-term academic, social, and vocational implications.

Table 2.5 Possible Indicators of Persistent Language Impairment

Age	Language Difficulties	Examples/Explanations
Preschool	Omission of grammatical morphemes (omission of finite morphemes in particular may be a red flag)	*I going home.* *The dog bark.* *Mary catch the ball.*
	Slow development and errors with pronouns	*Him do it.* *Us like cookies.*
	Shorter sentence length	Mean length of utterance significantly below age expectations
	Problems forming questions with inverted subjects/verbs	*Why you are going?*
	Significant pragmatic deficits	Major problems conversing with peers; unable to take two turns on a topic; child rarely, if ever, initiates conversation
	Excessive, protracted use of gesture for getting needs met	Child points to request juice, but does not attempt to verbalize
	Comprehension deficits	Child does not understand grammatically simple (*Hand me the orange stick*) or grammatically complex directions (*Find the blue caterpillar and stick it on the top of the picture*)
	Minimal or no narrative language skills	Child cannot begin to present a basic sequence of events
Elementary school age	Word finding problems, may be evidenced by lengthy pauses or circumlocutions ("talking around" the word)	*I want the round thing, um, ah, you know the thing that has the stuff on it.*
	Grammatical morpheme deficits	Brown's morphemes should be mastered by kindergarten

Table 2.5 Possible Indicators of Persistent Language Impairment (Continued)

Age	Language Difficulties	Examples/Explanations
	Does not use complex sentences	Child does not use a variety of multiple verb phrases conjoined (*I saw the girl and asked her to ride bikes with me*) or embedded sentences (*The one that has the red stripes is the prettiest*).
	Word naming errors	Saying *"bus"* when child means *"van"*
	Significantly delayed processing speed in language comprehension	
	Difficulty responding to indirect requests	Child does not appear to understand requests such as *"Would you mind ..."* or *"If it wouldn't be too much trouble ..."*
	Significant pragmatic deficits	Difficulty maintaining topics (5+ turns) Difficulty recognizing the need for conversational repair Not adjusting message to meet listener's needs
	Problems using and understanding nonliteral language	Child does not understand meaning of words with multiple meanings (e.g., *bat*); child does not understand implied meaning of idioms such as *"time flies when you're having fun"*
	Deficits in using or understanding abstract language concepts	Child does not demonstrate understanding of directions that involve exclusionary (instead, unless), temporal (first, after), or other higher-level concepts
	Deficits in narration; poor cohesion of narratives	Narratives that are devoid of organizational, sequential structure or story grammar

Table 2.5 Possible Indicators of Persistent Language Impairment (Continued)

Age	Language Difficulties	Examples/Explanations
Adolescence	Lack of metalinguisitic awareness	Child does not recognize grammatical errors in writing or oral language; child cannot explain linguistic thought processes; child does not use sentence cues to determine meanings of new words
	Age-inappropriate social use of language	Inappropriate comments; ineffective use of register; inappropriate topic selection; inability to take multiple turns on a conversational topic; redundancy; difficulty initiating to peers
	Word finding difficulties	See explanation in school age section

Adapted from: Pence, K. L., & Justice, L. M. (2008). *Language development from theory to practice*. Upper Saddle River: Pearson. (pp. 326–327).

References

Becker, J. (1986). Bossy and nice requests: Children's production and interpretation. *Merrill-Palmer Quarterly, 32,* 393–413.

Bever, T. G. (1970). The cognitive basis for linguistic structure. In J. R. Hayes (Ed.), *Cognition and the development of language.* New York: Wiley.

Bloom, L., & Lahey, M. (1978). *Language development and language disorders.* New York: John Wiley & Sons.

Bloom, L., Rocissano, L., & Hood, L. (1976). Adult-child discourse: Developmental interaction between information processing and linguistic interaction. *Cognitive Psychology, 8,* 521–552.

Bloom, P. (2000). *How children learn the meanings of words.* Cambridge, MA: The MIT Press.

Brinton, B., & Fujiki, M. (1984). Development of topic manipulation skills in discourse. *Journal of Speech and Hearing Research, 27,* 350–358.

Brinton, B., Fujiki, M., Loeb, D., & Winkler, E. (1986). Development of conversational repair strategies in response to requests for clarification. *Journal of Speech and Hearing Research, 29,* 75–81.

Brown, R. (1973). *A first language: The early stages.* Cambridge, MA: Harvard University Press.

Clark, E. V. (2004). How language acquisition builds on cognitive development. *Trends in Cognitive Sciences, 8,* 472–478.

Ervin-Tripp, S., & Gordon, D. (1986). The development of requests. In R. Schiefelbusch (Ed.), *Language competence: Assessment and intervention* (pp. 61–95). London: Taylor & Francis.

Garvey, C, (1984). *Children's talk.* Cambridge, MA: Harvard University Press.

Gee, J. P., Allen, A.-R., & Clinton, K. (2001). Language, class, and identity: Teenagers fashioning themselves through language. *Linguistics and Education, 12,* 175–194.

Gentner, D., & Rattermann, M. (1991). *Language and the career of similarity. Perspectives on language and thought: Interrelations in development* (pp. 225–277). New York: Cambridge University Press.

Goorhuis-Brouwer, S. M., & Knijff, K. A. (2003). Language disorders in young children: When is speech therapy recommended? *International Journal of Pediatric Otorhinolaryngology, 67,* 525.

Gropen, J., Pinker, S., Hollander, M., & Goldberg, R. (1991). Syntax and semantics in the acquisition of locative verbs. *Journal of Child Language, 18,* 115–151.

Horgan, D. (1978). The development of the full passive. *Journal of Child Language, 5,* 65–80.

Hulit, L. M., & Howard, M. R. (2006). *Born to talk: An introduction to speech and language development* (4th ed.) Boston: Allyn & Bacon.

Irwin, J. R., Carter, A. S., & Briggs-Gowan, M. J. (2002). The social-emotional development of "late-talking" toddlers. *Journal of the American Academy of Child & Adolescent Psychiatry, 41,* 1324–1332.

Justice, L., & Ezell, H. (2002). *The syntax handbook.* Eau Claire, WI: Thinking Publications.

Keegstra, A. L., Knijff, W. A., Post, W. J., & Goorhuis-Brouwer, S. M. (2007). Children with language problems in a speech and hearing clinic: Background variables and extent of language problems. *International Journal of Pediatric Otorhinolaryngology, 71,* 815–821.

Kemper, S., & Edwards, L. (1986). Children's expression of causality in their construction of narratives. *Topics in Language Disorders, 7,* 11–20.

Klee, T. (1985). Role of inversion in children's question development. *Journal of Speech and Hearing Research, 28,* 225–232.

Larsen, J. A., & Nippold, M. A. (2007). Morphological analysis in school-age children: Dynamic assessment of a word learning strategy. *Language, Speech, and Hearing Services in Schools, 38,* 201–212.

Leonard, L. B. (1998). *Children with specific language impairment.* Cambridge, MA: MIT Press.

McCabe, A., & Bliss, L. S. (2003). *Patterns of narrative discourse.* Boston: Allyn & Bacon.

McCabe, A., & Lipscomb, T. J. (1988). Sex differences in children's verbal aggression. *Merrill-Palmer Quarterly, 34,* 389–401.

McCabe, P. C. (2005). Social and behavioral correlates of preschoolers with specific language impairment. *Psychology in the Schools, 42,* 373–387.

Menyuk, P., Liebergott, J., & Schultz, M. (1995). *Early language development in full-term and premature infants.* Hillsdale, NJ: Lawrence Erlbaum Associates.

Mitchell-Kernan, C., & Kernan, K. (1977). Pragmatics of directive choice among children. In C. Mitchell-Kernan & S. Ervin-Tripp (Eds.), *Child discourse.* New York: Academic Press.

Newman, R. M., & McGregor, K. K. (2006). Teachers and laypersons discern quality differences between narratives produced by children with or without SLI. *Journal of Speech, Language, and Hearing Research, 49,* 1022–1036.

Nippold, M. A. (1998). *Later language development: The school-age and adolescent years* (2nd ed.). Austin, TX: PRO-ED.

Nippold, M. A., & Sun, L. (2008). Knowledge of morphologically complex words: A developmental study of older children and young adolescents. *Language, Speech, and Hearing Services in Schools, 39,* 365–373.

Owens, R. E. (2008). *Language development: An introduction* (7th ed.). Boston: Allyn & Bacon.

Pan, B. A., & Snow, C. E. (1999). The development of conversational and discourse skills. In M. Barrett (Ed.), *The development of language* (pp. 229–249). New York: Psychology Press.

Pence, K. L., & Justice, L. M. (2008). *Language development from theory to practice.* Upper Saddle River, NJ: Pearson.

Peterson, C., & McCabe, A. (1983). *Developmental psycholinguistics: Three ways of looking at a child's narrative.* New York: Plenum Press.

Sachs, J., Anselmi, D., & McMollam, K. (1990, July). *Young children's awareness of presuppositions based on community membership.* Paper presented at the 5th International Congress for the Study of Child Language, Budapest, Hungary.

Schober-Peterson, D., & Johnson, C. J. (1989). Non-dialogue speech during preschool interactions. *Journal of Child Language, 18,* 153–170.

Scott, C. (1984). Adverbial connectivity in conversations of children 6 to 12. *Journal of Child Language, 11,* 423–452.

Scott, C. (1988). Producing complex sentences. *Topics in Language Disorders, 8,* 44–62.

Siegel, M. E. (2002). Like: The discourse particle and semantics. *Journal of Semantics, 19,* 35–71.

Slobin, D. (1978). Cognitive prerequisites for the development of grammar. In L. Bloom & M. Lahey (Eds.), *Readings in language development.* New York: Wiley.

Sluckin, A. (1981). *Growing up in the playground: The social development of children.* London: Routledge & Kegan Paul.

Smith, P. T., Turner, J. E., Brown, P. A., & Henry, L. A. (2006). *The Quarterly Journal of Experimental Psychology, 59,* 2121–2134.

Stein, N., & Glenn, C. (1979). An analysis of story comprehension in elementary school children. In R. Freedle (Ed.), *New directions in discourse processing* (pp. 53–120). Norwood, NJ: Ablex.

Tager-Flusberg, H. (2005). Putting words together: Morphology and syntax in the preschool years. In J. Berko-Gleason (Ed.), *The development of language* (6th ed.) (pp. 148–179). Boston: Allyn & Bacon.

Tomblin, J. B., Records, N., & Zhang, X. (1996). A system for the diagnosis of specific language impairment in kindergarten children. *Journal of Speech and Hearing Research, 39,* 1284–1294.

van Daal, J., Verhoeven, L., & van Balkom, H. (2007). Behaviour problems in children with language impairment. *Journal of Child Psychology and Psychiatry, 48,* 1139–1147.

Warren, A., & Tate, C. (1992). Egocentrism in children's telephone conversations. In R. Diaz & L. Berk (Eds.), *Private speech: From social interaction to self-regulation* (pp. 245–264). Hillsdale, NJ: Erlbaum.

Wilkinson, L., Calculator, S., & Dollaghan, C. (1982). Ya wanna trade—just for awhile: Children's requests and responses to peers. *Discourse Processes, 5,* 161–176.

3
Communicating About Internal States

SHAYNA L. SKELLEY and KEITH A. CRNIC

As young children develop the ability to speak, they gain the ability to communicate their thoughts, beliefs, desires, and feelings. Language development advances at an exponential rate early in development, and with it, the tools for communicating open up the world as a place filled with social interactions and new information. Communication, and especially spoken language, is integral to facilitating a child's ability to think about his or her internal and external representations of the world.

We will address a number of complex questions in this chapter, exploring what young children know about their thoughts and emotions and at what age they can construct an understanding about the thoughts and feeling states of themselves and others. For clinicians, getting inside children's heads to understand how they think, what they think, and how they make sense of the connections between thinking and feeling is an important goal that enables the clinician to access critical material for therapeutic process and, eventually, therapeutic success. Indeed, children's internal states are central to their psychological experience, and may well guide the behaviors and emotions that represent normal and disordered functioning across childhood. Within this chapter, we discuss the development of cognitive awareness of a child's thinking and feeling, and the role of understanding others' mental states as critical to this emerging awareness. In addition, we will focus expressly on children's ability to both represent and express thoughts and emotions through language within the context of normal social discourse. As emotions are inherently social in nature, underlying internal cognitive and linguistic processes are critical to the experience of emotion and cognitive states.

What Are Internal States?

While it may seem easy to understand the idea of an individual's internal state, it has proven a surprisingly difficult construct for psychologists to define. There is no well-accepted "gold standard" definition in the study of internal states, so existing definitions of this term vary depending on the scientific or theoretical approach involved. From a neuroscientific perspective, internal states are defined as "brain information not directly related to a sensory input or motor output; for example, homeostatic information such as hunger, thirst or other motivational influences" (Nature Publishing Group, 2008). Those interested in emotional experience study internal states from an affective perspective and focus expressly on the experience of feelings states such as frustration or joy or sadness. Within cognitive theory, internal states are specified more as mental state processes, such as beliefs about the world and other people. Regardless of perspective, internal states provide clues about the ways in which internal representations form, change over the life span, and influence the course of development across major functional domains.

For this chapter, we will consider *internal states* to reflect both thoughts and emotions such as feeling, believing, and liking, which are experienced privately by an individual. We will discuss internal states from multiple perspectives, including cognitive, behavioral, and affective states that may be salient to the therapeutic or clinical context. For example, children are believed to experience a change in mental state over time in relation to desires (I want) versus beliefs (I think); as children develop over time, they talk about what they think more frequently and talk about what they want less frequently (Taumoepeau & Ruffman, 2008). It is this emerging sophistication that allows access to psychological material of interest to clinicians.

In the sections that follow, we first discuss the development of language within the context of cognitive processes to provide a foundation for understanding the emergence and function of internal states. Next, we consider the role of language in children's development of the ability to express their internal states and the capacity to think about internal states in oneself and others. Finally, we consider the key social factors that influence internal state comprehension and several specific clinical implications for children.

The Role of Language for Internal State Understanding

The Chicken or the Egg Debate (Part 1): Cognition or Emotion?

As we noted earlier, internal states can be represented across multiple domains, but emotion states and mental (i.e., cognitive) states are two basic representations. It is a natural process for humans to develop thoughts and beliefs about the world as well as about their own emotions. In fact, it seems impossible to feel an emotion without thinking about why you feel that way. Similarly, it seems impossible to feel an emotion without having first assessed your situation and possible adaptive threats to your well-being in the environment. Is it ever possible to experience emotions without some thought process preceding it? While most people agree that both cognition and affect occur in conjunction to produce meaning, there is a long history of debate regarding whether emotions can ever occur without any preceding cognitive process. Zajonc (1980, 1984) theorized that emotional arousal can occur without necessarily needing to think about it first, while Lazarus (1984) argued that some aware-ness of a situation is necessary in order for a person to react emotionally.

EXAMPLE

Danny was crossing a busy street when a car ran a red light and sped directly toward him. Filled with terror, Danny screamed and shrank back as a car screeched to a halt only feet in front of him. The fear and anxiety he experienced clung to him and he found it difficult to stop thinking about the near accident. Lazarus would argue that the boy's reaction indicates that he understood cognitively that his well-being was threatened by the speeding car. However, Zajonc would contend that the boy did not consciously assess the situation, but rather his autonomic nervous system was triggered through automatic, instinc-tual circuits.

Ultimately, the answer to this cognition-emotion debate is less impor-tant than the overarching agreement of both sides: Emotions and cognition are intertwined. Humans clearly think about the emotions they are having, whether or not they think before they feel them. Internal states, then, combine elements of cognition and affect even in very young children, although these integrations become progressively more complex as children develop across preschool, school age, and early adolescent periods.

The Chicken or the Egg Debate (Part 2): Language or Cognition?

Developmental questions don't simply end with the issue of cognition versus affect, though. When young children begin to speak, they also begin to express increasingly more complex thoughts about their beliefs and feelings about themselves and other people. It is still unclear whether language simply allows a child to express what he or she is already thinking or knows, or whether it has a more dynamic role that influences the ability to think about one's own feelings and states. When do language comprehension and language produc-tion start to match up? And is that connection important to understanding internal states? Do children understand their internal experiences before they learn to talk about them? Alternatively, does the acquisition of language stimulate the ability to comprehend one's internal states? Like many psycho-logical phenomena, the influences are most likely bidirectional. Attempting to disentangle these complex connections has occupied developmental scientists for many years. It may not actually matter that we have a final answer to this conundrum, but it does suggest that care must be taken to not overinterpret conversations with children about their internal states.

In the attempt to understand the connections between understanding and expression, several new experimental paradigms reflect the shift toward stressing the importance of assessing such connections. To this end, there has been more focus on infants who have not yet developed speech to explicate this process. One such new approach is the looking paradigm, which attempts to assess a child's ability to recognize novelty through linguistic stimuli. In this task, the infant is seated on his or her blindfolded mother's lap with an interesting light or toy revealed to draw in the child's focus. Then a phrase is uttered, such as "Look, he is kicking!" while two videos of visual scenes are displayed, one that shows a boy kicking an object and the other showing a person picking up an object. If the child looks longer at the scene that matches the spoken utterance, this preference is believed to provide evidence that comprehension has occurred. Another new paradigm for studying the learning of language is the "fast mapping" task, which introduces a novel object or action paired with a novel word in a few trials, followed by tests for comprehension, production, and memory for the novel association. Why are task methods important? Different task paradigms have produced evidence for comprehension of some complex cognitive concepts in infants as young as 13 months old, reflecting the importance of studying language acquisition in children even before language production emerges (Chapman, 2000). However, the fact that children might understand new words or concepts does not mean that they can represent them in some adaptive way that is critical to clinical process. Comprehension alone may not provide access for clinicians to the child's internal state, as children may not be able to communicate their state even though they have awareness of it. Spoken language may still be a key for such ability.

Given that language comprehension likely exists independently from production, it may be that children similarly think about their personal experience independently from the expression of it. This perspective proposes that preexisting conceptualizations about the world lead the child to seek out language and semantic development in the first place. New motor, cognitive, and social learning encourages the acquisition of language, and even before language has been acquired, young infants possess some awareness of internal states. Children's language learning is based on the theory that new motor, cognitive, and social learning develops before particular forms of language emerge, which could help the child express new thoughts (Chapman, 2000). Mobile infants and wobbly toddlers don't possess complex language expression; however, they do have access to emerging motor abilities that allow them to move toward objects and people, seek attention for their activities, and produce playful responses to parent's encouragement to engage their worlds. Their contagious laughter and bright eagerness to learn are indicators of states that may reflect a variety of emotion experiences (excitement, pleasure, joy, etc.) as well as cognitive ones (cause-effect, constancy, etc.). As infants and toddlers, they cannot express these states in spoken language, but the process of experiencing these activities and interactions encourages the development of language to represent these states as children move through the childhood periods.

However, there is evidence that language acquisition is the catalyst for children to think with more complexity about their own experiences. Research has shown that the usage of new linguistic forms leads to further development in cognitive realms. Thus, language may do more than just help a child talk about his or her growing knowledge about internal states; some argue that language actually aids the child in gaining an understanding of how, why, and when he or she feels a certain way. One study found that 70% of individual differences of emotion understanding in children were explained by age and language ability together (Pons, Lawson, Harris, & deRosney, 2003, cited by Vallotton, 2008), indicating that the development of new language skills influences how children think about their experiences and construct internal states.

In response to this debate, the modern interactionist perspective draws from both theories to explain the interplay of cognitive and linguistic development in a cyclical model. It states that a preexisting conscious understanding of one's thoughts about the world motivates young children to acquire language skills. In turn, the newly developed linguistic abilities influence the ways in which children form novel, more complex representations of their thoughts and experiences. Although we have yet to fully answer the question of whether language or cognition begins the process, children's language abilities clearly play a crucial role in the formation and understanding of internal states.

Thinking About and Expressing Internal States

If spoken language helps children develop more complex representations about internal states, do children understand emotion before they learn language? An interesting experiment (Vallotton, 2008) addressed this question by investigating whether preverbal children could learn to express internal states through gesture. Children as young as 11 months of age demonstrated the ability to successfully learn and spontaneously produce gestures that represented emotions. Gestures about feelings were also observed in children by as early as 15 months. These findings show promise for future study of internal state comprehension before language has emerged and open windows for understanding children's emotional states for those who may be delayed or impaired in language development. The clinical implications are potentially huge for identifying the ages at which interventions can be planned and carried out.

Models of Internal State Language

Hierarchical Acquisition

Given our limited knowledge on how preverbal children understand their emotions and feelings, language is often the best way to measure children's

Table 3.1 Six Categories of Internal State Language

Categories of Internal State Language	Description
Perception	Sight, hearing, taste, smell, skin senses
Physiology	Hunger, thirst, states of consciousness
Affect	Positive and negative emotions (joy, fear)
Volition/ability	Desires and needs to complete a task
Cognition	Knowledge, memory, uncertainty, dreams
Moral judgment/obligation	Conformity, permission, obligation

Adapted from Bretherton & Beeghly (1982).

cognitions of internal states. Since we are primarily interested in cognitive and emotional internal states, we must identify certain words that reflect such states (called internal state language, or ISL).

The development of ISL has been conceptualized from various perspectives. Bretherton and Beeghly (1982) broke ISL into six categories, all believed to emerge by three years of age (see Table 3.1).

More recently, Booth and colleagues (Booth, Hall, Robinson, & Kim, 1997) developed three features of cognitive internal state words that set certain criteria for identifying them. They must: (1) focus on internal state components; (2) refer to psychological—not physical—processes; and (3) label transitory states rather than long-term attitudes. These are qualities that actually define the cognitive nature of a specific internal mental state and differentiate the state from some larger or more characteristic aspects of the child's development. There are obvious parallels between the Bretherton and Beeghly and the Booth conceptualizations, and both reflect the potential to connect emotion and thought in internal states. Whether or not these models of ISL are universal is a reasonable question, and in the next section, we explore in more depth children's thoughts of their beliefs, feelings, and desires in a cultural context.

Cultural Effects

A focus on cross-cultural frames of reference improves our own understanding of language development that influences children's internal states. It is important to remember that research addressing English language development may not necessarily translate across other languages, especially across varying cultures. For example, English-speaking adults tend to speak to children in a style that uses objects (nouns) more often and with more meaning than actions (verbs). However, Korean-speaking adults interact with children in the opposite manner, with verbs taking priority in salience and frequency. Nonetheless, children of both cultures acquire nouns, specifically names of objects, more quickly than verbs. This indicates that there are certain universal constraints on children's learning of word meaning that can be useful for understanding semantic development across languages. Constraint theories are centered on the notion that a novel word is the starting point for children to search for meaning through several assumptions. The *whole object* assumption is based on the idea that a novel word refers to a whole object, rather than its parts or properties. Other constraints include a *mutual exclusivity* assumption that different words name different classes of objects; a *principle of contrast*, which assumes that no two words have the same meaning; and the *novel name-nameless category principle*, which assumes that new words refer to referents that previously had no other names (Chapman, 2000). These constraint theories identify several common features in the ways in which children approach and comprehend new words that are relevant to understanding internal state. Constraints may help children learn to recognize and then identify internal states, whether they represent new experience or well-formed ideas and affects.

Cultural differences do not stop at the issue of basic language development. Research has also begun to examine the role of key stylistic differences in mother-child interaction across populations, including such diverse groups as Papua New Guineans, Inuit, African Americans, Native Americans, and Latinos. Stylistic differences may determine the ways in which internal states develop. Further, it is important to remember that certain linguistic behaviors are valued differently from culture to culture; although one culture may stress the importance of learning to express one's thoughts and opinions, another teaches the asset of learning to be quiet. As such, children viewed as well taught or with well-developed language skills in one context may appear very different in another (Chapman, 2000). This not only has implications for the internal states that children experience, but also suggests that cultural competence in clinical practice may be facilitated by understanding the nature of these cultural differences in the ways that children can internally represent actions and meaning.

Cultures that are socially interdependent encourage children to value relationships with others rather than inner attributes. This can affect the expression of certain emotions that may threaten relationships with others. One example is the expression of anger among Ukta Eskimos, who are often said not to feel, express, or even talk about anger. While it is unlikely that these individuals lack the ability to feel anger, it seems that it is simply necessary to control and conceal it. In fact, when these Eskimos observe angry behavior in foreigners, they use a word that means "childish" to describe it. Thus, while children in Western culture are encouraged to express their inner feelings, Ukta Eskimo children are taught that the expression of anger is considered impulsive and inappropriate (Markus & Kitayama, 1991).

Systems that organize the acquisition of language and meaning are useful for conceptualizing the developmental process in children. There is wide agreement that internal state language begins broadly and simplistically, with increasing complexity as learning advances. We must remember that cultural differences in language structure and interaction style can affect the trajectory of children's developmental process. Nonetheless, while the pattern of language learning may differ based on cultural context, principles such as object versus verb differences and constraints show us some of the universal aspects of ISL acquisition that are not affected by culture. Thus, clinicians should work toward understanding the norms of the culture in which a child is reared, but only when appropriate; children with very different backgrounds can still develop ISL in similar ways even if expressions of internal states may vary. Next, we address the ways in which social factors affect children's ability to express internal states.

Social Influence on Internal State Language

As we discussed earlier, infants are at least somewhat aware of their internal states. But when are children capable of speaking about them? How does the social environment affect the emergence of internal state language? Language is primarily social in nature in that it allows people to communicate with one another. In this section, we discuss the typical milestones of internal state communication and how it can be affected by social processes, especially parents and the home environment.

Development of Internal State Language

While the environment plays an important role in the acquisition and production of language, it is important for clinicians to be familiar with the general timeline of healthy social communicative development, as this helps form the basis for the emergence of internal state awareness (see Table 3.2).

Before infants are even capable of speaking, there are cues that social comprehension has developed. By as early as nine months of age, infants begin to demonstrate a capacity to understand the meaning of interaction with others. As their cognitive skills evolve further, they begin to integrate social play with the mother with nonsocial play, such as using a toy for pretend play. At this age, infants often engage in intentional communication even though they have not yet developed the ability to talk (Bretherton & Beeghly, 1982).

From this point on, children gradually develop the capacity to think about their internal states over time. We often see this co-occur with gains in language abilities, allowing children to talk and share words about how they feel. Between 18 and 20 months of age, typically developing children begin to talk about emotions and internal feeling states. By two years, most children begin to use some basic internal state words, with articulation improving steadily (Bretherton & Beeghly, 1982; Dunn, Bretherton, & Munn, 1987). By age 3, some children begin to differentiate past and present experiences and emotions about them, and by about five years old, children have a well-developed understanding that others have mental processes that differ from their own, or theory of mind (ToM)

Table 3.2 Developmental Timeline of Internal State Language

Age	Milestone	Specific Words
9 months	Understanding of meaningful interaction; social and pretend play	
10–14 months	First words emerge; complex language comprehension develops; emotional gestures emerge	
18–20 months	First internal state language emerges (physiology, perception, affect)	Need, want, feel
2 years	Telegraphic speech, cognitive state language, knowledge of others' actions but not internal states	Know (most simple uses)
3 years	Use of past and present emotions and experiences; all six of Bretherton's (1982) ISL categories achieved (perception, physiology, affect, volition/ability, cognition, moral judgment/obligation)	Remember, believe, seem,
3.5 years	Beginning of verbal pretend play	Be wrong, imagine
4 years	More fluent language structure; simple meanings to phrases; application of broad grammatical rules to novel words	Understand, guess, be acquainted with, mean, learn
4.5 years	Active expression of likes and dislikes	Realize, decide, feel like
5 years	Theory of mind emerges; false belief; complex language structure	Worry, think, get to know, pretend, know (most advanced uses), would have
6–8 years	Consideration of intentions of others to explain their behavior; use of scripts, stories, and personal narratives	

Note: Ages of milestones are estimates; opinions vary greatly.
Adapted from Bretherton & Beeghly (1982), Booth et al. (1997), McCabe & Peterson (1991), Chapman (2000), MacRory (2001), Pascual, Aguado, Sotillo & Masdeu (2008), and Vallotton (2008).

(Vallotton, 2008). Several other aspects of children's cognitive development in relation to theory of mind are discussed in Chapters 5 and 6.

While the majority of internal state language development has been achieved by age 5, children typically do not fully consider the intentions and feelings of others as explanation for their actions until at least age 6, and often continue to increase in complexity until eight years of age. Further, children at this age begin to formulate scripts and narratives to tell complete stories of experiences. From this point on, older children expand their linguistic abilities to express increasingly complex cognitive processes related to exploring the world from the perspective of others, as well as themselves. Indeed, vocabulary expands, which offers school-aged children a wider range of expressive words to convey meaning and experience. But it is increasingly complex cognitive abilities that allow children to address more sophisticated understanding of internal state thoughts and beliefs, as well as more subtle and complex affective experience.

Context is critical to understand language-mediated social interactions. There are several settings in which young children are exposed to and practice internal state language. A wealth of data have been gathered from conversations between children and adults during free play and narrations of events by children. Pretend play allows language to be used naturally in relation to many cognitive and social situations, which provides a wealth of information about a given child's sophistication in language expressivity as well as internal state awareness (Youngblade & Dunn, 1995). Shared picture book reading between a parent and child is an often used context for studies that examine parent-child interaction, as it provides another context for free-flowing conversation that encourages internal state talk. This is especially true for discussing the perspectives of the characters in the story (Adrian, Clemente, Villanueva, & Rieffe, 2005), which suggests that clinicians could use similar techniques to explore internal states with their child clients (and the processes need not be limited to picture books). Siblings also serve an important role in teaching a young child to think about internal states. There are research findings that suggest that pretend play with siblings may affect later understanding of others' feelings (Youngblade & Dunn, 1995). Scripts from everyday activities are also useful, such as taking the bus, requesting toys, and making purchases, for example, especially for providing information from children with social deficits (Chapman, 2000). Indeed, the use of social scripts suggests that even when children may be undiagnosed, clinicians have tools available to guide their entry to children's internal states. Natural language samples acquired from social interaction contexts provide rich sources of information for detailing children's emerging language skills and the nature of the internal state cognitions that can be represented by the language. For clinicians, the implications for involving families in both assessment and treatment processes are clear in attempting to understand a child's internal state language and experience.

Since children spend a great deal of their time at home, the communicative environment of the family affects several aspects of internal state language acquisition. For example, we know that the number of times a child is spoken to on a daily basis can have dramatic effects on subsequent production vocabulary and rate of syntactic development, and a family's socioeconomic status is one critical determinant of the amount a child is spoken to over the first four years of life. In fact, children from low-income families are generally exposed to fewer spoken utterances than other children. More specifically, some of this research indicates that children from low-income families hear about 12 million utterances across a full developmental period, while those in working-class families hear about 28 million, and those in high-income, professional families hear about 48 million utterances. Given the disparity in exposure to language and the importance of language as a mediator for internal state, children from disadvantaged environments are less likely to have the range and depth of descriptors for representations of internal state processes, and this will be true across each developmental period. In turn, clinicians must consider the socioeconomic context of their clients as a potential limitation of the ability to fully utilize internal state processes as a window into the child's experience.

Clearly, the overwhelming differences in parental input contribute to the rate of development of language comprehension, production, and even verbal IQ, all of which dictate children's internal state representations across developmental periods. Family and social partners are therefore important contributors to emerging internal state abilities and the conditions that limit or facilitate their functions.

Caregiver Interaction

Parent-child conversation likely provides the most salient opportunity for children to learn and practice talking about their own internal states as well as the internal states of others. Here we discuss the effects of parental influence on children's internal state communication, but it is important to keep in mind that most of our knowledge reflects mothers' behavior and perspectives. We do not yet know whether the processes by which fathers influence children's internal state language and their respective effects will be similar or distinct.

With respect to basic cognitive ability, verbal IQ may be among the most important facets for internal state, as it represents skills in both basic cognitive functioning and the ability to use language to represent critical constructs or concepts. Three important factors have typically been identified to account for a large percentage of verbal IQ differences: the amount of parent participation with children, parents' performance as a social partner, and the qualitative content of parents' utterances. The quality of content includes language diversity, feedback tone, symbolic emphasis, guidance style, and responsiveness to the child.

EXAMPLE

As parents, we are often attending to the cues that our children are providing about their internal states. We are incredibly curious to know what's going on in their heads: What are they thinking? Are they upset? What's behind that mischievous smile? Typically, we give some context for exploring our child's internal state: "You're frowning ... what are you thinking about?" "You have a far away, pensive look on your face ... what is on your mind?" This encourages our child to not only attend to internal state experience, but to express that state. And despite the fact that our questions to children about internal states are often met with little more than "nothin'" as a response, it is important to continue to show an interest in the child's response and to be patient. Sometimes, the reward is a rich understanding of the complexity of our children's experience.

It seems apparent that certain patterns of parent-child communicative interaction result in faster language acquisition for children and, therefore, earlier emergence of ISL. These include increasing the frequency of appropriate language *modeling* (e.g., effectively using language to model appropriate uses), recasting the child's utterances in new forms (e.g., correcting grammatical errors with correct linguistic forms), expanding on the child's semantic and grammatical range (e.g., using forms that expand children's abilities to the next developmental level or near the top of their zone of proximal development), following the child's lead on topics and actions, and requesting that the child imitate an uttered word (Chapman, 2000).

EXAMPLE

Sonja was just picked up by her mom from a birthday party. She says, "The funny clown runned around!" Her mom responds, "He ran around? What did he do while he ran around?" Sonja, jumping up and down, shrieks, "He ran around with balloons and blowed them!" Mom responded, "Oh, he blew up balloons for all the kids? Did he make shapes?" Sonja said, "Yeah. He blew up funny animal shapes!" Sonja is learning to use verbs correctly and elaborate on details from her mother's responses.

As parents hold conversations with their children, their style of interaction evolves as the child gains new skills for thinking about the world. They expose their children to internal state language in several ways. They often include events that brought about certain emotional reactions in the child, positive or negative (Burch, Austin, & Bauer, 2004). In addition, conversations include how the child has felt in relation to time (the past vs. present) (Burch et al., 2004) as well as the internal states of a certain person (self vs. other) (Bretherton & Beeghly, 1982). Mothers speak more about desires (e.g. "You want milk") when the child is younger, while more talk regarding beliefs emerges as the child reaches near age 3 (e.g., "I think the ball is over there"). In addition, when mothers use desire language at early ages, children tend to use mental state language more often and perform better on emotion tasks given at later ages. This indicates that desire language used by mothers helps children express internal mental experiences through a sort of "emotional scaffolding." Further, mother talk that refers to others' thoughts earlier in the child's life (by about two years old) increases the likelihood that he or she will demonstrate an understanding of the idea of self versus other by three years of age (Taumoepeau & Ruffman, 2008).

The importance of the quality of the early parent-child relationship is hard to ignore, which raises the issue of attachment security, a developmental benchmark important for children to generate more diverse internal state language. Children who have more secure attachments to their parents produce more words that reflect positive emotion, ability, morals, and cognition. Secure children also utter more negative emotion vocabulary than insecure children at 17 and 23 months, and fewer negative words than insecure (at 30 months) and disorganized children (36 months). Similarly, connectedness is also associated with more mother-child conversations about emotions and with children's social understanding (Ensor & Hughes, 2008).

Nonetheless, it is important to remember that parents play an integral role in teaching their children that other people have their own thoughts through their conversations about internal states. From a very young age, children are filtering meaning through what they believe other people are thinking, which includes their beliefs, objects of their attention, and their intended goals (Chapman, 2000). Clearly, there is a strong influence of parental conversation upon a child's knowledge and attention to his or her internal states and his or her subsequent awareness of emotional understanding and expression.

EXAMPLE

Bobby picks up a book and shows it to his mother. She glances up from the TV and flashes a brief smile. When she doesn't respond to him, he says, "I'm going to read a book to you!" Mom says, "OK." He opens the book and starts reading, "Once upon a time there was a p ... pr ...," stuck on a word. Mom keeps watching but says, "Try again." Frustrated,

Bobby brings the book to his dad. In contrast to his mom's response, Bobby's dad becomes animated and says, "Oh, I love that book! Is this your favorite?" Bobby responds, "Yep I love it." Then Dad asks, "Do you think you can you read it all by yourself? Give it a try." This time when Bobby trips over the word again, his dad encourages him, "Sound it out. Prin-cess. Great job! What happens next?" While Bobby missed out on the interaction and support he wanted from his mom, this brief time with his dad provided him with a social opportunity to learn to discuss his likes, expand his language, and judge his abilities.

Clinical Implications

There is a great deal that can be learned from studying children with specific impairments in comprehension and communication skills. Disorders that affect only certain aspects of communicating about internal states help to illustrate the ways that children develop skills needed to use language to describe their thoughts, beliefs, and emotions. These conditions are likely to have genetic, neurobiological, and psychological origins, and shed light on processes that interfere with understanding internal states as well as the language skills needed to communicate them. In this section, we discuss several types of disorders that address various questions regarding the ways that children engage in internal state communication.

Developmental Language Impairments

The range of what is considered to be normative language development is quite large. Consequently, what might appear to be language delays or language impairments may fall within the typical range of children's language use at various developmental periods (see Chapter 2 for a more comprehensive review of basic language development). Many children experience difficulties with acquisition of expressive vocabulary, syntax, morphology, or phonological awareness in reading and spelling, each of which can undermine the formation of skills necessary to establish accurate and detailed internal state understandings. However, language disorders do not necessarily affect cognitive development as a whole. For instance, children with apraxia, a motor disorder characterized by poor language production, still demonstrate a strong grasp of representational thought by using gestures and showing comprehension to others' speech (Downey et al., 2002). Children with congenital deafness also appear to understand emotional expression. In a study by Hosie, Gray, Russell, and Hunter (2004), deaf children performed comparably well in identifying emotional expressions in faces compared to children with intact hearing. The authors suggest that this may be possible due to children's heightened attention to nonverbal cues as compensation for an inability to rely on spoken communication. Therefore, children with hearing impairments can develop similar internal state processes as children with intact hearing. Moreover, while language is clearly an important tool for learning to think about one's internal states, the inability to speak does not necessarily interfere with all aspects of internal state communication and understanding.

When Children Aren't Talking

Often clinicians encounter children who, for a variety of reasons, do not want to talk about how they feel. Should there be concern about the child's cognitive development as a result of this language inhibition? Children with selective mutism (SM), which is characterized by children (more often females) who withhold speech in social situations despite physical capability, are often diagnosed upon entering school. Some of the symptoms and associated features most often reported include shyness, mother-child enmeshment and interdependence, anxiety disorders, and the occurrence of traumatic incidences within the first three years (Anstendig, 1999). In the DSM-IV (American Psychiatric Association, 2000), SM is classified under "other disorders of infancy, childhood, and adolescence," but some psychologists argue that there is evidence that SM would be best classified as an anxiety disorder. Despite these questions, the fact remains that children with SM demonstrate symptoms related to their language development, with research indicating that these children's narratives are shorter and less linguistically complex than those of other children (McInnes, Fung, Manassis, Fiksenbaum, & Tannock, 2004). Based upon these findings, it is reasonable to speculate that SM children may also demonstrate impaired internal state comprehension and production (aspects of their emotion understanding). This potential deficit suggests that clinicians working with these children may not be able to make typical age-relevant inferences about internal state. It is therefore important for clinicians to consider this in working with SM children.

Developmental Disorders

Children with developmental disabilities often have trouble forming an understanding of mental states (including internal states) compared to typically developing children. While children with developmental disorders do not always display language difficulties, issues with language development may be present and vary across conditions. For example, children with autism have difficulty taking on the perspective of another person in order to understand their thoughts and feelings, even when they are highly functioning and verbally fluent (Ciccetti, Rogosch, Maughan, Toth, & Bruce, 2003). This observation suggests that autism is associated with specific neurobiological anomalies that result in impaired ability to represent internal states as well as many of the other known impairments characteristic of autism. Research has also revealed that mothers do not engage in conversations reflecting on their own and others' mental states when their child has autism, most likely because the children do not respond to such a communication style. The extent to which children on the autistic spectrum are aware of and comprehend internal states, either mental or emotional, is not entirely well understood, but the key deficits associated with functioning on the spectrum place children at risk for deficits in internal state awareness.

It is important to note, however, that communicative skills alone are not a sufficient basis on which to judge internal state function or ability. Some children with autistic spectrum disorder (ASD), and even some children who are typically developing, may be quite articulate but lack a foundational understanding in emotional and social domains critical for internal state awareness.

In addition, children with Down syndrome experience difficulty forming effective theory of mind, although this difficulty is not as severe as that found in autism. Given the known impairments with abstract thought and general cognitive ability, self-reflection through metacognition is difficult, and these difficulties can be seen in proportionally less use of internal state language. Interestingly, however, Down syndrome children appear to use a higher proportion of affective words, but fewer words about volition, ability, and cognition, compared to typically developing children (Ciccetti et al., 2003). In this light, it is noteworthy that mothers of children with Down syndrome use fewer (and a smaller variety of) internal state words, which may contribute to the children's lower use as well. In contrast, children with mental retardation of undifferentiated etiology exhibit fewer impairments in internal state language use and are more successful in completing theory of mind tasks than children with Down syndrome (Ciccetti et al., 2003). Thus there seems to be some specificity to the features that are associated with both Down syndrome and autism, and these features may affect awareness and understanding of internal states. What seems clear is that disorders are not uniform in their effects on internal state understanding and expression, requiring clinicians to attend to the particulars of the disorder under consideration.

Maltreatment

Maltreatment is of great concern to clinicians, not only for the physical and psychological well-being of the child, but also because of the wide array of developmental difficulties that are also associated with such disruptive and harmful contexts. Parenting styles in such homes are often characterized by chaos, chronic stress, disorganization, and less overall empathy and child sensitivity. The result is that children in maltreating homes have difficulty predicting how parents will act from situation to situation and confusion over emotional expression by parents (Ciccetti et al., 2003). In addition, maltreated children often have difficulty developing effective internal state comprehension and theory of mind, which are likely a function of the more frequent insecure attachments that are formed with care providers and deficits in internal state language between the child and caregivers. We have noted earlier how critical attachment security is to children's internal states and the working models they form about themselves, their caregivers, and the world. Children with insecure attachments are at risk not only for compromised internal state development, but more negative cognitive and emotional internal state functions.

Internal state awareness and false belief understanding (see Chapter 6) share some critical cognitive underpinnings, and maltreatment has shown some informative associations with both children's false belief understanding and internal state awareness. Maltreated children exhibit impaired theory of mind in false belief tasks and also experience deficits in internal state language. Further, physical abuse seems to be particularly harmful to the development of both false belief understanding and children's perspective-taking ability (see Chapter 5). A number of factors are believed to be the cause for such effects, including parenting style, psychological intimidation, and even neuroanatomical changes that occur over time as a result of maltreatment, especially when it occurs early in life. In fact, there is evidence that children with physical abuse, sexual abuse, or a combination of three types of maltreatment are most likely to have irregularities in brain structure and function (Ciccetti et al., 2003) that underlie these critical cognitive abilities. These findings demonstrate that the pervasive effects of child maltreatment may extend to the development of children's communications about internal states. These difficulties understanding the thoughts, feelings, and beliefs of themselves and others may lead to impaired social skills and functioning across childhood and into adulthood.

Conclusions

An internal state, whether cognitive or emotional, provides a critical frame of reference by which children both understand their world and may be understood by the world. Language or communicative skills form the basis for the development of these internal states, and the ties between cognition and language are instrumental in the development of children's awareness of internal state and their eventual understanding of internal state (their own as well as others). Internal state awareness and understanding are critical features of clinical process and are often the explicit targets of clinical practice. This makes understanding the nature, development, and role of cognition and language in the formation and function of internal states a valuable aid to clinicians and educators working with children across a variety of professional settings.

References

Adrian, J. E., Clemente, R. A., Villanueva, L., & Rieffe, C. (2005). Parent-child picture-book reading, mothers' mental state language and children's theory of mind. *Journal of Child Language, 32*, 673–686.

American Psychiatric Association. (2000). *Diagnostic and statistical manual of mental disorders* (4th ed. rev.). Washington, DC: Author.

Anstendig, K. D. (1999). Is selective mutism an anxiety disorder? Rethinking its DSM classification. *Journal of Anxiety Disorders, 13*, 417–434.

Booth, J. R., Hall, W. S., Robison, G. C., & Kim, S. Y. (1997). Acquisition of the mental state verb know by 2- to 5-year-old children. *Journal of Psycholinguistic Research, 26*, 581–603.

Bretherton, I., & Beeghly, M. (1982). Talking about internal states: The acquisition of an explicit theory of mind. *Developmental Psychology, 18*, 906–921.

Burch, M. M., Austin, J., & Bauer, P. J. (2004). Understanding the emotional past: Relations between parent and child contributions in emotionally negative and nonnegative events. *Journal of Experimental Child Psychology, 89*, 276–297.

Chapman, R. S. (2000). Children's language learning: An interactionist perspective. *Journal of Child Psychology and Psychiatry, 41*, 33–54.

Ciccetti, D., Rogosch, F. A., Maughan, A., Toth, S. L., & Bruce, J. (2003). False belief understanding in maltreated children. *Development and Psychopathology, 15*, 1067–1091.

Downey, D., Mraz, R., Knott, J., Knutson, C., Lenore, H., & van Dyke, D. (2002). Diagnosis and evaluation of children who are not talking. *Infants and Young Children, 15*, 38–48.

Dunn, J., Bretherton, I., & Munn, P. (1987). Conversations about feeling states between mothers and their young children. *Developmental Psychology, 23*, 132–139.

Ensor, R., & Hughes, C. (2008). Content or connectedness? Mother-child talk and early social understanding. *Child Development, 79*, 201–216.

Hosie, J. A., Gray, C. D., Russell, P. A., & Hunter, N. (2004). The matching of facial expressions by deaf and hearing children and their production and comprehension of emotion labels. *Motivation and Emotion, 22*, 293–313.

Lazarus, R. S. (1984). On the primacy of cognition. *American Psychologist, 39*, 124–129.

MacRory, G. (2001). Language development: What do early years practitioners need to know? *Early Years: Journal of International Research and Development, 21*, 33–40.

Markus, H. R., & Kitayama, S. (1991). Culture and the self: Implications for cognition, emotion, and motivation. *Psychological Review, 98*, 224–253.

McCabe, A., & Peterson, C. (1991). *Developing narrative structure*. Hillsdale, NJ: Lawrence Erlbaum Associates.

McInnes, A., Fung, D., Manassis, K., Fiksenbaum, L., & Tannock, R. (2004). Narrative skills in children with selective mutism: An exploratory study. *American Journal of Speech-Language Pathology, 13*, 304–315.

Nature Publishing Group. (2008). *Nature reviews neuroscience: Glossary*. Retrieved September 24, 2008, from http://www.nature.com/nrn/journal/v1/n1/glossary/nrn1000_059a_glossary.html

Pascual, B., Aguado, G., Sotillo, M., & Masdeu, J. C. (2008). Acquisition of mental state language in Spanish children: A longitudinal study of the relationship between the production of mental verbs and linguistic development. *Developmental Science, 11*, 454–466.

Pons, F., Lawson, J., Harris, P., & deRosney, M. (2003). Individual differences in children's emotion understanding: Effects of age and language. *Scandinavian Journal of Psychology, 44*, 347–353.

Taumoepeau, M., & Ruffman, T. (2008). Stepping stones to others' minds: Maternal talk relates to child mental state language and emotion understanding at 15, 24, and 33 months. *Child Development, 79*, 284–302.

Vallotton, C. D. (2008). Signs of emotion: What can preverbal children "say" about internal states? *Infant Mental Health Journal, 29,* 234–258.

Youngblade, L. M., & Dunn, J. (1995). Individual differences in young children's pretend play with mother and sibling: Links to relationships and understanding of other people's feelings and beliefs. *Child Development, 66,* 1472–1492.

Zajonc, R. B. (1980). Feeling and thinking: Preferences need no inferences. *American Psychologist, 35,* 151–175.

Zajonc, R. B. (1984). On the primacy of affect. *American Psychologist, 39,* 117–123.

4

General Guidelines for Talking With Children

SARAHBETH GOLDEN

A clinician can help a child to the extent that he or she understands that child's subjective concerns. The interview is one way clinicians get to know their young clients. In conversing with a child, an interviewer hopes to hear about the child's experienced events and interpretations of those events. The goal of most clinical interviews is to assess the child's needs as well as his or her cognitive and emotional processes. What makes one interview more useful than another? While an interview's quality is related to the amount of information the child shares, the accuracy/reliability of what is shared is just as, if not more, important. How can a clinician elicit the most reliable information from a young interviewee? What steps can a clinician take to maximize the likelihood that a child understands the interviewer? And to what extent can a clinician trust that a child's report is reliable? Knowing what to expect from the young interviewee—the child's cognitive capabilities and limitations, as well as the child's *own* expectations for the interview—will give a clinician some necessary tools for conducting a useful interview.

Through their own interactions with parents at home and teachers at school, children are primed to have certain expectations regarding conversations with adults. A typical conversation between a child and an adult has two main characteristics: the adult has the directive role, and the adult knows the answers. This dynamic is referred to as adult-to-child language (ACL; Poole & Lamb, 1998), and children come to expect that adults will lead the way in conversations. Thus, children may be reluctant participants in an interview, and base the information they share on what they believe the adult expects to hear. Children may also "be on the lookout" for any cues from an adult about what might be the correct response to a question or comment. It is a novel experience indeed when a child is faced with determining the course of a conversation! The child will most likely look to the interviewer for "game rules" on how to approach the situation. Orienting the child to the interview process, in addition to establishing rapport, is an important first step.

Starting Off: Orienting to the Interview

As mentioned previously, children typically look to adults to guide a conversation. This phenomenon will be apparent in an interview as well. It is common for children to wait and watch *you* for cues regarding what this interview business is all about. Interviewers should take care to avoid "running the show," however, because a perceived lack of control can inhibit a child's disclosure (Steward & Steward, 1996). It is essential to first orient the child to the interviewing experience. This involves introducing yourself, calling the child by name, explaining your role, and emphasizing the child's role in giving the interviewer information (rather than the other way around). This takes *time*. Children are more responsive to adults who attempt to communicate on the child's level. This includes using developmentally appropriate language and sentence structure, being aware of a child's understanding of abstract concepts (which is very limited; lean toward being more concrete), and even manipulating your use of physical space and body posture (e.g., sitting or lying on the floor, or entering a child's fantasy play world). Many children won't be ready to talk right away. Interviewers should use the child's reticence as an opportunity to watch and listen—don't command the child to converse with you. An example of entering the child's world before starting an interview was provided in an interaction I had with four-year-old Liam, whose plans did not involve talking with me:

EXAMPLE

Liam was sitting in his room playing with his trains.

Me:	Liam, can I see Marlin? (*Marlin is Liam's new pet fish.*)
Liam:	No.
Me:	Oh, but I was hoping to meet him.
Liam:	He's busy right now.
Me:	Okay. Could you tell me when he's ready for a visitor?
Liam:	Yeah.

About five minutes pass; I quietly watch Liam continue with his trains.

Liam:	Okay.
Me:	He's ready now?
Liam:	Yeah.

Some interviewers use drawing or play in the initial phases of an interview to help the child become comfortable. The literature seems split on the utility of this approach; therapeutic interviewers, in an effort to build rapport, may allow a child to draw while talking, while forensic interviewing experts have expressed concern that young children could be distracted from the interview if they simultaneously draw and speak (Poole & Lamb, 1998). The *purpose* of allowing/encouraging a child to draw is important here; are you helping the child become more comfortable with you and the interview process, or are you looking for information to be shared through the drawing? Drawing can be a helpful warm-up for a child, facilitating his or her comfort with you. It could even help start some rapport-building conversation:

EXAMPLE

Interviewer:	What's that?
Child:	A bunny.
Interviewer:	Oh, I see it!
Child:	Yeah, I made some big ears!
Interviewer:	Wow those ears *are* big! That bunny must hear every-thing! What other animals do you like?
Child:	Dogs! I have a dog at home! My sister named him Brownie!

Some interviewers encourage children to draw or play while relaying a narrative in an effort to increase the amount of information shared by the child. The rationale here is that children are limited in their linguistic and cognitive ability, and they may be more likely to *show* an interviewer their experience than *tell* about it. At the same time, a child's free play may not be a form of communication (with you, anyway). Interpreting a child's drawing or play opens the door for errors due to the subjective nature of such interpretations. You may have a hunch about the cause of a child's problem, for example, and be on the lookout for "evidence" supporting that hunch. The risk here is that you may interpret some clinical issue that isn't really there. Take this example:

EXAMPLE

Three-year-old Abby is playing with a dollhouse. You notice that she has put the brother doll and sister doll up on the dollhouse roof, while the mother and father doll have been stuffed under the sofa. You know that Abby's mother and father have been having marital problems.

You:	Oh, the brother and sister are up on the roof. What are they doing up there?
Abby:	Playing.

| *You:* | And, how about the mommy and daddy? Where are they? |
| *Abby:* | They're at work. They have to work all the time and don't ever have time to play with them. |

You formulate a clinical picture in your head of Abby and her relationship with her parents. As you make a mental list of questions to ask Abby's parents, you suddenly notice that Abby has started singing to herself:

| *Abby:* | Chim Chimminy Chim Chimminy Chim Chim Cheree … |

As it turns out, Abby watched Mary Poppins the day before your meeting. It is a Thanksgiving tradition in her family—after dinner, the whole family sits down to watch it together.

I have observed my friend Liam crash trains together, "drown" a genie in the bathtub, and hide Cinderella under a pile of blankets. In addition to having a vivid imagination, Liam also loves to recreate scenes from his favorite movies. It's doubtful that these recreations are his attempts at communicating something to me other than his enthusiasm for these movies. It is definitely more developmentally appropriate for him to convey his enjoyment this way than by giving me a verbal Roger Ebert-style review of his favorite movies. Playing comes a bit easier to my four-year-old friend than conversation.

Children's Language Limitations

Around 18 months of age, children display a dramatic increase in vocabulary known as the word spurt (Benedict, 1979). Despite this giant growth in vocabulary, children may not always know the meanings of the words they're saying, or they may know the meaning but struggle with correct pronunciation of a word. It is common for an adult to misunderstand a child due to errors in that child's pronunciation (particularly children with whom the adult rarely interacts). In an interview, mistaking one word for another can lead the conversation down an irrelevant, confusing, or erroneous path. For example, a child may say, "I saw a bicycle," and the adult hears, "I saw a popsicle!" In day-to-day conversation, this misunderstanding may provide an amusing story, but in an interview the ramifications could be more serious; the focus of an interview may shift according to how the word or phrase was perceived. Without being aware of it, the interviewer can change the course of the interview based on a misunderstood word or phrase. A great example of this was provided by one of the editors of this book; it took place during her daughter's visit to the family doctor.

EXAMPLE

Liliana (age 4) talking to the pediatrician at a routine physical.

Pediatrician: So Liliana, have you been a healthy girl lately?

Liliana: Well, yes, mostly. I had to spend some time with the nurse because of my ear whack.

Pediatrician: Your ear whack?

Liliana: It hurt so bad and I couldn't even hear right. It was all Dad's fault.

Pediatrician: It was your dad's fault?

Liliana: It was! He couldn't tip it right.

Pediatrician is now confused and totally engaged in the line of questioning. It takes several more exchanges plus a bit of maternal help to decode: "Ear whack" is the singular form of "ear wax," which caused suffering in one ear as a perceived result of failed parental Q-tip intervention.

A few simple steps can help an interviewer avoid this dilemma. First, note any difficulties the child has with pronunciation during initial, rapport-building conversations. Second, identify (and write down phonetically) any questionable word uttered, rather than assuming that it sounded "close enough" to your interpretation. You should *not* suggest a specific interpretation to the child, since children often go along with adults' interpretations (Poole & Lamb, 1998). Next, follow up with a clarifying question, asking the child to either repeat the word or say what they know about it. You'll find that what a child understands and what a child expresses are two different things; children are typically able to understand more than they can articulate. This is demonstrated when an adult mimics a child's pronunciation, only to be corrected by the child. An example of this occurred in an interaction with my five-year-old nephew, Gavin.

EXAMPLE

Gavin: (*appearing upset*) He broke my chip!

Me: That's okay, you can still eat it!

Gavin: No! He *broke* it!

Me: He broke your chip?

Gavin: No!!! My ch-i-i-i-i-p!

(Gavin's mother translated that he was upset because his toy jeep was broken.)

An interviewer may also discover semantic differences between one's own understanding and a child's understanding of a word. Each may use the same word but mean different things. For example, a child may complain that his head hurts when experiencing a toothache. Or, an interviewer may inquire about whether a child was touched, but the child understands *touch* to only involve contact with someone else's hands (Poole & Lamb, 1998). It is also common for children to "overextend" their words well into their grade school years (Fabes & Martin, 2000). An error of overextension involves referring to something with a word that is outside the realm of that object's true meaning. For example, a child may describe seeing a man wave a *stick* in the air until his mother explains that the man was a magician waving a magic *wand*. Another language error commonly committed by children involves the use of words that carry double meanings. A six-year-old only considers the word *warm* to refer to temperature, and is not aware that it can also be an emotional disposition. It isn't until age 11 or so that children can both comprehend and correctly utilize words with double (or triple) meanings. Interviewers should not assume that a young interviewee grasps the "adult meaning" of words used in their conversation. It is best to choose words that generally have just one meaning, and in the event of confusion, follow up with the child to clarify what he or she means when saying _____. Children can also be confused by adults' use of idioms, largely due to children's tendency to interpret statements literally. Piaget pointed out that children under age 8 (and sometimes up to age 11) have difficulty understanding abstract ideas and rely on concrete interpretations of statements. Interviewers should avoid using idioms for this reason. An amusing example of this took place in an interaction between my Aunt Ann and my younger brother when he was six years old.

EXAMPLE

Aunt Ann had just arrived in town for a visit; she hadn't seen us for close to a year.

Ann: Garrett! Look at you! You've grown a foot!
Garrett: (*looking down in a panic*) What?! I have not!

The adults found this wildly funny. Garrett did not see the humor, and I actually recall not getting it either (I was probably 9).

A common interview goal is to seek information regarding when certain events took place. Depending on their age, children can have great difficulty providing accurate timelines due to their limited understanding of temporal terms. For example, two-year-olds have a hard time distinguishing between yesterday, today, and tomorrow, while three-year-olds know that yesterday is simply "not today" (Poole & Lamb, 1998). Meanwhile, four-year-old children may understand the difference between yesterday and tomorrow, but may say an event that took place one week ago happened "last year." In general, children have a limited understanding of temporal terms until about age 8. Poole and Lamb encourage interviewers to select an event that is salient to a child (birthday, Halloween, etc.) as a "bookmark" for time orientation. Although this can help narrow down the time frame for an event, one problem with this is that the younger the child is, the more difficulty he or she has with concepts such as *before* and *after*.

While care should be given to word choice in an interview, adults must also attend to limitations in a child's syntactic understanding. Syntax refers to word order and "voice" used in sentences. A typical pattern of speech observed in children is subject-verb-object, such as: "The boy drank the juice." Meanwhile, adults tend to use more complex sentence constructions, and may frame questions in a passive voice: "Did you get hit with a block?" Using a passive voice can confuse a child. Many children could respond to this block question with a resounding no, interpreting it as if *they* had performed the hitting. Children do not achieve full understanding of the passive voice until about ages 10 to 13 (Poole & Lamb, 1998).

EXAMPLE

Gavin, my five-year-old nephew, was once outraged when he thought I sympathized with his dog (Tucker) rather than with him following an accidental injury. Gavin and Tucker had been playing outside when one of Tucker's toenails scraped Gavin's arm. Gavin ran into the house crying.

Gavin:	Ow! He stabbed me!
Me:	Oh no! Did you get scraped by Tucker?
Gavin:	(*furious*) No!! Tucker scraped *me*!

Due to my use of the passive voice, poor Gavin assumed I was taking the dog's side.

Due to children's limited ability to understand complex sentence structure, the passive voice, or even basic vocabulary, interviewers are encouraged to keep their questions as simple as possible. It is also essential to be aware of children's attention limitations. Interviewers do not have a guarantee that children (or adults for that matter) pay attention to details in experienced events. Unfortunately, many interviewers feel pressed for time and embed several questions within one sentence or string several questions together.

For example: "Were you there when John spilled the milk? Was it after you got home from school, and did anyone else see it too?" Questions like this are confusing to children, who frequently still offer a response in an effort to be helpful: "Yes!" This hypothetical exchange would leave most interviewers confused as well, or worse yet, convinced that the child saw John spill the milk after school, along with at least one other witness! Keep your questions simple, ask one question at a time, and *wait* for the child's response.

Children's Narratives

A personal narrative is an account or story of one's experience with an event or set of events. The hallmarks of a good narrative include accuracy, completeness, and consistency across time (Steward & Steward, 1996). Adults typically will supply all sorts of details about their experiences if asked to simply "tell about the time when you...." Due to the ongoing nature of child cognitive development, young interviewees are far less likely to volunteer many details, or to offer a coherent and organized narrative. In addition, depending on the nature of questioning and the age of the child, his or her narratives are open to error. However, this does not mean that children cannot be reliable reporters of their experience. Interviewers must be aware of the extent to which a child's report can be influenced by the frequency and ways that questions are framed, the length of time between an event and the interview, and the child's expectations for the interview.

An adult's (and an older child's) personal narrative is generally story-like, with a beginning, middle, and an end, a protagonist, and possibly an antagonist. Additionally, adults' personal narratives often include spatial-temporal information (whether the event occurred before/after another event); a social context, for instance who else was present; and evaluative information, such as why the event is important/meaningful (Haden, Haine, & Fivush, 1997). In contrast, young children's narratives do not typically contain all of these elements, making their stories somewhat skeletal or incomplete. Young children, especially those under age 6, have a harder time offering sequential accounts of their experience, and they tend to rely on adults to keep them focused on the topic/event. By the school age years, children volunteer more information in their narratives, because their memory is more advanced, their language is more sophisticated, and they have more experience with storytelling (hearing stories and telling them).

EXAMPLE

The differences between preschool and school age narratives can be seen in the joint storytelling of two siblings, Zach, age 8, and Dylan, age 4.

Dylan:	(*to Mom*) Do you 'member when Zach broke his head on his bed?
Zach:	I didn't *break* my head; I just *cut* my head. I fell when I was jumping on my bed.
Mom:	Of course I remember. Do *you* remember what happened, Dylan?
Dylan:	No.
Mom:	Do you remember *when* it was?
Dylan:	It was last year.
Zach:	No it wasn't! It was during the summer. When the men were painting our house. What month was that Mom?
Mom:	August. Good remembering! (*To Dylan*) Do you remember what happened next?
Dylan:	Zach bleeded and had to go to the hospital.
Zach:	Yeah … they put three staples in my head. They had to stay there for a whole week. It really hurt when they took them out.

As demonstrated in the example above, preschool age children are likely to need a series of guided questions ("Who was there?" "What did they do next?" "How did you feel after that?" "Where was your brother?") to provide a complete account of a specific event. Unfortunately, the younger the child is, the more difficulty he or she may have with responding to an adult's attempts to draw out a personal narrative due to other developmental limitations in children's perspective taking (see Chapter 5) and memory (see Chapters 7 and 8). Although these topics are covered in greater detail elsewhere, in light of the relevance of this issue for children's interviewing, the remainder of the chapter is devoted to some of the most common challenges with guided interviewing and suggestions for minimizing sources of interviewing error.

Topic Drift

It is common for children under six years old to struggle with *event recognition*, or knowing which event is being discussed. Some children, in responding to general queries, will offer answers that don't relate to the event in question. It is difficult for children to focus on a conversation; they are easily distracted and often can't discriminate between important and unimportant information (Lane & Pearson, 1982). In addition, children are probably aware that the adult interviewer expects a response, so they'll comply by giving one—regardless of its relevance. An alert interviewer will refer to the event frequently to keep the child on track.

Another related source of interviewing error is a result of young children's tendency to "topic drift." Topic drift refers to an unannounced shift in focus within one topic of conversation, common among children ages 4 and younger (Poole & Lamb, 1998). Problems may arise when a topic drift is so subtle, it leads the interviewer down an inaccurate/irrelevant path (and also results in the interviewer assuming the child is an unreliable reporter).

EXAMPLE

Me: How did you get that boo-boo on your back, Liam?
Liam: I don't know.
Me: You don't know what happened to your back?
Liam: I fell down at Daddy's house.
Me: Oh no! How did that happen?
Liam: At daycare!
Me: You fell down at daycare?
Liam: Yeah! And I get to see Mickey Mouse for Halloween!!

Liam had indeed fallen down at his father's house. Pursuing a line of questioning about Liam's daycare could have led to a narrative full of inaccuracies and confusion on both our parts (I later found out that Liam was excited about seeing Mickey Mouse at daycare for a Halloween treat). Another source of confusion can be found in children's frequent inability to understand the difference between their experience and someone else's.

Self-Other Differentiation

A good story involves knowing one's audience, and communicating that story within the confines of that audience's ability. Doing this requires differentiating one's own experience from another's. Children begin developing a sense of separateness from their caregivers as early as 15 months (Mahler, 1967), eventually leading to an understanding of the subjective nature of personal experience. Piaget (1960) proposed that young children's speech is egocentric, and they cannot take into consideration others' perspectives. Departing from egocentric thought and fully understanding that his or her experience is separate and unique from others' comes much later, perhaps as late as the elementary school years. When giving an account of their experiences, young children are likely to assume that if they understand what they're saying, so will a listener. For this reason, young children are often unaware when their message is inadequate or confusing to their audience (Steward & Steward, 1996). This phenomenon is observed regularly in children ages 4 and younger (Bjorklund, 2005), but can happen to even the most articulate first graders.

EXAMPLE

Aiden:	Mom, can you download that song from school?
Mother:	What song from school?
Aiden:	The one that I liked.
Mother:	I need more information than that. What song was it that you liked?
Aiden:	The one about Argentina.
Mother:	Ummm ... Argentina? Can you sing it for me?
Aiden:	No, but Mrs. Canava can.
Mother:	Who is Mrs. Canava? Someone who visited your class?
Aiden:	No. The substitute art teacher.
Mother:	And she taught your class a song about Argentina?
Aiden:	No.
Mother:	(*breathes deep*) Can you tell me any of the words?
Aiden:	It's about Argentina. People don't cry there.

The back-story: Aiden overheard two teachers singing lyrics from Evita while his class was waiting in line for admission to the music classroom.

Young children also have difficulty identifying or articulating when they themselves are confused! The ability to recognize when one is confused or confusing another requires the development of theory of mind, which develops over the course of several years, from preschool (age 3) into first grade and through the elementary school years. Theory of mind involves the understanding of inner mental events, acknowledging that people think, imagine, and wonder about the world around them (Fabes & Martin, 2000). Another way that children demonstrate theory of mind during interviewing or conversation is when they self-monitor their speech (Evans, 1985). Children as young as five years old will edit their statements—frequently mid-sentence. They may do this by adding details, making slight modifications, or repeating certain elements. This demonstrates the child's awareness that his or her message *could* be clearer to the audience, and his or her edits reflect his or her attempt to clarify and improve the message. Self-monitoring may sound a bit like this: "My dog ate it ... the turkey, my dog ate the turkey when nobody was looking! And he got mad, my dad got real mad at my dog when he ate it ... when my dog ate the turkey!"

Many times children's attempts to self-monitor speech come in reaction to observing a quizzical or confused look on the listener's face, thereby demonstrating an understanding that the listener's perspective differs from his or her own. Developing the understanding that others hold different perspectives of the same event is a fluid, ongoing process—it doesn't happen overnight (see Chapter 5). If we observe children self-monitoring their speech, we can assume that they have some perspective-taking abilities (albeit potentially limited). Self-monitoring speech should be heard with patience—wait for children to make their edits, and ask for clarification if necessary. If a child does *not* self-monitor speech, this does not necessarily mean that he or she is ignoring our cues, particularly if the speaker is a young child. It is more likely an indicator that the ability to take another's perspective is only beginning to develop. Deficiencies in perspective taking can certainly impact the quality of a narrative. Another significant contributor to narrative errors is memory—or rather, developmental limitations in memory.

Memory Errors

Another source of error during interviewing comes from the inability to monitor one's memory source (see Chapters 7 and 8). Source monitoring refers to knowing *how* one knows something, including the ability to differentiate between experiencing something from simply hearing about it. Preschool-aged children in particular struggle with this. Although some three-year-olds can distinguish between seeing an object and imagining it in their minds, they have great difficulty recognizing that imagined events do not reflect reality (Woolley & Wellman, 1993). In fact, asking a child to imagine an event introduces the possibility that, at a later date, the child will "remember" what they imagined as something that actually happened (Ceci, Huffman, Smith, & Loftus, 1994). Children up to six or seven years old regularly struggle with source monitoring, sometimes claiming to have done something when they only imagined doing it (Foley & Ratner, 1998).

To minimize source monitoring errors, interviewers should use open-ended rather than closed-ended questions. Questions like "Tell me more about _____" or "What happened?" reduce errors of source monitoring by allowing children to elaborate on their own experiences without the influence of the interviewer's perspective (however unintended). Research has shown that responses to open-ended questions tend to be more accurate than responses to specific questions, regardless of the interviewee's age (Dale, Loftus, & Rathbun, 1978; Hutcheson, Baxter, Telfer, & Warden, 1995). In fact, when open-ended techniques are used, there are no differences in the accuracy of accounts reported by very young children compared to adults (Fanetti & Boles, 2004). Additionally, a specific or closed question can imply to a child that there is one correct answer. In an effort to comply with the adult interviewer, young children may give the "answer" despite not knowing it—or even understanding the question (Poole & Lamb, 1998).

One drawback to using free recall with children is that young children tend to leave out important details (called *omission* errors); the younger the child, the less information he or she is likely to offer (Fanetti & Boles, 2004). After hearing a child's account, an interviewer may want to ask the child some more specific questions to give that child an opportunity to expand on the narrative. Remember, children (especially young children) have difficulty understanding that what they know does not always match what the listener knows. Young children also lack the cognitive skills to organize elements of an event, which contributes to their difficulty with providing detailed and cohesive accounts (Saywitz & Snyder, 1996). Asking some direct follow-up questions is one way to illuminate a child's experience.

Let's say four-year-old Annie has told you about seeing her brother Billy fall down while playing at the park, but she doesn't elaborate. You might try an open-ended question by requesting that she "Tell me how Billy fell down." Other open-ended prompts you could give Annie are: "Tell me everything you can about Billy falling" or "You said that Billy was crying. Tell me more about what happened."

You may consider using more specific questions to help Annie remember information about Billy's fall. For example, asking Annie, "Where was your mom when Billy fell?" or "Who else saw Billy fall?" could help Annie to provide more information. On the one hand, asking specific questions can assist retrieval from memory, but on the other hand, it can open the door for *commission* error, which involves adding an inaccurate detail or including an event, person, object, and so forth, that was not part of the original experience. Commission errors are particularly likely to occur if specific questions contain cues introduced by the interviewer *before* the child mentions them. Both of the specific questions above introduce "someone else" to the event. Annie may wrack her brain for other people she could put at the scene in response to the question "Who else saw Billy fall?" One result: Suddenly you're hearing about Aunt Susan and Mr. Thompson being present at the park as well.

Specific questions can therefore have similar results as *leading questions*, because they both increase the risk of commission errors. However, leading questions are different from specific questions, because they imply an answer, and they are even more likely to pull for inaccurate information. For example, you could ask Annie, "You pushed Billy by accident, didn't you" or "You felt sad after he started crying, huh?" Meanwhile, asking Annie, "What did you do to Billy after he fell?" is more specific than leading. In Chapter 9 you will find extensive recommendations about how to elicit information from children when accuracy is tantamount (e.g., in criminal investigations).

By posing questions that introduce new variables (people, places, actions), the interviewer increases the risk that the child integrates the cues into her narrative. When this happens, there is a risk that the cues change not only her story, but her memory for the event. Try to elicit information from a child first with an open-ended question, followed by more specific questions that build off the child's narrative: "You said that Billy shouted at you and grabbed his knee. Tell me more about what Billy did."

Interviewers may also be tempted to repeat questions multiple times throughout an interview, in an effort to maximize information obtained. Repeated questions also contribute to commission errors. With each repetition, the child may infer that he or she is giving incorrect or inadequate information (Steward & Steward, 1996). In an effort to comply with the interviewer, both preschoolers and elementary school-aged children may provide inaccurate information. Poole and Lamb (1998) point out that older children may add information they simply heard about in order to demonstrate their knowledge. For example, the child could offer something they heard from a parent, the interviewer, or he or she may even speculate on what *might* have happened. In addition, the more frequently one tells a story, the more open it is to confabulated or false memory—even in adults (Roediger, Wheeler, & Rjaram, 1993)! Because memory is largely a constructive process, each time a person shares a narrative, it is open for reconstruction (see Chapter 8).

A great deal of forensic research has been dedicated to understanding children's suggestibility (Kulkofsky & Klemfuss, 2008; Haden et al., 1997; Saywitz & Snyder, 1996; see Chapter 9). Even if an interviewer is not compiling information for legal purposes, it is still essential to be aware of conditions contributing to children's suggestibility. Children's suggestibility involves both cognitive and social factors (Poole & Lamb, 1998). Cognitive factors include the integration of inaccurate information due to source monitoring or memory errors. Social factors involve children providing information that they think the interviewer wants or expects. Many of these conditions (following a topic drift, introducing cues prematurely) could be committed unintentionally by an interviewer, and therefore require considerable self-discipline and self-monitoring. Interviewers need to be cognizant of their own behavior (i.e., whether their questions are neutral or leading) and of the developmental level of the young interviewee.

One empirically supported method of assisting children's narrative production comes in the form of Saywitz and Snyder's (1996) "narrative elaboration" procedure. In an effort to compensate for children's developmental limitations in memory and communication, this procedure uses reminder cards to help children structure their narratives. This innovative idea is based on the notion that children need to be *taught* how to organize event elements. In Saywitz and Snyder's study on the efficacy of this memory method, children were taught to include five categories when recalling an event: participants, setting, actions, conversation/affective states, and consequences. The authors used simple line drawings on cards, each depicting a different event category. After hearing the child's free recall response to the question "What happened?" the researchers presented each card and asked, "Does this card remind you to tell something else?" They found that training children in the use of generic visual cues and

basic interviewing procedures promoted more complete and accurate narratives. It seems that in teaching children how to access their memories in an
organized fashion, interviewers can facilitate the sharing of detailed, accurate
narratives, even with young children.

Interviewers may take direction from this study and employ a similar method for helping children organize and recall narratives. At the very
least, Saywitz and Snyder's work demonstrates strong evidence that children's narratives benefit from the introduction of an organizational structure.
Interviewers will benefit from showing children *how* to tell their stories; more
work done on the instructional "front end" of an interview is likely to result
in children providing fuller, more accurate narratives. While this method has
been validated by several recent studies (Camparo, Wagner, & Saywitz, 2001;
Dorado & Saywitz, 2001; Saywitz, Snyder, & Lamphear, 1996), other methods of employing props, such as anatomically detailed dolls and human figure
drawings, are a bit more controversial.

Using Props: Dolls and Drawings

Interviewers are all too familiar with the rather sparse narratives children provide on their own. Faced with the challenge of eliciting a complete and detailed
account, interviewers may integrate props into the interview process. The most
commonly used props, particularly when assessing for physical or sexual abuse,
are anatomically detailed (AD) dolls and human body drawings. Although there
is some evidence reflecting the utility of props, an increasing number of experts
are urging child interviewers to use caution when employing them.

A recent study with five- to seven-year-olds found that using human figure drawings to assess being touched led to an increase in erroneous reports
of touching (Brown, Pipe, Lewis, Lamb, & Orbach, 2007). The authors noted
that children offered false reports of touching, including those children who
had been instructed in how to use the drawings (i.e., by touching a child on
his elbow, then asking him to indicate the elbow on a human figure drawing). Brown et al. suggested that the children may have been responding to
demand characteristics; the children may have perceived that the interviewers expected to hear about the child being touched. A previous study using
figure drawings with younger children (ages 3 to 6) reported similar findings
(Steward & Steward, 1996). Poole and Lamb (1998) recommend only using
drawings after a child discloses being inappropriately touched. This advice is
extended to the use of dolls as well.

Children who have been abused often lack the vocabulary to provide
detailed descriptions of what happened to them. Many clinicians are tempted
to use anatomically detailed dolls to facilitate children's disclosure of sexual
abuse. Unfortunately, the use of these dolls can elicit more inaccurate accounts
than accurate ones. One reason for this is children do not grasp the concept
of dual representation; a child may not understand that the doll is supposed to

be a model for that child's body. Dual representation of objects can be difficult for children under age 5, and it is particularly hard for children three years old and younger (DeLoache & Marzolf, 1995).

Researchers have yet to develop or validate a method of interpreting children's interaction with AD dolls. One might assume that a child's spontaneous touching of an AD doll's genitals means that he or she has been touched that way. On the contrary, research has demonstrated that even nonabused children will touch and examine genitals on anatomically detailed dolls (Koocher et al., 1995; Glaser & Collins, 1989). It is difficult, if not impossible, to distinguish between a child's curiosity and an actual depiction of abuse using dolls alone. Based on a comprehensive review of research using AD dolls, experts discourage the use of the dolls without first employing open-ended questions (Koocher et al., 1995). Fortunately, interviewers may get all the information they need from skillful open-ended questions. A recent study reported that three- to twelve-year-old alleged sexual abuse victims gave as many details responding to open-ended questions *without* dolls as they did with dolls (Thierry, Lamb, Orbach, & Pipe, 2005). Remember that children can pick up on an interviewer's expectations; simply introducing a doll into the interviewing dynamic can implicitly suggest to the child that he or she should use it. We are only beginning to understand the ramifications of using AD dolls. A consistent rule of thumb presented by researchers is to use open-ended questions first, and only consider using an AD doll if the child has clearly made a disclosure of abuse.

Concluding Remarks

Many people (clinicians included) consider children to be unreliable reporters of their experience. Hopefully, after reading this chapter, you have a more optimistic view of children's capabilities as interview participants. Yes, children are limited in their ability to pronounce and understand words, remember events, and take another's perspective. However, children are the experts of their experiences and *can* be reliable reporters—especially when interacting with a skilled interviewer who understands their developmental strengths and limitations.

This may sound obvious, but it is so important to remember *who* you're talking to when interviewing a child. This is a person who is not used to being interviewed and likely has no idea that they know more about an event than you do. It is important to orient the child to who you are and what the interviewing process is about. Remind the child that you want to learn about them. Keep your questions simple, your words basic, and *wait* for the child's response. Avoid making assumptions about pronunciation or semantics—ask the child to clarify by describing what they mean.

Be on the lookout for ways that children differ from adults in conversation. Topic drift and source confusion can happen frequently among children four years old and younger. Unless you stay on your toes and watch for these error sources, you could end up confused, or worse, convinced that the child is an unreliable reporter. Keep in mind that most young children are limited in their understanding of different perspectives. They may omit information from a narrative or response because they assume since they know it, you do too! Watch for nonverbal cues indicating confusion; most children won't interrupt an interviewer to express it on their own.

It will be tempting to use specific questions and to rapidly go from one question to the next; you want to find out as much about the child you're interviewing as possible! Unfortunately, this inclination is not the best for eliciting the most accurate responses. Instead, use open-ended questions and build your subsequent questions from the child's original response. Remember that children aren't quite used to the process of telling their story. You may try teaching them how to organize their experience so they can better share it with you.

In interviewing children, there seems to be a delicate balance to strike between giving children credit for what they are capable of doing and not assuming that they can do it as well as adults. By considering developmental limitations in a child's cognitive abilities, you can form realistic expectations for yourself, the child being interviewed, and the interviewing process as a whole.

References

Benedict, H. (1979). Early lexical development: Comprehension and production. *Journal of Child Language, 6*, 183–200.

Bjorklund, D. F. (2005). *Children's thinking: Developmental function and individual differences*. Belmont, CA: Wadsworth/Thomson Learning.

Brown, D. A., Pipe, M. E., Lewis, C., Lamb, M. E., & Orbach, Y. (2007). Supportive or suggestive: Do human figure drawings help 5- to 7-year-old children to report touch? *Journal of Consulting and Clinical Psychology, 75*, 33–42.

Camparo, L. B., Wagner, J. T., & Saywitz, K. J. (2001). Interviewing children about real and fictitious events: Revisiting the narrative elaboration procedure. *Law and Human Behavior, 25*, 63–80.

Ceci, S. J., Huffman, M. L. C., Smith, E., & Loftus, E. F. (1994). Repeatedly thinking about a non-event: Source misattributions among preschoolers. *Consciousness and Cognition, 3*, 388–407.

Dale, P. S., Loftus, E. F., & Rathbun, L. (1978). The influence of the form of the question on eyewitness testimony of preschool children. *Journal of Psycholinguistic Research, 7*, 269–277.

DeLoache, J. S., & Marzolf, D. P. (1995). The use of dolls to interview young children: Issues of symbolic representation. *Journal of Experimental Child Psychology, 60*, 155–173.

Dorado, J. S., & Saywitz, K. J. (2001). Interviewing preschoolers from low- and middle-SES communities: A test of the narrative elaboration recall improvement techniques. *Journal of Clinical Child Psychology, 30*, 566–578.

Evans, M. A. (1985). Self-initiated speech repairs: A reflection of communicative monitoring in young children. *Developmental Psychology, 21,* 365–371.

Fabes, R., & Martin, C. L. (2000). *Exploring child development: Transactions and transformations.* Needham Heights, MA: Allyn & Bacon.

Fanetti, M., & Boles, R. (2004). Forensic interviewing and assessment issues with children. In W. O'Donohue & E. Levensky (Eds.), *Handbook of forensic psychology: Resource for mental health and legal professionals* (pp. 245–265). San Diego: Elsevier Academic Press.

Foley, M. A., & Ratner, H. H. (1998). Distinguishing between memories for thoughts and deeds: The role of prospective processing in children's source monitoring. *British Journal of Developmental Psychology, 16,* 465–484.

Glaser, D., & Collins, C. (1989). The response of young, non-sexually abused children to anatomically correct dolls. *Journal of Child Psychology and Psychiatry, 30,* 547–560.

Haden, C. A., Haine, R. A., & Fivush, R. (1997). Developing narrative structure in parent-child reminiscing across the preschool years. *Developmental Psychology, 33,* 295–307.

Hutcheson, G. D., Baxter, J. S., Telfer, K., & Warden, D. (1995). Child witness statement quality: Question type and errors of omission. *Law and Human Behavior, 19,* 631–648.

Koocher, G. P., Goodman, G. S., White, C. S., Friedrich, W. N., Sivan, A. B., & Reynolds, C. R. (1995). Psychological science and the use of anatomically detailed dolls in child sexual-abuse assessments. *Psychological Bulletin, 118,* 199–222.

Kulkofsky, S., & Klemfuss, J. Z. (2008). What the stories children can tell about their memory: Narrative skill and young children's suggestibility. *Developmental Psychology, 44,* 1442–1456.

Lane, D. M., & Pearson, D. A. (1982). The development of selective attention. *Merrill-Palmer Quarterly, 28,* 317–337.

Mahler, M. S. (1967). On human symbiosis and the vicissitudes of individuation. *Journal of the American Psychoanalytic Association, 15,* 740–763.

Piaget, J. (1960). *The child's conception of the world* (J. Tomlinson & A. Tomlinson, Trans.). Paterson, NJ: Littlefield, Adams & Co. (Original work published 1926)

Poole, D. A., & Lamb, M. E. (1998). *Investigative interviews of children: A guide for helping professionals.* Washington, DC: American Psychological Association.

Roediger, H. L., III, Wheeler, M. A., & Rajaram, S. (1993). Remembering, knowing, and reconstructing the past. In D. L. Medin (Ed.), *The psychology of learning and motivation: Advances in research and theory: Vol. 30,* (pp. 9–134). Orlando, FL: Academic Press.

Saywitz, K. J., & Snyder, L. (1996). Narrative elaboration: Test of a new procedure for interviewing children. *Journal of Consulting and Clinical Psychology, 64,* 1347–1357.

Saywitz, K. J., Snyder, L., & Lamphear, V. (1996). Helping children tell what happened: A follow-up study of the narrative elaboration procedure. *Child Maltreatment, 1,* 200–212.

Steward, M. S., & Steward, D. S. (with Farquhar, L., Myers, J. E. B., Reinhart, M., Welker, J., Joye, N., Driskill, J., & Morgan, J.). (1996). Interviewing young children about body touch and handling. *Monograph of the Society for Research in Child Development, 61* (4–5, Serial No. 248).

Thierry, K. L., Lamb, M. E., Orbach, Y., & Pipe, M. E. (2005). Developmental differences in the function and use of anatomical dolls during interviews with alleged sexual abuse victims. *Journal of Consulting and Clinical Psychology, 73*, 1125–1134.

Woolley, J. D., & Wellman, H. M. (1993). Origin and truth: Young children's understanding of imaginary mental representations. *Child Development, 64*, 1–17.

II

Understanding Others' Perspectives

Children learn to communicate their needs and wants to others before they come to appreciate that "others" are different, in very fundamental ways, from the "self." The preschool years are a busy time for discovering what is and is not automatically known, *de facto*, by others.

Developing appreciation of the boundaries between one's own mind and the minds of others allows room for alternative viewpoints. As chronicled by Kose and Fireman (Chapter 5), initially these are physical—understanding that successfully showing Mommy your book requires more than simply moving the book closer to her. But even this is not an easy task! Consider what it is like for you to walk into a room to discover that someone has taken *your* seat—the place where you always sit—thereby forcing you to move somewhere else. Shifting perspectives can be challenging and uncomfortable, even for adults. And yet, with advances in children's perspective taking come developments in problem solving and social understanding.

Understanding of visual perspectives also paves the way for more abstract conceptualizations of the way others might "see" things. This, coupled with advancing representational skills, leads to being able to appreciate that others might believe untrue things to be true. This knowledge is powerful, for it enables the child to engage in deception—a skill that serves us well in so many ways. In Chapter 6, Spritz, Fergusson, and Bankoff outline the development of children's false beliefs and deception with an emphasis on practical implications for working with children.

5

Perspective Taking

GARY D. FIREMAN and GARY KOSE

Consider how much time we spend thinking of others. Almost every expressive act of communication (except maybe for exclamations!) requires that we think of the listeners or readers of our messages. All forms of social interaction demand some thought of those around us; we need to consider their expectations and anticipate their reactions. Failure to think of others is often problematic. And, when it comes to analyzing events or situations, a complete understanding often involves looking at a problem from different points of view. Considering different points of view is so common that many of us may take perspective-taking skills for granted. Yet, the ability to take the perspective of others is not always an obvious part of our psychological response, and very young children often show marked limitations in being able to see the world from another's point of view.

The game of hide-and-seek is a consummate example of the need for perspective taking. One child covers her eyes while a second child finds a hiding place; after a prearranged time (say, until the count of 10), the first child seeks the second child, who should be hidden out of view. In order to successfully hide you need to think of what the seeker can and cannot see; in order to successfully seek, you need to imagine where someone might hide outside of your perspective. When very young children play hide-and-seek, sometimes their lack of perspective taking is obvious.

EXAMPLE

While two-year-old Ella covers her eyes and counts to 10 (with the help of her Grammy), her brother, four-year-old Owen, hides under the cushion of a chair. When Ella turns to seek Owen, immediately she is awestruck by the deformed piece of furniture with two legs sticking out from under the cushion (it looked as if her brother was being eaten by the chair). When she sheepishly peeks under the cushion, Owen jumps up to surprise her. Owen knew that you can't see under a chair cushion— hence you could hide there. But he failed to consider that you could see parts of him under such a cushion: The displaced cushion was an obvious clue, not to mention his legs extending out from underneath.

Successful hiding is not simply a matter of knowing about possible hiding places, but requires consideration of an appropriate hiding place in which all possible perceptual cues are out of view. When it's Ella's turn to hide, while Owen counts to 10 (all by himself), she runs to the chair and simply hides her face in the cushion and giggles, apparently pleased with her ability to hide and trick her brother. Owen turns and says, "That's not hiding!" Of course, Ella doesn't care. She's having fun and, for Ella, if she can't see Owen, then "Owen can't see her," despite the fact that she is simply standing by the chair with her face pressed in the cushion.

This example captures the range of cognitive changes that children go through in the toddler and preschool years. At first, very young children, around two years of age, seem to lack any understanding of different perspectives. What they see, everyone can see; what they can't see, no one else can see either (hence, if two-year-old Ella can't see Owen, then Owen can't see her). By the time children reach four to five years of age, they know about the existence of different perspectives. They come to understand that different people may see things differently from how they see things. However, the four- or five-year-old lacks the capacity to imagine what the different perspective might look like from a point of view different from his or her own (thus, Owen knows you can't see under a chair cushion but fails to consider that when hiding there his legs will be in clear view). Through the school years, children gradually come to appreciate perspectives other than their own. Along with increased intellectual abilities, children become better able to anticipate and envision how the world can look from someone else's point of view. This course of development for perspective taking was first documented and described in the seminal work of Jean Piaget and Barbel Inhelder.

Early Studies of Perspective Taking

Piaget first noted children's lack of perspective taking with regard to communication. In this early research, Piaget (1926) found that before seven or eight years of age, children tend to communicate *egocentrically*, that is, without taking account of what their listeners need to know. As Piaget put it, "The younger child always gave us the impression of talking to himself, without bothering about the other child. Very rarely did he succeed in placing himself at the listener's point of view" (1926, p. 115). Piaget noted preschool children's tendency to engage in "egocentric speech," that is, to communicate without considering the perspective of the listener and to leave out vital information (e.g., using a pronoun without first having specified a referent: "He hit me!") or to talk when no listener is present (e.g., preschool children will often engage in monologues that accompany play activities but are not directed toward anyone in particular).

In 1956, Piaget and Inhelder documented marked improvements with age in children's ability to infer how spatial displays would look to other observers who viewed them from different positions. For example, in a famous series of studies, Piaget and Inhelder made use of a scale model of three mountains, photographs of the model taken from various positions around it, and a doll observer who viewed the model from various positions. Children from four to eleven years of age had to guess what the doll saw from various perspectives around the three-mountain model. Younger children made a variety of errors indicative of poor perspective-taking skills. Some kept selecting the photographs depicting their own view of the mountains regardless of where the doll was placed. Others seemed to think that a number of different photographs could all represent what the doll saw from a given position. With increasing age, children became aware that only one photograph could depict a particular point of view, and that how the display looks changes systematically with changes in the viewer's position. Children also became increasingly skilled at predicting the details of the observer's view, for example, correctly identifying which mountain would appear behind or to the right of another mountain from the observer's perspective.

Piaget and Inhelder described a sequence of stages in the development of perspective-taking ability: Children four years of age do not understand the meaning of the questions being asked of them; six-year-olds consistently fail to distinguish between their own view and the doll's—they always choose their own view regardless of the position and perspective of the observer; between seven and eight years of age, children begin to distinguish different points of view but cannot specify what an alternative perspective looks like; next they begin to understand the relationship between their point of view and that of an observer with regard to being in front of or behind the mountains, but right and left transformations remain problematic; and only after eight years of age can children deal with all changes in perspective.

Piaget and Inhelder found young preschool children to be "rooted in their own position," being unable to imagine any position other than their own. In general, Piaget and Inhelder perceived this egocentrism as a limitation in the child's ability to differentiate what is subjective (i.e., what is strictly private and personal) from what is objective (i.e., a matter of public knowledge certain to be true from any perspective). In this sense, egocentrism is a limitation in reasoning, and it does not refer to selfishness as a personality trait or a lack of knowledge of others. Egocentrism is simply the unconscious adoption of one's own perspective through a failure to realize that other perspectives exist. Growing out of egocentrism is not just a matter of visual discovery—discovering for oneself that scenes look different from different positions.

Rather, nonegocentric perspective taking requires the imaginative ability to transform and represent spatial relationships from the child's point of view to that of another's perspective.

For the next 20 years, this Piagetian conception of childhood egocentrism sparked a great deal of research. Much of the early research confirmed Piaget and Inhelder's observations that young children are rooted in their own perspective and cannot take the perspective of another person. For example, John Flavell and colleagues (Flavell, Bodkin, Fry, Wright, & Jarvis, 1968; also see Flavell, 1966, 1974) published an extensive series of studies that examined children's ability to adapt their communication to their listener's perspective, and their ability to infer how object displays look to others who view them from different perspectives. In one study, children were shown an ordered series of pictures that, in comic strip fashion, illustrated a story. After a child narrated the story, three pictures were removed from the series, leaving a four-picture sequence that suggested quite a different story to someone who might see only those four pictures. The child was told that another person would be entering the room who had never seen any of the pictures before. The child was then asked to predict the story this new person would tell based on seeing just those four pictures. It was expected that the younger children would have difficulty suppressing their own perspective based on the original seven pictures when asked to infer the other person's story. In fact, 60% of the younger children either just repeated their original seven-picture story or spoiled the correct four-picture story by intruding seven-picture elements in their responses.

In another study, children from grades 2 through 11 learned to play a game and were then instructed to tell an adult listener how to play the game. For half of the children at each grade level, the adult listener was blindfolded, and for the other half the listener was sighted. In addition, a subgroup of second and eighth grade children described the game to both blindfolded and sighted listeners. For the eighth graders, the mean number of words per message was substantially higher in the messages directed to the blindfolded listener than in those directed to the sighted listener. In contrast, for the second grade children, the mean length of their messages was identical for both blindfolded and sighted listeners. The younger children also demonstrated the consequence of failing to keep the listener's perspective in mind where, in a few instances, the children spoke of picking up "this" or putting it "over there" when trying to explain the game to the blindfolded listener.

Flavell et al. (1968) concluded their series of studies by identifying four component skills young children need to acquire in order to take the perspectives of others: existence, need, inference, and application. First, the *existence* component refers to the child's knowledge that distinct mental states exist that correspond to different perspectives; *need* refers to the recognition that certain situations call for an effort to obtain knowledge about another person's mental state; *inference* refers to the ability to obtain this knowledge of other persons' perspectives by way of reasoning processes; and finally, *application* refers to the actual ability to apply that knowledge to the situation at hand.

There were also, however, a number of critics of the Piagetian view of egocentrism. Many studies raised questions about the competency of young children to appreciate perspectives other than their own. An increasing number of commentators came to believe that observed egocentrism may have been a result of Piaget and Inhelder's strangely worded questions and abstract tasks. Rather than demonstrating young children's limited ability to appreciate different perspectives, some believe that the children's failure may just reflect the children's misunderstanding of the questions and the experimental situation. For example, Margaret Donaldson argued in her book *Children's Minds* (1978) that traditional Piagetian tasks make little sense to preschool children (also see Siegal, 1997, for a more recent review). Donaldson claimed that preschool children are much more competent than Piaget gave them credit for. She suggested that the Piagetian tasks are too abstract and do not connect with young children's everyday, social experience. Consequently, children's ability is often underestimated. Donaldson suggested instead that children should be tested in situations that make "human sense" to them (i.e., tested on problems that are couched in the social terms familiar to the child's everyday life). One example she discussed at some length in her book was an experiment concerning egocentrism in which the child had the task of "hiding" a doll from a policeman doll (Hughes, 1975; Hughes & Donaldson, 1979). The scene was comprised of two intersecting walls (Figure 5.1). Children from three to five years of age were asked to hide a doll in one of the quadrants formed by the walls so that the doll could not be seen by the policeman doll. In Figure 5.1a, two quadrants were visible and two hidden from the policeman's position. In Figure 5.1b, with two policemen, only one hiding location is concealed from

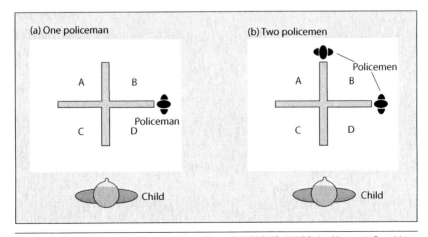

Figure 5.1 Egocentrism and perspective. From CHILDREN'S MINDS by Margaret Donaldson. Copyright© 1978 by Margaret Donaldson. Used by permission of W.W. Norton & Company, Inc.

the gaze of the policemen. The results showed that even three-year-old children were 90% correct in identifying whether the policeman doll(s) could see the boy doll. In a more complex arrangement, with up to six sections of wall and three policemen stationed at various positions, over 90% of the four-year-olds still identified correct hiding places.

These findings, at first, seemed impossible to reconcile with any extreme characterization of young children as egocentric. Such results seemed to provide convincing evidence that even the youngest children could appreciate the possibility of different viewpoints. At the very least, these findings can be explained by knowledge of the lines of sight and how to hide. Young children may be able to say whether the boy would be visible or invisible from various positions of the policeman simply by working out whether the policeman's line of sight is blocked by a wall.

On the other hand, this task is much easier than Piaget and Inhelder's three-mountain task, in which the question is not whether something can be perceived but rather what can be perceived from positions other than the child's own. The three-mountain task requires that the child imagine what someone else would see from a different position. Cox (1980) argued that the three-mountain task requires the simultaneous consideration and transformation of a number of spatial relations. Thus, while children may have the capacity to appreciate that points of view can be different for people looking at the same scene from different positions, they still may have difficulty determining precisely what can be seen and experienced from a different perspective. Here the problem is that different perspective-taking tasks may be of differential difficulty. For example, a doll has an easily identifiable front, back, and sides that could help children specify what would be seen from particular perspectives. In the three-mountain task, not only are the mountains symmetrical (not having fronts and backs) but also the children must imagine the relationships between them. Furthermore, the mountains occlude each other differently from different viewpoints. Cox concluded that Piaget and Inhelder's three-mountain task is much more complex than Donaldson's "hide from the police" task. Knowing how more complex scenes of this kind appear to another observer, according to Cox, is rather a late-appearing ability. Nonetheless, Donaldson's study demonstrates that young children appreciate that different viewpoints do exist, despite their inability to specify exactly what can be seen from any particular viewpoint other than their own. Also, Donaldson's position underscores the importance of contextual effects of social interaction and language on children's performance.

Starting in the 1980s, the study of the development of perspective taking became part of a larger inquiry. Given that it is first necessary for children to recognize that distinct mental states are associated with particular visual experiences, and that different people with different perspectives will have differing states of mind, it was quite natural for the study of perspective-taking skills to become part of the broader inquiry into children's awareness and knowledge of the mental states of others.

Perspective Taking and the Child's Theory of Mind

When do young children realize that what we see creates distinct mental states? When do children understand that if others see things differently, they are likely to have different mental states from their own? When can children begin to imagine what those different mental states might be like? Such questions are at the heart of the inquiry into children's *theory of mind*—that is, an intuitive folk theory about their own mental states and those of others.

There is considerable evidence showing that children's awareness and recognition of others begins in infancy. Infants are highly attentive to human faces and voices, and they seem to expect people to behave differently from objects (Ellsworth, Muir, & Hains, 1993; Legerstee, 1991). Young infants can also distinguish among people. At birth, they can discriminate their mother's voice from the voice of other women. Early in the first year, infants recognize their caregivers and develop emotional attachments to them (DeCasper & Fifer, 1980). From about two months of age, infants display contingent interactions—reciprocal actions and reactions that resemble the mutual give-and-take of conversations (Bates, Benigni, Camaloni, & Volterra, 1979; Trevarthen, 1979). Such interactions suggest that infants anticipate certain types of behavior from their partners. For example, when caregivers display a "still face," not moving or speaking, infants smile less and avert their gaze, heart rate changes, and some infants cry and fuss (Kisilevsky et al., 1998; Toda & Fogel, 1993). Furthermore, from early in the first year, infants are able to discriminate emotional expressions. Walker (1982) showed five-month-old infants two films of an unfamiliar adult. In one, the adult spoke in an angry tone with angry facial expressions and gestures; in the other, the adult spoke in a happy tone making happy facial expressions and gestures. The sound tracks on the films were matched with the video or not. Infants looked longer at the films with matching sound tracks, regardless of whether it was angry or happy, showing that infants have some knowledge about different emotions and how they are expressed facially or vocally. By the second half of the first year, infants gauge the emotional reactions of other people in order to evaluate situations or objects as safe or risky. Social referencing has been demonstrated in infants as young as six months of age (Walden & Ogan, 1988). In a classic study, one-year-old infants were willing to cross the deep side of a visual cliff when caregivers posed happy expressions, but none of the infants crossed over when the caregivers posed frightened expressions. In toddlers and throughout the preschool years, you see this in children checking with their parent when they take a tumble to determine if they should cry or pick themselves up and continue to play, or when children look to a parent's facial expression when a stranger enters the room to be reassured about the relationship. Thus, from infancy, children show clear signs of an intuitive sense of other people.

With the development of language and cognitive skills, children form concepts of others focusing on their external, observable characteristics (physical appearance, possessions, activities, and behavior relevant to themselves). While young children will refer to emotional states of others, such psychological attributions are generally situation specific (Lillard & Flavell, 1990). Throughout the preschool years, children come to understand that people have goals, intentions, and expectations. Children understand that people know some things and not others, and that some of this knowledge may be different from what the child believes and knows.

To some extent, becoming aware of mental states begins with our consciousness of our self. An awareness of the workings of our own minds can serve as a basis for generalizing to the minds of others (Harris, 1992). In fact, it has been proposed that an awareness of mental psychological states constitutes a core domain, and that young children are predisposed to form reasonable theories about how the mind works (Gelman, 2003; Gopnik & Meltzoff, 1997; Wellman & Gelman, 1998). Wellman (1990) has suggested that from about three years onward, children have a naïve theory of how the mind works. The central tenet of this belief-desire theory of mind is that internal beliefs and desires lead to overt action. It is from this core theory that the child will develop a complete theory of mind in which it is understood that mental states, such as beliefs, desires, and fantasies, are internal entities distinct from reality, and that these mental states may relate to the world in particular ways. In essence, the child must come to understand that the mind is a representation of reality that could allow individuals to predict and explain the actions of themselves or others. A true theory of mind involves at the most basic level a child understanding that the belief that cookies are in the cookie jar is the reason she will search for cookies in the jar. Perhaps, more importantly, the young child will develop an understanding that others may have beliefs different than her own and will consequently act differently—so, her brother, for example, will look elsewhere for cookies if he does not share her belief and thinks differently.

While adults typically take all this for granted, children must come to the realization that intentions, desires, and beliefs are related to actions, and that such a theory of mind can come to serve them in understanding themselves and the social world around them. Wellman, Cross, and Watson (2001) maintain that a full theory of mind is achieved when children can understand the relationship between beliefs and actions, which occurs between three and four years of age. Most notability, the standard for having achieved a theory of mind is the child's ability to succeed on a false belief task (discussed further in Chapter 6). This task involves a story in which the location of an object is changed: "Sally puts her marble in to the basket. She goes out to play. While she is outside she can't see that Anne comes and transfers her marble to a box.

She then leaves to visit a friend. When Sally comes home to get her marble, where will she look for it?" (Wimmer & Perner, 1983, p. 107). Most children younger than three years of age will respond that Sally will look in the box, where the marble actually is. By age 4, most children respond that Sally will look in the basket, where she originally put the marble. This basic experimental paradigm has given rise to a great number of studies. The finding is robust and has been replicated beyond Western cultures (Avis & Harris, 1991). Several factors affect performance: Children succeed at the task if they understand that deception is involved; also, children improve performance if they carry out the displacement themselves; and, performance is better if the child's initial mental state or the time between the first and second locations is stressed.

However, a general developmental trend is consistently seen: Children progress from below chance performance to above chance performance on false belief tasks during the preschool years. There is considerable controversy over the cause of this development. One group of researchers maintains that preschool children fail the task because they lack competence with regard to a theory of mind. In other words, the children do not understand that other people may have representations that can differ from their own (Astington & Gopnik, 1991; Flavell & Miller, 1998; Perner, 1991). Other researchers argue that children who fail the task possess the competence but fail because of the demands of the verbal skills needed to respond to the question (Lewis & Osbourne, 1990; Siegal & Peterson, 1994). This alternative emphasizes the general information processing demands of the task.

A second indication of the development of a child's theory of mind involves understanding the distinction between *appearance* and *reality*. Flavell, Flavell, and Green (1983) presented preschool children with deceptive objects, such as a sponge that had been painted to look like a rock. After the children played with the objects, the children were asked about what the objects looked like and what they "really, really were." While most of the four- and five-year-olds could answer these questions correctly, most three-year-olds claimed that the sponge looked like a rock and, in fact, was a rock. Interestingly, when the children looked at the objects through a magnifying glass, the four- and five-year-olds differentiated the magnification from the actual size of the objects; three-year-olds believed that objects appearing larger through the magnifying glass were, in fact, larger. This line of research suggests that part of any theory of mind must include an awareness of vision and the differing mental states that can arise from changes in perspective.

Seeing as a Psychological Event

Given the impressive evidence showing how infants attend to the gaze of others (e.g., Butler, Caron, & Brooks, 2000; Mumme & Fernald, 2003), the question remains as to when children take gaze as an action accompanied by distinct subjective experience. Here the emphasis is on knowing not only that the gaze refers to an object but also that the gaze gives rise to a unique subjective experience of seeing. And, when does the young child realize that "seeing" leads to a certain kind of knowing? O'Neill (1996) had two-year-olds ask a parent for help in retrieving a toy dropped into one of two identical containers that were placed out of reach. With the child watching, the parent had either seen where the toy was dropped or not. In the children's request for help, they gestured significantly more often when the parent had not seen which container held the toy. By around two years of age, children seemed to understand that seeing leads to knowing. There is other evidence that shows that when asked to show a picture to an adult who is covering her eyes with her hands, 18-month-olds will move the adult's hands or try to put the picture between the adult's hands and eyes (Bretherton & Beeghly, 1982). It seems that by the end of infancy, children have an intuitive understanding that seeing leads to knowing.

Beyond such a rudimentary understanding of the relationship between vision and knowledge, Flavell (1992, 2004) has distinguished two further levels of perspective taking that develop in early childhood. First, at Level 1, the child comes to understand that the other person need not see something just because the child saw it, and visa versa. Children at this level will recognize, for example, that while they can see what is on their side of a vertically held card, another person, seated opposite, does not. However, they do not yet conceptualize and consciously represent the fact of perspective and derive differences between their view and the other person's visual experience of something they both can see. Level 1 children know others also see things and that they need not see the same things at any given moment. They may also be capable of inferring exactly what things cannot be seen from the other perspective given adequate cues. Level 2 children are aware that the same things may look different to another viewing from a different position, and they are better at inferring how things appear from that different position. Flavell and colleagues demonstrated that when sitting across from an adult, looking at cards with different pictures on either side of the cards (e.g., a cat on one side and a dog on the other), three-year-olds could easily indicate which animal the adult sees. However, when presented with a Level 2 task, such as a picture of a turtle placed in such a way that the turtle appears upside down from one side and right side up from the other, three-year-old children always correctly reported how the turtle appeared to themselves (as either upside down or right side up, demonstrating that they knew the difference), but only a third consistently attributed the opposite orientation to the adult. In contrast, four-year-old children performed the task without error. Flavell noted that the younger children did not improve even when given relevant experience or provided with correct answers.

Thus, for Flavell, Level 1 children seem to know that a person's eyes must be open; the person's eyes must be aimed in the general direction of the target;

there must be no obstructions in the person's line of sight; and what the child sees has no bearing on what the other person sees. To this extent, children two to three years of age can be said to have an understanding about the relationship between vision and knowing. With a Level 2 conception, children develop a more representation-centered (how it is perceived) knowledge of vision and perspective. Thus, Flavell (2004) points out that four- and five-year-old children can acknowledge basic perspective-taking rules: Objects will appear the same if viewed from the same perspective; objects will appear different if two observers view objects from different sides; and certain objects (e.g., cylinders) will appear the same if viewed from different sides. Further, Flavell noted that Level 2 concepts also may involve knowledge of attention; in other words, that attention is selective, constructive, and may be limited. Flavell, Green, and Flavell (1995) showed that between four and eight years of age, children understand that when a person is mentally focused on one thing, he or she will devote little or no simultaneous attention to other totally irrelevant aspects of the situation. Such rules lead to more accurate representations of what constitutes a particular perspective.

For example, this type of distinction can be found in children attempting to cheat at a game or in school. At Level 1, the child is most concerned with whether he is in the teacher's direct line of sight or can be seen cheating. At Level 2, the child is concerned not only with the teacher's gaze or line of sight, but also with the teacher's point of view. At this level, the child may try to provide a distraction or use some deceptive technique such as feigning a yawn while looking at a neighbor's work.

As children develop through middle childhood, they increasingly come to understand that the mind does not merely copy impressions of objects and events as they are presented to the senses. Rather, the mind is construed as selective, representational, and interpretive, and children come to understand that vision and perspective taking are actions (or techniques) that help construct an understanding of the world around them. A rather obvious example of young children's difficulty in accurately representing perspective can be found in their drawings (see Golomb, 2004, for an extensive review). While drawing is a favored activity of preschool children, they tend to depict people, objects, and scenes with little regard for orientation or perspective. Their primary concern is with the topographical boundaries of figures, ignoring size, shape, and the relationship between figures depicted in the picture. Piaget and Inhelder (1969) described these limitations as a *synthetic incapacity*. Up until the age of four years, children's drawings increasingly include greater detail and complexity, yet they are still limited in terms of perspective. Often a scene will be depicted without much concern for actual shape, size, and proportion. Piaget has characterized this stage of drawing as *intellectual realism,* in that children tend to draw figures in terms of what they know about the object they are trying to represent, regardless of how the object actually appears. For example, *transparencies* are quite common, in which drawings depict both what is visible and not visible in a scene, showing aspects of a variety of perspectives in a picture. So, for example, a house will be drawn from the outside with the interior in juxtaposition, or a pregnant mommy will be drawn with a baby inside her body, or a car will be drawn showing all four wheels while only two wheels can actually be seen from a given perspective. *Visual realism* emerges through middle childhood where children tend to show a greater ability to depict scenes realistically as they appear from a particular station point. Children at this stage develop a variety of rules specific to graphic depiction. The relations between left and right, and in front and behind can now be represented; straight lines, angles, and curves are maintained across distances and transformations; and objects are depicted accurately with some degree of fidelity and the viewpoint of the observer is respected.

Taking Perspectives

"Perspective is a Latin word (*perspicere*) that means seeing through." This was how the Renaissance artist Albrecht Düer began to explain perspective (Panofsky, 1927/1994, p. 27). From the late 14th century, perspective was a technique developed in the visual arts in which artists could achieve pictorial realism. The technique is based on the fact that we can only see in straight lines, and we cannot see around corners. As long as we look with one stationary point of view, we see objects from one side and have to guess, or imagine, what lies behind. We see only one aspect of an object, and it is not very hard to work out exactly what this aspect will be from any given point. All you have to do is to draw straight lines from that point to any part of the object's surface. Anything behind an opaque body will be hidden; anything falling within the lines will be seen. Moreover, the fact that we only see in straight lines accounts for the apparent change in size of an object at a distance. Realizing a perspective, for a Renaissance artist, was not merely a visual discovery but rather a way of "rationalizing sight," and was developed with geometric precision. Creating a realistic-looking picture was a matter of first applying the formula or concept of perspective to a pictorial representation by establishing a particular point of view at a particular moment and then attending to the "space, light, and mood" between the objects and figures in the scene (Panofsky, 1955). As a result of the development of this technique, Renaissance art in Europe was revolutionized, making possible a pictorial realism never before achieved (Gombrich, 1972).

Similar to the development of perspective in the visual arts, young children develop the ability to establish perspective, which then revolutionizes the way they see and understand the world around them. A young child must first become aware of his or her own unique point of view and differentiate it from different points of view. Beyond recognizing that there are different points of view, children, like artists, must attend to the spatial relationships between the objects and figures within the perspective in order to achieve an accurate representation of a scene. With time, children can take the imaginative leap to envision different points of view and the vista from within a particular perspective.

In discovering perspective, Renaissance artists had to suppress what they knew about the world around them and learn to depict the world as it appears. We know the world is made up of three-dimensional objects, with fronts, backs, and sides, with objects that do not change shape or size as they (or we) move around in space. Yet, in order to depict a scene in perspective, we must represent the scene as it appears according to the geometric laws that determine light and sight (Gombrich, 1972). Perhaps it is no coincidence that the discovery of perspective occurred in the arts, because establishing perspective is immanent to any form of representation. All representations are about something (they have content) and all representations present the content in a particular way (Brentano, 1874/1955; Frege, 1892/1960; Goodman, 1976; Dretske, 1988). So, for example, a photo would have to be a photo of something (say, a horse); further, this photo of a horse would have to depict the horse in a particular way (say, at a gallop or grazing, front-on or profile). Thus, any form of representation implicates the establishment of perspective: whether pictorial, narratives, or mental representations in the form of beliefs and desires, or an understanding of differences in point of view.

Perner, Brandl, and Garnham (2003) have outlined the nature of perspective and the problems entailed in its development. For Perner et al., the development of cognitive perspective in young children requires an understanding that something—an individual, event, situation, or scene—can be described differently depending on one's point of view. In fact, as they see it, it is the development of perspective that is fundamental to understanding false beliefs, the distinction between appearance and reality, and in establishing a theory of mind. In the broadest sense, perspective is defined as "a way something is represented in a representational medium" (p. 357). Perspective, then, is the "aspectual shape" or "mode of representation." A difference in perspective occurs when individuals represent the same content but differ in the mode representation.

Understanding the concept of differences in perspective, according to Perner et al., is a relative notion because it can be defined only relative to a fixed content or point of view. It may be that this relativity is why perspective seems to be vague and elusive and requires time to develop. Perner et al. delineate three cognitive requisites that must develop to fully achieve perspective taking. The first is to appreciate *switching perspectives*, that is, to recognize that things can be seen differently. This requirement is achieved early in development and is likely to be a result of the different visual experiences that come with movement or over time. Thus, for example, children as young as 18 months or two years of age appreciate that you must have visual access to find a toy or communicate with another person.

The second requirement is the *task of integrating information from different perspectives.* In the simplest cases, this can be achieved by integrating different visual cues and information into a single image of a scene from different angles or at different times. This second requirement is a later developmental accomplishment and is dependent on the representational medium that can allow this kind of integration without incompatibilities. Thus, a three-year-old can realize that a card has two sides and the view of the back is different from the view of the front of the card.

Finally, the third requisite is the *ability to represent different information as different ways of representing the same thing or scene.* What is involved here is the understanding by the child that different representations can arise from the fact that different perspectives comprise the same objective referent. This means knowing about different visual experiences, which result in different representations, and then coordinating the different representations into a coherent understanding of the scene. At this point, the older child, around four years of age, can begin to imagine exactly how alternative perspectives differ from his or her own.

Achieving perspective—"seeing through" in other words—is not a direct extension of perception. Perspective is not a mere reading or apprehension of the properties of objects or of natural scenes. Rather, perspective is a technique or a cognitive action that restricts the view of objects and figures within a spatial array. Perspective is a representation achieved through a developmental process, and all representations are richer in content than perception because representations incorporate knowledge of the possible transformations of objects. This capacity to represent objects in perspective transcends perception since a representational image is not a simple copy but comprises elements of a cognitive reconstruction.

References

Astington, J. W., & Gopnik, A. (1991). Theoretical explanations of children's theory of mind. *British Journal of Developmental Psychology, 9,* 7–31.

Avis, J., & Harris, P. L. (1991). Belief-desire reasoning among Baka children: Evidence for a universal conception of mind. *Child Development, 62,* 460–467.

Bates, E., Benigni, L., Camaloni, L. & Volterra, V. (1979). *The emergence of symbols: Cognition and communication in infancy.* New York: Academic Press.

Brentano, F. von. (1955). *Psychology from an empirical standpoint* (O. Kraus, Ed.; L. L. MacAllister, Trans.). London: Routledge and Kegan Paul. (Original work published 1874)

Bretherton, I., & Beeghly, M. (1982). Talking about inner states: The acquisition of an explicit theory of mind. *Developmental Psychology, 18,* 906–921.

Butler, S. C., Caron, A. J., & Brooks, R. (2000). Infant understanding of the referential nature of looking. *Journal of Cognition and Development, 1,* 359–377.

Cox, M. V. (1980). Visual perspective taking in children. In M. V. Cox (Ed.), *Are young children egocentric?* New York: St. Martin's Press.

DeCasper, A. J., & Fifer, W. (1980). Of human bonding: Newborns prefer their mother's voices. *Science, 208*, 1174–1176.

Donaldson, M. (1978). *Children's minds*. New York: W.W. Norton & Co.

Dretske, F. (1988). *Explaining behavior: Reasons in a world of causes*. Cambridge, MA: MIT Press.

Ellsworth, C. P., Muir, D., & Hains, S. M. J. (1993). Social competence and person-object differentiation: An analysis of the still-face effect. *Developmental Psychology, 29*, 63–73.

Flavell, J. M. (1966). Role taking and communication skill in young children. *Young Children, 21*, 164–177.

Flavell, J. M. (1974). The development of inferences about others. In T. Mischel (Ed.), *Understanding other persons*. Oxford: Blackwell.

Flavell, J. M. (1992). Perspectives on perspective taking. In H. Beilin and P. Pufall (Eds.), *Piaget's theory: Prospects and possibilities*. Hillsdale, NJ: Erlbaum.

Flavell, J. M. (2004). Development of knowledge about vision. In D. T. Levin (Ed.), *Thinking and seeing: Visual metacognition in adults and children* (pp. 13–36). Cambridge, MA: MIT Press.

Flavell, J. H., Bodkin, P. T., Fry, C. L. Wright, J. W., & Jarvis, P. E. (1968). *The development of role-taking and communication skills in children*. New York: Wiley.

Flavell, J. M., Flavell, E. R., & Green, F. L. (1983). Development of appearance reality distinction. *Cognitive Psychology, 15*, 95–120.

Flavell, J. M., Green, F. L., & Flavell, E. R. (1995). The development of children's knowledge about attentional focus. *Developmental Psychology, 31*, 706–712.

Flavell, J. M., & Miller, P. H. (1998). Social cognition. In D. Kuhn & R. S. Siegler (Eds.), *Handbook of child psychology: Cognition, perception, and language* (5th ed., Vol. 2, pp. 851–898). New York: Wiley.

Frege, G. (1960). On sense and reference. In P. Greach & M. Black (Eds.), *Philosophical writings of Gottlob Frege* (pp. 56–78). Oxford: Basil Blackwell. (Original work published 1892)

Gelman, S. A. (2003). *The essential child: Origins of essentialism in everyday thought*. New York: Oxford University Press.

Golomb, C. (2004). *The child's creation of a pictorial world*. Mahwah, NJ: LEA Publishers.

Gombrich, E. H. (1972). *Art and illusion: A study of the psychology of pictorial representation*. Princeton, NJ: Princeton University Press.

Goodman, N. (1976). *Languages of art*. Indianapolis, IN: Hackett Publishing Co.

Gopnik, A., & Meltzoff, A. N. (1997). *Words, thoughts, and theories*. Cambridge, MA: MIT Press.

Harris, P. L. (1992). From simulation to folk psychology: The case for development. *Mind & Language, 7*, 120–144.

Hughes, M. (1975). *Egocentrism in preschool children*. Unpublished doctoral dissertation, University of Edinburgh.

Hughes, M., & Donaldson, M. (1979). The use of hiding games for studying the coordination of perspectives. *Educational Review, 31*, 133–140.

Kisilevsky, B. S., Hains, S. M. J., Lee, K., Muir, D. W., Xu, F., Fu, G., et al. (1998). The still-face effect in Chinese and Canadian 3- and 6-month-old infants. *Developmental Psychology, 34*, 629–639.

Legerstee, M. (1991). The role of person and object in eliciting early imitation. *Journal of Experimental Child Psychology, 51*, 423–433.

Lewis, C., & Osbourne, A. (1990). Three-year-olds problems with false-belief: Conceptual or linguistic artifact? *Child Development, 61*, 1514–1519.

Lillard, A. S., & Flavell, J. M. (1990). Young children's preference for mental state versus behavioral descriptions of human actions. *Child Development, 61,* 731–741.

Mumme, D. L., & Fernald, A. (2003). The infant as onlooker: Learning from emotional reactions observed in a television scenario. *Child Development, 74,* 221–237.

O'Neill, D. K. (1996). Two-year-olds' sensitivity to a parent's knowledge state when making requests. *Child Development, 67,* 659–677.

Panofsky, E. (1994). *Perspective as symbolic form.* New York: Zone Books. (Original work published 1927)

Panofsky, E. (1955). *Meaning in the visual arts.* New York: Doubleday & Co.

Perner, J. (1991). *Understanding the representational mind.* Cambridge, MA: MIT Press.

Perner, J., Brandl, J. L., & Garnham, A. (2003). What is the perspective problem? Developmental issues in belief ascription and dual identity. *Facta Philosophica, 5,* 355–378.

Piaget, J. (1926). *The language and thought of the child.* New York: Harcourt, Brace.

Piaget, J., & Inhelder, B. (1956). *The child's conception of space.* London: Routledge & Kegan Paul.

Piaget, J., & Inhelder, B. (1969). *The psychology of the child.* New York: Basic Books.

Siegal, M. (1997). *Knowing children: Experiments in conversation and cognition.* Hove, UK: Psychology Press.

Siegal, M., & Peterson, C. C. (1994). Children's theory of mind and the conversational territory of cognitive development. In C. Lewis & P. Mitchell (Eds.), *Children's early understanding of mind: Origins and development* (pp. 22–43). Hillsdale, NJ: Erlbaum.

Toda, S., & Fogel, A. (1993). Infant response to the still face situation at 3 and 6 months. *Developmental Psychology, 29,* 532–538.

Trevarthen, C. (1979). Communication and cooperation in early infancy: A description of primary intersubjectivity. In M. Bullowa (Ed.), *Before speech: The beginning of human communication.* Cambridge, UK: Cambridge University Press.

Walden, T. A., & Ogan, T. A. (1988). The development of social referencing. *Child Development, 59,* 1230–1240.

Walker, A. S. (1982). Intermodal perception of expressive behaviors by human infants. *Journal of Experimental Child Psychology, 33,* 514–535.

Wellman, H. M. (1990). *The child's theory of mind.* Cambridge, MA: Bradford Books/ MIT Press.

Wellman, H. M., Cross, D., & Watson, J. (2001). Meta-analysis of theory-of-mind development: The truth about false belief. *Child Development, 72,* 655–684.

Wellman, H. M., & Gelman, S. A. (1998). Knowledge and acquisition of functional domains. In D. Kuhn & R. Siegler (Eds.), *Handbook of child psychology: Cognition, perception, and language* (5th ed., Vol. 2, pp. 523–573). New York: Wiley.

Wimmer, H., & Perner, J. (1983). Beliefs about beliefs: Representation and constraining function of wrong beliefs in young children's understanding of deception. *Cognition, 13,* 103–128.

6
False Beliefs and the Development of Deception

BECKY L. SPRITZ, ART S. FERGUSSON, and SARAH M. BANKOFF

> Much to learn, you still have.
>
> **Yoda,** *Star Wars Episode II: Attack of the Clones*

Such is the case with children's theory of mind in early childhood. In Chapter 5, we learned that the way children see the world undergoes dramatic transformations in early childhood, making it possible for them to view situations from alternate viewpoints. However, like the Jedi warriors from the *Star Wars* series, simply having special powers does not mean that one is a Jedi master. Viewing the world from another person's perspective, and using that information to understand, predict, and act upon the world requires practice and maturation. In this chapter, we focus on two skills that directly build upon children's basic perspective-taking abilities: understanding false beliefs and deception.

Children's False Belief Understanding

What Is a False Belief?

To consider children's development of false belief understanding, it is important to be clear about what is meant by a false belief:

EXAMPLE: A FALSE BELIEF

Like many parents, once my (BLS) children are in bed I return the toys scattered throughout the house to their rightful places. This sometimes creates issues the next morning when someone is looking for a favorite toy. On one occasion, Sam left his Spiderman action figure in the bathtub. After he was in bed, I moved it from the bathroom to the playroom (where it belongs!). The next morning, Sam searched every corner of the bathroom looking for his beloved toy. Because he thought he knew where he had left it, it never occurred to him to look someplace else.

Sam's erroneous belief that his Spiderman was in the bathroom is a classic example of a false belief—a belief about something that is, in reality, incorrect (Wimmer & Perner, 1983). From Sam's perspective, there was only one possible place for Spiderman to be because he had no knowledge that he had been moved to a new location. But, the fact that we recognize that Sam's belief is false is important because it demonstrates our understanding that beliefs (and thoughts and emotions) are mental representations, not facts. And, when you add together the knowledge that

1. people view the world from different perspectives, with
2. beliefs are mental representations, and
3. mental representations can be wrong or inaccurate,

what follows is that people have *different* thoughts, beliefs, and emotions, all of which can be manipulated. The practical implications of children being armed with this knowledge will be covered later in the chapter; for now, let's further consider the development of false belief understanding.

In the Spiderman example above, my (BLS) false belief understanding is demonstrated by my knowledge that (1) Sam would wake up believing that his Spiderman was still in the bathtub (even though I had moved it to the playroom), and (2) he would go to the bathroom to look for it (because that's where he falsely believed it was). Eventually, Sam also realized that his belief about his Spiderman was mistaken:

EXAMPLE: ACCEPTING ONE'S OWN FALSE BELIEF (REPRESENTATIONAL CHANGE)

Later, Sam described the incident to his younger sister, Alison. "So, when I woke up, I thought Spiderman was still in the bathtub and I looked everywhere, but he wasn't there! Then, Mom told me that she had cleaned up the bath toys, and I said, 'Duh! She put him back with the superheroes.' But, I wasted all that time, when I could have been fighting bad guys!"

Psychologists distinguish between two types of false beliefs; "other" false beliefs and representational change (Gopnik & Astington, 1988). *Other false beliefs* refer to the type of false belief described at the outset of the chapter; a situation in which, as an onlooker, we recognize that another person possesses and acts upon an erroneous belief. By contrast, *representational change* refers to the understanding that one's own beliefs were *previously* false or inaccurate, but *now* reflect accurate information, aka "the truth." This is illustrated by Sam's "duh" moment in the example above. The primary distinction between these types of false beliefs is the person referent (whether the child had a false belief or whether the false belief was held by another) and the time referent (whether the belief is presently false or whether the belief used to be false). Demonstrations of both types of false belief (other false beliefs and representational change) are required for a child to have fully achieved false belief understanding (Curenton, 2003).

Developmental Issues in False Beliefs

The majority of research on the development of false belief understanding has been examined through the use of distinct research paradigms, commonly known as false belief tasks. Over the years, a number of standard tasks have been developed to assess false belief understanding (Wimmer & Perner, 1983) and representational change (Gopnik & Astington, 1988) in children. Across both types of tasks, research has consistently shown that children younger than age 4 struggle with and often fail at false belief tasks (Wellman, Cross, & Watson, 2001). For instance, children under age 4 are likely to report that a puppet will look for the piece of fruit in a different box (location 2), despite watching someone move the piece of fruit from the original location and despite knowing that the puppet believed the piece of fruit was in the basket (location 1).

Why do three-year-olds have difficulty with false belief tasks? Perner (1991) suggested that young children lack an understanding that thoughts, beliefs, and feelings are representations of the world. He labeled this lag in perspective taking a *representational deficit*, a concept somewhat akin to Piaget's *egocentrism* described decades earlier. In contrast to Piaget, however, Perner observed that around age 4, children undergo a shift in their thought processes that allows them to view their own and other people's mental states not as a reflection of things as they really are, but rather as representations of the world. It is this shift in children's representational world that characterizes changes in children's perspective taking and the emergence of children's false belief understanding (Perner, 1991).

A number of other factors have been shown to influence children's false belief understanding. In a meta-analytic review of 178 studies, Wellman and his colleagues (2001) demonstrated that subtle changes within the research protocol affect children's performance on false belief tasks. For example, children performed better when the protagonist's mental state was clearly articulated. Providing a temporal marker such as "Where will Tasha look first?" also provided clarity that seemed to aid older children in responding more accurately to false belief questions.

But, wait! False belief understanding does not end there! Children's false belief understanding becomes increasingly sophisticated with respect to *second-order false beliefs*—false beliefs about another's beliefs, as illustrated by the following:

EXAMPLE: SECOND-ORDER FALSE BELIEFS

It is school vacation week. I (BLS) call my mother to vent. And I do, complaining about everything: the noise level, the constant layer of crumbs on the kitchen floor, the general clutter.... Mom listens, and then launches into her own set of complaints: my father's snoring, the dishes in the sink, the general clutter. I hang up the phone, feeling completely vindicated. Later, much to my surprise, my mom calls to apologize. I say, "For what, Mom?" And she responds, "I was worried that you might feel I was minimizing your situation!"

This example illustrates the complex nature of second-order false beliefs: Person A has a false belief about Person B's belief about Situation X (Perner & Wimmer, 1985). In the example, after my mother hung up the phone, she (Person A) got to thinking about our conversation (Situation X), and what I (Person B) might be thinking about it (Situation X). While second-order false beliefs are challenging to map out, they have tremendous practical significance with respect to interpersonal misunderstandings (*You mean you didn't really think that? I thought that you thought that ...*).

In comparison to traditional false belief tasks, second-order false beliefs are much more difficult for children (and adults!) to comprehend, with children's understanding of second-order false beliefs emerging gradually between the ages of five and ten years (Parker, MacDonald, & Miller, 2007). Children's difficulties with second-order false beliefs may explain a lot, particularly in relation to the children's relationships with parents, teachers, and peers. Consider the drama of a preadolescent female: "You thought that Mimi was mad at you? I thought that you knew that Mimi was mad at Hannah." There is also research to suggest that second-order false beliefs may be related to the development of children's deception, discussed later in the chapter.

False Beliefs and Emotional Perspective Taking

Traditional false belief tasks assess children's false belief understanding in relation to a specific type of situation: their beliefs about the physical world (the location of a toy, the physical contents of a box). This begs the question: Do the developmental norms and limitations of children's false belief understanding generalize to other types of mental representations, such as desires and emotions? Consider the following example:

EXAMPLE: FALSE BELIEFS ABOUT EMOTIONS

Janice promised her children she would take them ice skating on Saturday. During the week, the temperature plummets such that by the weekend it is bitter cold. She is dreading the skating outing, but does not want to break her promise to her children. Suddenly, her ten-year-old son comes running into the kitchen, announcing that the city has had to temporarily close the rink for safety reasons. Despite her inner joy, she puts on her best disappointment face and says, "Oh! And I was so looking forward to it!"

In the above example, Janice's son has a false belief about her emotion. He mistakenly believes that she is disappointed about the rink being closed, when in fact she is not. Compared to traditional false beliefs, research on false beliefs about emotions is considerably more scant and somewhat inconsistent in its findings, although the general trends indicate that false beliefs about emotions are somewhat more difficult for children than false beliefs about beliefs (Bradmetz & Schneider, 2004; Parker et al., 2007). Why?

Returning to a discussion of theory of mind and perspective taking (Chapter 5), children display a basic understanding of desires and emotions prior to beliefs (Wellman, 2002). Even infants and toddlers reference other people's emotions and make decisions based on their emotional expressions (Denham, 1998). Preschool-aged children can also take the emotional perspective of someone else, as demonstrated by their understanding of disappointment (Cole, 1986). These findings are important because children who perform well on emotional perspective-taking tasks have been shown to be more effective communicators and show greater emotion understanding (Dunn & Hughes, 1998). It is for this reason that emotional perspective-taking strategies are often incorporated within social skills programs (Domitrovich, Cortes, & Greenberg, 2007).

Given that emotional perspective taking emerges early in development, why might children have more difficulty on tasks involving false beliefs about emotions than those involving false beliefs about beliefs? The answer is not yet clear; however, it may be related to basic processes involved in the development of theory of mind (de Rosnay, Pons, Harris, & Morrell, 2004). Children are more likely to base their judgments about emotions on the *desires* of others (she wants ice cream, so she feels happy) rather than on the *beliefs* of others (she believes there is ice cream, so she feels happy). To this end, false beliefs about emotions may represent a less natural connection for young children.

Despite this, children's understanding of emotional false beliefs does have important practical implications for children's social and emotional competence and the development of deception, the foci of the remainder of the chapter.

Practical Implications of False Belief Understanding

Several studies have demonstrated a connection between language development and children's false belief understanding (Farrar, Ashwell, & Maag, 2005; Lohmann & Tomasello, 2003). Researchers have also demonstrated that opportunities for talking about mental states (i.e., beliefs, desires, emotion) with parents are positively related to the development of false belief (Ruffman, Slade, & Crowe, 2002). Consider the interchange children experience when conversing with adults about knowledge and beliefs: *Robert thinks he is getting a bicycle for his birthday,* or *Amanda says she doesn't like parties.* When children hear adults speak in this way, they begin to learn that what people think or say are mental representations and, therefore, do not necessarily reflect a fixed reality. Interactions with siblings and peers also promote false belief understanding by providing opportunities to encounter different perspectives (Jenkins, Turrell, Kogushi, Lollis, & Ross, 2003). Thus, one way of helping children perform better on false belief tasks is to increase children's exposure to mental state language through social interactions, coaching, and modeling. In fact, any number of activities involving communications about mental states, such as children's make-believe play, could potentially improve performance on false belief tasks (Riggs & Peterson, 2000).

One of the practical challenges for professionals working with young children is that young children may be unaware that they hold false beliefs or that previously held beliefs may be false. Moreover, young children who do not yet understand the *concept* of false beliefs likewise cannot understand that some of *their own* beliefs may not be true. And, being confronted with this reality can be very embarrassing and frustrating.

EXAMPLE: LACK OF FALSE BELIEF UNDERSTANDING IN YOUNG CHILDREN

For Christmas, my (BLS) children received a game called *Feed the Kitty,* a game designed for preschool age children with no reading required. It comes equipped with a plastic kitty bowl and plastic mice. Children roll a die with pictures that tell the player what to do: (1) Feed kitty (put a mouse in kitty's bowl), (2) take away from kitty (remove a mouse from kitty's bowl, or (3) pass a mouse to the person on your left.

What the designers of the game failed to consider is that when played with preschool age children sitting across from one another,

developmental limitations in perspective taking result in intense disagreements about "which way is left"! One day, after the holidays were
behind us, I joked with my children about this—their false belief about
which way was left. Sammy (age 6) agreed that it was amusing; Alison
(age 4) became quite offended. She rose to her feet, her right finger in the
air, and proclaimed, "I *did too* know that this is left, and don't you say
that ever again!"

This is a good example of what *not* to do when confronting a child about
her false beliefs. Alison perceived this explicit discussion of her false beliefs
as mocking her cognitive limitations, even though it occurred considerably after the initial event. As an alternative, an attempt should be made
to explain to her that beliefs are not always true and that different people
can hold different beliefs. In helping children understand and acknowledge
representational change, one may appeal to children's current and accepted
representations of the world. Using what they already know to be true, an
attempt can be made to challenge their false belief in a manner that they can
logically follow and understand. However, depending on the child's level
of development, such explanations may or may not be understood. Some
of children's difficulty accepting and acknowledging false beliefs may also
be related to children's inability to differentiate false beliefs from deception
(Berthoud-Papandropoulou & Kilcher, 2003). Research indicates that very
young children (ages 3 to 5) often have difficulty distinguishing between
false beliefs and deception. These children may think that by having a false
belief they are doing something morally wrong! Helping children to understand this difference can further promote their understanding of the com-
plexities of social interactions. It is with this in mind that we now turn to a
consideration of deception.

Children's Understanding and Use of Deception

Differentiating False Beliefs From Deception

As described in the previous section, false belief understanding involves an
awareness that someone (oneself or another) has (or had) an erroneous belief
that the person tried to act upon in some way. In contrast, deceptive strategies
are defined as communications or behaviors enacted with the intent of instilling false beliefs in others (Chandler, Fritz, & Hala, 1989). Deceptive strategies
can be either verbal (i.e., lying, withholding information) or nonverbal (i.e.,
hiding the evidence, covering one's tracks).

EXAMPLE: A CLASSIC EXAMPLE OF DECEPTION

Timothy (age 8) sat at the dinner table, a heaping serving of peas still on his plate. Timothy was all too familiar with this situation; he would remain at the table until he finished his vegetables. Yet, as soon as his mother turned to clear the table, Timothy took a handful of peas and tucked them in his pocket. Whenever his mother's glance shifted back in his direction, Timothy pretended to be chewing with a look of disgust on his face. This continued until Timothy transferred all of the peas from his plate. Then, he carried his empty plate to the sink and handed it to his mother.

In the above example, we may be impressed by the various strategies Timothy used to fool his mother. But what makes Timothy's behaviors in this example different from the type of false belief understanding discussed earlier in the chapter?

According to Lee and Cameron (2000), the meaning and function of a person's communications are determined by the intentional states or representations of the speaker, referred to as the *expression-representation distinction*. This distinction differentiates between how something is expressed (i.e., how it was said) and how it was intended to be represented (i.e., what was meant). Using this paradigm, verbal communications can be classified along five dimensions (see Table 6.1).

Examining consistencies and inconsistencies across these dimensions reveals important information about a speaker's verbal communications. For instance, using Sam's false belief about his Spiderman from the beginning of the chapter, if someone had asked Sam where his Spiderman was located, he would have (mistakenly) answered "the bathtub." Sam's communication of this false belief could be illustrated as shown in Table 6.2.

Table 6.1 Dimensions of Verbal Communications

Factuality	The extent to which the statement is reflective of the true state of affairs (true or false)
Speaker's belief	What the speaker believes about the statement in relation to reality (true or false)
Speaker's intention	How the speaker intends for the listener to understand the statement (intent to deceive)
Literal meaning	What the speaker means (manifest content). Is it consistent with other dimensions?
Deeper meaning	What the speaker means (latent content). Is it consistent with other dimensions?

Adapted from: Lee and Cameron, 2000.

Table 6.2 Verbal Communication Dimensions in Children's False Beliefs

Factuality	False (Spiderman is not in the bathroom)
Speaker's beliefs	True (Sam believes Spiderman is in the bathroom)
Speaker's intention	Consistent with the speaker's beliefs (Sam wants us to believe what he believes)
Literal meaning	Consistent with the speaker's beliefs (On the surface, Sam means what he says)
Deeper meaning	Consistent with the speaker's beliefs (On a deeper level, Sam means what he says)

Here the speaker's beliefs, the speaker's intent, the literal meaning, and the deeper meaning are all consistent; only the factuality of the statement is false. It is for this reason that Lee and Cameron (2000) referred to false beliefs as "honest mistakes"—while the speaker is mistaken (in reality), there is no intent by the speaker to deceive.

This is, of course, in sharp contrast to Timothy's efforts to fool his mother into thinking he ate his peas (see Table 6.3).

The key aspect here is that deception involves inconsistency between what is intended by the speaker and what is believed by the speaker. This inconsistency between the speaker's intention and the speaker's belief is referred to as the *intent to deceive* (Lee & Cameron, 2000). False beliefs and deception differ on the critical dimension of intentionality. While a false belief is unintentional, deception is quite intentional, with the purpose of reaching an identified goal (Wilson, Smith, & Ross, 2003).

Lying, Joking, and Pretending

Lying, a specific type of deception, also necessarily involves the intent to deceive (Wilson et al., 2003). While some forms of deception may involve

Table 6.3 Verbal Communication Dimensions in Children's Lies

Factuality	False (Timothy did not eat his peas)
Speaker's beliefs	False (Timothy knows he did not eat his peas)
Speaker's intention	Inconsistent with the speaker's beliefs (Timothy wants his mother to believe that he ate his peas)
Literal meaning	Inconsistent with the speaker's beliefs (On a surface level, Timothy means what he says)
Deeper meaning	Inconsistent with speaker's beliefs (On a deeper level, Timothy means what he says)

exclusively nonverbal strategies (e.g., hiding a candy wrapper), lying involves at least some verbal deception:

- "I didn't do it."
- "Emma broke the vase."
- "Tucker hit me first; I just hit him back."

In contrast to the examples of deception and lying, consider a variation on the pea-hiding scenario, this time between Jackson (age 9) and his parents:

EXAMPLE: JOKING

Jackson sat at the dinner table with his parents. "OK, Jackson, let's finish up," his father prompted. As his father turned away, Jackson placed his napkin over his plate, covering his peas. When his father looked back he said, "All done, Dad!" with a mischievous smile on his face. His dad chuckled, "Nice try, Jackson, but you can't fool me!"

There is an important distinction between deception and joking. As in instances of deception, jokes may involve an explicit attempt to convey false information. Indeed, in the previous example, Jackson makes a clear, false statement to his father about being finished with his peas. However, jokes differ from deception because the individual does not intend for the recipient of the false information to believe that information beyond the immediate situation (Wilson et al., 2003). When jokes are *shared* between individuals, this agreement is explicit. Alternatively, when jokes are *played* on individuals, this agreement is implicit and known only to the speaker. Sometimes, particularly with older children in peer situations, children will fool or trick another child and will attempt to pass off the situation as a "practical joke." When the intent is for the recipient to believe that it is true, particularly at the recipient's expense, then the act is clearly an act of deception (and a malicious one at that!):

EXAMPLE: JOKING WITH THE INTENT TO DECEIVE

It is school spirit week at the middle school. Derek, a shy and awkward preteen, innocently asks one of the girls in his class what the theme is for tomorrow. Without hesitation and with apparent sincerity, she answers, "Tomorrow is pajama day!" Their teacher, Mr. Jones, overhears her and scolds her for lying to Derek. The young lady denies intending Derek any harm and claims that it was all an innocent joke.

Like joking, deception can also be distinguished from pretense, for instance, in the context of children's fantasy play (Taylor, Lussier, & Maring, 2003). Joking and pretense are similar in that the speaker does not intend for the recipient to believe information beyond the immediate social interaction. Interestingly, however, Taylor and her colleagues have demonstrated that the distinction between deceiving and pretending involves more than merely the presence or absence of deceptive intent. To specifically identify a situation as an example of pretense, individuals—both children and adults—require explicit knowledge of the playful intentions of the social partner. This suggests that, unlike jokes, pretense involves an acceptance of falsities between communicative partners based upon the particular functions of the social interaction (Taylor et al., 2003).

The Functions of Deception

Lies and other acts of deception serve many different social functions (Wilson et al., 2003). Sometimes the functions of deceptive acts are self-serving; for example, a child lies about breaking his mother's laptop because he knows he will be severely punished. Other times, however, we engage in deception for other reasons; such as to enhance an interpersonal relationship or to protect the feelings of another:

EXAMPLE: THE SOCIAL FUNCTIONS OF DECEPTION

Jeremy, age 10, plays soccer, although by all objective accounts not very well. His father, who is away on a business trip, calls to get the play by play of this week's game. When talking to his father, Jeremy lies in a dramatic fashion, telling his father that he scored several goals and was the player of the game. Jeremy's mother overhears him and gently confronts him about his deception. After some hesitation, Jeremy explains, "I know Dad wants me to be good at soccer and I want him to be happy."

From a moral perspective, deception is wrong based upon its intent to disguise the truth from another (see Chapter 11). This view is vehemently endorsed by young children, but also to some extent by adults. Still, there is a general distinction between "white lies" and other forms of deception, with the former implicating a more altruistic, accepted purpose for deceiving another (Bussey, 1999). Naturalistic studies of family interaction likewise confirm that children's deception serves a range of functions, which include both positive social functions, such as protecting another, and negative social functions, such as avoiding responsibility (Wilson et al., 2003). As discussed in the chapter on moral reasoning, however, children's moral judgments about lies differ across both age and culture (Fu, Xu, Cameron, Heyman, & Lee, 2007). This further suggests that it is important to consider developmental changes in both children's production and understanding of deceptive strategies.

Developmental Issues in Deception

Most professionals working with young children are aware of the fact that, even at an early age, young children actively employ deceptive strategies. However, many professionals underestimate children's capacity for deception (Stromwall, Granhag, & Landstrom, 2007). In a classic study of children's deception, Chandler and colleagues used a hide-and-seek game to assess the deceptive strategies of preschool children between ages 2½ and 4 (Chandler et al., 1989). The task involved a puppet hiding pieces of "treasure" in various locations. As the puppet moved, it left footprints in its track that could, under the discretion of the child, be wiped away or used to lead someone to a deceiving location. Their findings revealed that children as young as 2½ routinely engage in deceptive strategies, such as withholding and destroying evidence. By contrast, lying is less common and is mastered more gradually. Recent studies have revealed that the frequency with which children employ lying increases with age, with 65% of two-year-olds, 85% of four-year-olds, and 95% of six-year-olds having lied on some occasion (Wilson et al., 2003). Taken together, these findings demonstrate that deception and lying are normal developmental phenomena among young children.

In real-world situations, lying involves the use of multiple verbal and nonverbal deceptive strategies, particularly if adults or other children challenge the liar on the initial claim. So, if a child claims "I didn't do it," a parent or teacher may follow with "Really?" or "Then tell me what really happened." To be an effective liar, the child must coordinate his or her verbal elaborations on the initial lie with nonverbal cues. Research on developmental changes in children's lying indicates that these skills emerge gradually during the school age years. With regard to verbal strategies, preschool age children tend to lie using denials (e.g., I didn't do it) or simple elaborations (e.g., Sarah did it), but when pressed further have considerable difficulty maintaining consistencies between the initial lie and subsequent statements. As a result, young children are likely to blurt out or leak information that reveals the truth, or at the very least, that they are lying. Talwar and Lee (2002) referred to this as children's *semantic leakage control* and noted that it improves from preschool age (three to five years), when children appear to be virtually incapable of semantic leakage control, to early school age (six to seven years), when children utilize semantic leakage control approximately half the time (Talwar & Lee, 2002).

EXAMPLE: SEMANTIC LEAKAGE CONTROL

Lili, age 6, was caught playing a computer game well after her allotted time had passed. Her mother says, "Lili! I told you to close your game!"

Lili looks distressed; her eyes dart from side to side and her brow furrows. After a few seconds pass her mother says, "Well?"

Lili says, "I can't think of what I want to say! I would rather not speak."

Children's ability to construct, control, and manipulate their verbal statements to maintain a lie continues to develop through school age and into adolescence, coinciding with the development of second-order false beliefs and improvements in executive functioning (see Chapter 12) (Talwar, Gordon, & Lee, 2007). Likewise, children's use of nonverbal strategies for deception (e.g., manipulating the environment, gaze aversion) also improves with age. While children can utilize nonverbal deceptive strategies as early as age 2 (Chandler et al., 1989), children become increasingly able to use nonverbal deceptive cues such as a person's gaze and gaze aversion both to fool a person and to detect when others are trying to fool them (Einav & Hood, 2008). For instance, while both six-year-olds and nine-year-olds accurately use eye contact as a cue to detect when people are lying (i.e., people are more likely to be lying if they avoid eye contact), only nine-year-olds are able to explicitly report using that strategy. Einav and Hood have suggested that these changes may reflect children's growing understanding of the mental states and emotions that accompany lies, such as anxiety. So, in response to the example of Lili from above, a nine-year-old might say, "She looked away because she was thinking about what to say and was feeling scared about being caught" (Einav & Hood, 2008).

Children's awareness of what it takes to be a good liar is further refined as they approach adolescence, as demonstrated by Table 6.4, a list of self-reported strategies used by children ages 11 to 13 (Stromwall et al., 2007).

Table 6.4 Self-Reported Lying Strategies by Eleven- to Thirteen-Year-Olds

Nonverbal Strategies	Verbal Strategies
Staying calm	Elaborating the story based upon other previous experiences (of oneself or of another)
Acting normal	Providing details about the event
Not laughing	Boosting credibility by using proper language
Don't look away	Using memory as an excuse (I was young, so I don't remember a lot)

Adapted from Stromwall et al. 2007.

Thus, as many professionals working with children are aware, it becomes increasingly difficult to detect when children are lying (Bond & DePaulo, 2006). By the time children reach ages 11 to 13, they have become such skilled liars that an adult's ability to accurately detect children's lies is just above chance, ranging from 57 to 59% across studies (Bond & DePaulo, 2006). Under conditions in which children "prepare" (practice) their lies, accuracy decreases even further. And, accuracy is no better for adults familiar to children (parents, teachers, therapists) than for strangers.

Taken together, these findings demonstrate that the developmental changes in children's deception during the school age years result in children being masters of the art of deception, a reality that has important practical and clinical implications.

Practical Implications

One of the themes of this chapter is that deception is a normal developmental phenomenon; even young children *can* and *do* lie. From a layperson's perspective, deception is often viewed as evidence of immoral behavior or a symptom of child psychopathology, but in reality, experimenting with deception provides opportunities for weighing the pros and cons of different courses of action. This serves as an important context for the development of moral reasoning in children (see Chapter 11). In addition, as discussed earlier in the chapter, deception may serve a variety of social functions. Thus, when deception is employed in concert with social expectations for behavior or for altruistic reasons, it may in fact improve the quality of children's relationships.

This is not to say, however, that adults should endorse lying and deception in children. Adult responses to children's deceptive acts are important for communicating expectations regarding moral behavior and establishing consequences for children's transgressions. Naturalistic studies of deception with young children have demonstrated that when parents allow lying in older siblings, there is an increase in deceptive behavior by all children in the family across time (Wilson et al., 2003). Of course, as outlined in the previous section, one of the challenges with this is that adults are not particularly good at detecting lies and deception, especially as children approach later school age and adolescence. To make matters worse, adults possess a *truth bias* when it comes to children—an assumption that children are generally truthful (rather than deceptive) (Stromwall et al., 2007). Thus, to effectively deal with children's deception, adults must take into consideration both children's cognitive development (false belief understanding, development of deception) and their own cognitive biases and limitations (their ability to detect children's deceptive strategies, the truth bias).

It is relatively common for parents and teachers to raise questions about a child's lying and deception as either a primary or secondary clinical concern.

Often, these individuals are seeking advice regarding how to deal with children's lying. So, how *should* a parent respond when confronted with a three-year-old who denies flushing his underwear? Or a ten-year-old who is caught walking across town with her friends (against her parents' rules)? Let's consider each in turn.

Dealing With Deception I: Preschool Age Children. Many parents of preschool age children are reluctant to confront children about their deceptive behavior.

EXAMPLE: DECEPTION IN A PRESCHOOL AGE CHILD

Bob and Maria Wilson are seeking advice regarding their three-year-old son, Michael. Michael, who is resisting potty training, has taken to flushing his underwear whenever he has an accident. When confronted about his behavior, Michael vehemently denies both the accident and the flushing. Because Michael is an only child, the Wilsons have no doubt that Michael is the culprit, but they are unclear about whether to challenge him about his lying and if they should punish him for his deception.

Studies of lying with children ages 2 to 6 have revealed that while parents challenge children's lies fairly often (38% of the time), they ignore lies as often as they punish them (18%), and only rarely respond by telling the child not to lie (0.3%) (Newton, Reddy, & Bull, 2000; Wilson et al., 2003). In clinical practice, we have likewise encountered many parents who, even when catching a young child "red-handed," minimize the child's wrongdoing. Parents may be resistant to label a child's behavior as "deception" because of the child's age, as demonstrated by a mother who, despite catching her child hiding empty chocolate candy wrappers, said, "She's too young to know what she was doing" and "She doesn't *intentionally* lie." Other times, parents recognize children's motives for their deceptive behavior and feel sympathetic, as in the case of Michael above.

Still, preschool age children should be gently confronted about their deceptive behavior and, when known, the truth of the situation ("We know that you flushed your underwear, Michael"). Because children reference adults' emotions at a very early age (Denham, 1998), they are likely to be keenly aware of adults' emotional responses to their transgressions. Efforts should be made to remain neutral so as not to induce excessive fear, shame, or guilt in the child. To facilitate moral reasoning, adults should acknowledge the child's motive or inquire about it ("We know you were embarrassed about having an accident" or "Tell us why you put your underwear in the potty").

Should preschool age children *ever* be punished for their lies and deception? Yes. When an adult provides a child with a clear rule that the child intentionally violates and tries to cover up, it is imperative that adults follow through with an age-appropriate consequence. Natural consequences, those that follow directly from a transgression, are often most effective (child breaks a coveted Hummel doll and helps clean up the mess; child steals a piece of candy and must return it to the store owner with an apology). However, other meaningful consequences (taking away a special snack or television time) are also reasonable approaches. Although limitations in children's reasoning (Chapter 10) and understanding of internal states (Chapter 3) make it unlikely that preschoolers will fully comprehend this process, this type of sensitive approach will set the stage for dealing with future transgressions (there will almost certainly be some!).

Dealing With Deception II: School Age Children. With school age children, some of the same issues remain; others change:

EXAMPLE: DECEPTION IN A SCHOOL AGE CHILD

Charlene, age 10, has been repeatedly instructed by her parents not to walk to town without an adult. One day two of Charlene's friends decide to walk to town after school for ice cream; they invite Charlene to come. Charlene calls her mom and tells her that she will be going to Tabby's house after school. Later, when Charlene's mother calls looking for her, Tabby's mother reveals that the girls went to town.

Although Charlene's premeditated lie is indicative of her emerging cognitive abilities, deceit at more advanced ages should be addressed quickly and directly. Because an understanding of concepts of morality is now within the child's capacity, children can be expected to consistently follow established expectations for moral behavior (i.e., we expect you not to lie, to cheat, to steal, etc.). Children who repeatedly engage in deceptive acts will quickly lose the trust of parents, teachers, and peers to the point that it negatively impacts their social relationships. Adults must therefore confront children about their transgressions and implement age-appropriate consequences for behavior.

While Charlene's deception is distressing for her parents and teachers, in the majority of cases such isolated incidents do *not* represent a cause for concern. Generally, such situations are linked to specific environmental circumstances with strong social motives (in Charlene's case her parents' seemingly unfair rule about walking to town paired with the strong pull of her peer group). By trying to discern the function of the deception in relation to the social situation, adults can gain a better understanding of children's motives and perhaps better address the situation ("We know you really wanted to walk to town with your friends, but it is dangerous to walk along Middle Highway").

In contrast to the isolated example of Charlene above, frequent lying and deception across contexts (home and school) have been linked with children's behavior problems (Gervais, Tremblay, Desmarais-Gervais, & Vitaro, 2000). Although it is not clear whether telling lies leads to problem behaviors or if the presence of problem behaviors justifies the need to lie, lying has been linked with aggression, defiance, delinquency, and other antisocial behaviors (stealing, vandalism, etc.) (Loeber, Burke, Lahey, Winters, & Zera, 2000). In fact, lying is one of several symptoms required for oppositional defiant disorder (ODD) and conduct disorder (CD), two of the most common childhood disruptive behavior disorders (American Psychiatric Association, 2004). While we have emphasized throughout the chapter that lying does not necessarily represent deviant behavior, when lying is a part of a larger pattern of disruptive or aggressive behavior, further evaluation and treatment are highly recommended.

Conclusions

We conclude by returning to Yoda, the wise and powerful Jedi master from the *Star Wars* series. Like all Jedi warriors, Yoda possessed telepathic powers: the ability to read and control another's mind. While mind *control* is beyond the scope of this chapter, mind *reading*, at least as it pertains to understanding, predicting, and acting based upon the thoughts and feelings of another, is a fundamental part of children's cognitive development. Consider one final example:

EXAMPLE: MIND READING, FALSE BELIEFS, AND DECEPTION

Sam, age 6½, religiously has a peanut butter and jelly sandwich for lunch. One day, rather than asking him what he wanted, I (BLS) simply prepared his PB&J and served it to him. He was indignant and commented, "How did you even know that I wanted peanut butter and jelly?" To which I jokingly responded, "I must be a mind reader!" Later I was working on the computer when Sam entered the room and stood silently staring at me. I turned to him and said, "What's up, Sam?" No response. I repeated, "Sam, what is it?" Finally, I insisted, "Sam, tell me what you need!" To which he calmly responded, "I guess you're not a mind reader after all!"

Clearly, my musings about mind reading did not go unnoticed by Sam. Why? Because Sam has made considerable advancement in his theory of mind—his understanding that others have thoughts, feelings, and beliefs different from his own. Sam's awareness that his mom *possesses* different thoughts and beliefs, that she might *act* on those beliefs, and that he can *manipulate* those thoughts and beliefs demonstrates his mastery of the two important cognitive skills that are the focus of this chapter: false belief understanding and deception. Sam's efforts to "test" his predictions about her beliefs also demonstrate his fairly advanced reasoning skills, but that is beyond the scope of this chapter, so see Chapters 10 and 11 for more on that topic.

References

American Psychiatric Association. (2004). *Diagnostic and statistical manual of mental disorders IV-TR*. Washington, DC: Author.

Berthoud-Papandropoulou, I., & Kilcher, H. (2003). Is a false belief statement a lie or a truthful statement? Judgments and explanations of children aged 3 to 8. *Developmental Science, 6*, 173–177.

Bond, C. F., Jr., & DePaulo, B. M. (2006). Accuracy of deception judgments. *Personality and Social Psychology Review, 10*, 214–234.

Bradmetz, J., & Schneider, R. (2004). The role of the counterfactually satisfied desire in the lag between false-belief and false-emotion attributions in children ages 4–7. *British Journal of Developmental Psychology, 22*, 185–196.

Bussey, K. (1999). Children's categorization and evaluation of different types of lies and truths. *Child Development, 70*, 1338–1347.

Chandler, M., Fritz, A. S., & Hala, S. (1989). Small-scale deceit: Deception as a marker of two-, three-, and four-year-olds' early theories of mind. *Child Development, 60*, 1263–1277.

Cole, P. M. (1986). Children's spontaneous control of facial expressions. *Child Development, 57*, 1309–1321.

Curenton, S. M. (2003). Low-income preschoolers' false-belief performance. *Journal of Genetic Psychology, 162*, 411–424.

Denham, S. A. (1998). *Emotional development in young children*. New York: Guildford Press.

de Rosnay, M., Pons, F., Harris, P. L., & Morrell, J. M. B. (2004). A lag between understanding false belief and emotion attribution in young children: Relationships with linguistic ability and mothers' mental-state language. *British Journal of Developmental Psychology, 22*, 197–218.

Domitrovich, C. E., Cortes, R. C., & Greenberg, M. T. (2007). Improving young children's social and emotional competence: A randomized trial of the preschool 'PATHS' curriculum. *Journal of Primary Prevention, 28*, 67–91.

Dunn, J., & Hughes, C. (1998). Understanding mind and emotion: Longitudinal associations with mental-state talk between young friends. *Developmental Psychology, 34*, 1026–1037.

Einav, S., & Hood, B. M. (2008). Tell-tale eyes: Children's attribution of gaze aversion as a lying cue. *Developmental Psychology, 44*, 1655–1667.

Farrar, J. M., Ashwell, S., & Maag, L. (2005). The emergence of phonological awareness: Connections to language and theory of mind development. *First Language, 25*, 157–172.

Fu, G., Xu, F., Cameron, C. A., Heyman, G., & Lee, K. (2007). Cross-cultural differences in children's choices, categorizations, and evaluations of truths and lies. *Developmental Psychology, 43,* 278–293.

Gervais, J., Tremblay, R. E., Desmarais-Gervais, L., & Vitaro, F. (2000). Children's persistent lying, gender differences, and disruptive behaviours: A longitudinal perspective. *International Journal of Behavioral Development, 24,* 213–221.

Gopnik, A., & Astington, J. W. (1988). Children's understanding of representational change and its relation to the understanding of false belief and the appearance-reality distinction. *Child Development, 59,* 26–37.

Jenkins, J. M., Turrell, S. L., Kogushi, Y., Lollis, S., & Ross, H. S. (2003). A longitudinal investigation of the dynamics of mental state talk in families. *Child Development, 74,* 905–920.

Lee, K., & Cameron, A. (2000). Extracting truthful information from lies: Emergence of the expression-representation distinction. *Merrill-Palmer Quarterly, 46,* 1–20.

Loeber, R., Burke, J. D., Lahey, B. B., Winters, A., & Zera, M. (2000). Oppositional defiant and conduct disorder: A review of the past 10 years. Part I. *Journal of the American Academy of Child and Adolescent Psychiatry, 39,* 1468–1484.

Lohmann, H., & Tomasello, M. (2003). The role of language in the development of false belief understanding: A training study. *Child Development, 74,* 1130–1144.

Newton, P., Reddy, V., & Bull, R. (2000). Children's everyday deception and performance on false-belief tasks. *British Journal of Developmental Psychology, 18,* 297–317.

Parker, J., MacDonald, C., & Miller, C. (2007). "John thinks that Mary *feels* … " False belief in children across affective and physical domains. *Journal of Genetic Psychology, 168,* 43–61.

Perner, J. (1991). *Understanding the representational mind.* Cambridge, MA: MIT Press.

Perner, J., & Wimmer, H. (1985). "John *thinks* that Mary *thinks* that …" Attribution of second-order beliefs by 5- to 10-year-old children. *Journal of Experimental Child Psychology, 39,* 437–471.

Riggs, K. J., & Peterson, D. M. (2000). Counterfactual thinking in preschool children: Mental state and causal inferences. In P. Mitchell & K. J. Riggs (Eds.), *Children's reasoning and the mind* (pp. 87–99). Hove, England: Psychology Press/Taylor & Francis.

Ruffman, T., Slade, L., & Crowe, E. (2002). The relation between children's and mothers' mental state language and theory-of-mind understanding. *Child Development, 73,* 734–751.

Stromwall, L. A., Granhag, P. A., & Landstrom, S. (2007). Children's prepared and unprepared lies: Can adults see through their strategies? *Applied Cognitive Psychology, 21,* 457–471.

Talwar, V., Gordon, H., & Lee, K. (2007). Lying in the elementary school years: Verbal deception and its relation to second-order belief understanding. *Developmental Psychology, 43,* 804–810.

Talwar, V., & Lee, K. (2002). Development of lying to conceal a transgression: Children's control of expressive behavior during verbal deception. *International Journal of Behavioral Development, 26,* 436–444.

Taylor, M., Lussier, G. L., & Maring, B. L. (2003). The distinction between lying and pretending. *Journal of Cognition and Development, 4,* 299–323.

Wellman, H. M. (2002). Understanding the psychological world: Developing a theory of mind. In U. Goswami (Ed.), *Blackwell handbook of childhood cognitive development* (pp. 167–187). Malden, MA: Blackwell Publishing.

Wellman, H. M., Cross, D., & Watson, J. (2001). Meta-analysis of theory-of-mind development: The truth about false belief. *Child Development, 72,* 655–685.

Wilson, A. E., Smith, M. D., & Ross, H. S. (2003). The nature and effects of young children's lies. *Social Development, 12,* 21–45.

Wimmer, H., & Perner, J. (1983). Beliefs about beliefs: Representation and constraining function of wrong beliefs in young children's understanding of deception. *Cognition, 13,* 103–128.

III
Children's Memory

Without memory, we have nothing. Memory allows us to learn, memory serves as the foundation for building new cognitive architecture, and our memories define who we are. Memory is a place, a process, and a product all bundled into one tiny system (that fits neatly in the palm of your hand!).

The processes associated with storing information in the short- and long-term are described by Reeder, Martin, and Turner in Chapter 7. What emerges is an appreciation of children's memory as a fluid, dynamic cognitive process with implications for clinical and educational practice.

Retrieving information from memory is not nearly as analogous to computers as we like to believe. You can trust that, once saved, a document or photo on your computer will look exactly the same every time you access it. We make the same assumptions about children's memories. In Chapter 8 we have tried to highlight the truly astonishing malleability of children's memory—autobiographies built up from many sources that coalesce into the entity of what is "remembered."

In light of this, when there is a pressing need to draw accurate factual accounts from the mind of a child (like accessing a hard drive!), extreme care must be taken not to corrupt the files. In Chapter 9, Gregory, Carol, and Compo translate the tools of the forensic interview to the needs of all professionals working with children who strive to "establish truth."

7

Memory Development in Childhood

JOHN A. REEDER, SARAH E. MARTIN, and GEOFFREY F. W. TURNER

Newborn infants whose mothers read aloud from *The Cat in the Hat* during their final six weeks of pregnancy displayed a stronger preference for the story than other babies who had not been read to (DeCasper & Spence, 1986). Like Dr. Seuss's fictional feline, their memory of the cat came back! It might have been a simple form of memory and probably not a conscious one, but it demonstrated the delayed influence of specific prior experiences and sensations no longer present. It revealed the first rudimentary functions of memory.

An early capacity to retain specific information contradicts common intuitions about the unreliability of children's memory, but developmental psychologists have found evidence for complex memory processes even in young children, and increasingly dependable and versatile systems in older ones. To be fair, children do recall the past in less detail than adults, and they are susceptible to certain kinds of memory errors that could be of concern to clinicians in particular. They will never completely outgrow that susceptibility. After all, a memory is not simply stored information. It is an echo of the way information was originally processed, shaped by the way it is later retrieved. Thus, as the cognitive processes of infancy develop into those of childhood, adolescence, and adulthood, memory formation changes too. Memories can never be any more sophisticated or reliable than the processes that produced them, however.

From a developmental psychopathology framework (e.g., Cicchetti, 2006), understanding normative memory development is necessary to identifying atypical development and working effectively with children in clinical settings. Some familiarity with normative memory development is necessary for appropriately interpreting children's accounts of past events. It is of particular importance to a clinician who seeks to understand a child's subjective experience of the world.

Overview of Memory Systems

Researchers have identified a wide variety of memory functions that involve different kinds of information, processed in different ways, over different intervals of time. Traditionally, these functions are organized into three memory systems (based on the modal model of Atkinson and Shiffrin, 1968; see Figure 7.1).

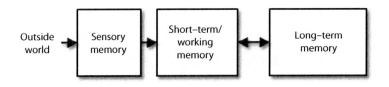

Figure 7.1 The "box" model of memory systems.

First, impressions of the outside world are acquired by the senses and transferred to *sensory memory*. The rapidly changing input is held in temporary registers just long enough to be transferred to *short-term memory* (STM), where it is stored, organized, and integrated. For this reason, the system is generally identified as *working memory* (WM) and associated with ongoing thought.

WM serves as a gateway to *long-term memory* (LTM), where information is stored indefinitely. The wealth of information in LTM is compromised, however, by limited accessibility. Certain details may elude conscious attempts at retrieval, then suddenly spring to mind when a sufficient cue is provided.

LTM is depicted as a single box in Figure 7.1, but it is useful to partition it in various ways that reflect functional distinctions within the system. For example, LTM is the repository of *semantic memory*, meaningful information that is not identified with any particular time or place, and *episodic memory*, the traces of specific events that comprise an individual's personal experience. Another distinction involves our awareness of LTM: *Explicit memory* refers to the purposeful retrieval of information into conscious thought, and *implicit memory* refers to the *un*conscious influence of prior experiences on cognition. That description might sound psychodynamic, but most of these unconscious influences are mundane, like improved performance on a practiced skill, or solving a puzzle with the word *butter* because someone said *bread* earlier, even though that connection escapes awareness.

Developmental Changes in Memory

There is no evidence to suggest that children acquire the memory systems in Figure 7.1 in any sequence. Instead, all of the systems appear to be available at an early age, but they only function to the extent allowed by the child's general developmental progress. Memory is primarily a *constructive* process, in which fragmentary details from the past are assembled and embellished based on the rememberer's expectations. Consequently, children's overall cognitive development affects the way they remember things.

In particular, two categories of developmental change influence children's memory function. First, children's cognitive processes become more efficient and sophisticated with age. Second, children continually accumulate world knowledge and personal experience. Together, these complementary factors support more elaborate operations in WM that leave richer and more easily retrievable traces in LTM.

The Increased Efficiency and Sophistication of Cognitive Processes

A developing child gradually performs mental tasks faster, and with less effort and attention. In part, this improvement reflects biological maturation, but it also arises from the increased efficiency and sophistication of the child's mental processes (Case, 1985). These changes occur across the various memory systems in Figure 7.1, but they are especially apparent and important in WM.

The most obvious developmental difference in WM is an age-related increase in *span*, the number of pieces of information that the system can maintain at once. Two-year-olds can hold only about two unrelated "chunks," whereas preteens can store about seven, the same as adults. Further, because a chunk is simply a meaningful unit, as meaning changes, so too does a chunk. For example, F, B, and I are simply three letters to most five-year-olds. But to older children and adults with knowledge of government bureaus, FBI represents one chunk. In this way, chunks are scalable in capacity. In addition to maintaining more of them at once, older children and adults can use their knowledge to reorganize the information in WM so that each chunk stores a greater amount of detail.

Most research suggests that span does not reflect WM capacity, exactly, but the rate at which information *decays* or is forgotten due to interference from other information competing for attention. By the time a child reports a couple of chunks, the remaining contents of WM have been forgotten. One of the main factors that determine WM span is *rehearsal*. By repeating pieces of information over and over (maintenance rehearsal), or thinking about each one more deeply (elaborative rehearsal), a person can postpone the decay of information indefinitely. Children cannot rehearse information as quickly as adults, and rehearsal speed is correlated with WM capacity (Towse, Hitch, & Horton, 2007). The problem for young children is that they may not be capable of *any* rehearsal before age 5 or 6. Even at age 7 or 8, when they *are* able to rehearse, they do not do so spontaneously. Not surprisingly, this development reflects the acquisition of language skills.

The Accumulation of General Knowledge

Interacting with the environment leads to a more comprehensive and well-organized body of knowledge about the world. As Berndt (1997) points out, increasing knowledge allows for more efficient encoding of new material. Further, having a rich semantic network full of interrelated concepts and facts facilitates memory because recalling one detail spontaneously activates others that are semantically related. And once children become aware of these interactions, they are more likely to exploit them strategically.

One of the more famous examples of why a large knowledge base leads to superior memory performance comes from Chi and Koeske (1983). These authors examined one boy's dinosaur knowledge in intimate detail. They were interested in whether he would remember more new information concerning dinosaurs he knew a lot about or those he knew less about. Their investigation demonstrated that memory was greater for higher initial levels of knowledge. The difference in retention for high- and low-knowledge lists was even greater when tested a year later. This effect is explained by the number of links that can be formed between new information and existing information. There are more concepts, more links, and more high-quality links between concepts for an expert (Chi, 1978).

It goes without saying that children possess less general knowledge than adults. In order to fully understand memory development, therefore, it is necessary to disentangle the effects of knowledge from age-related changes in memory processes. In groundbreaking work, Chi (1978) documented the impact of knowledge on memory in children and adults. The children she studied were accomplished chess players. As expected, the adults could keep track of more random digits than the children, but when memory for the positions of chess pieces during real matches was measured, children outperformed the adults. Although their general memory capacity was smaller, the child experts could store more information about chess in each chunk. This finding has been replicated in many other domains of expertise, and in LTM as well as WM (for example, see Gaultney, Bjorklund, & Schneider, 1992).

Knowledge is also more important than aptitude. Schneider, Körkel, and Weinert (1989) divided children into "expert" and "novice" groups based on their knowledge of soccer, and into "low-aptitude" and "high-aptitude" groups on the basis of a standardized test. Regardless of aptitude, experts at all grade levels outperformed novices in terms of the amount of a soccer story they could remember, their ability to draw correct inferences from the text, and their ability to detect contradictions in it.

Taken together, these findings stress the importance of knowledge over age as a critical factor in memory development. Knowledge provides the basis for "filling in the blanks," where information stored in memory is insufficient to provide a coherent record of what was learned or experienced. From an early age, children begin to exploit their knowledge in several ways that make it more useful: as scripts, schemas, insights of meta-memory, and strategies.

Scripts. One way that children organize their knowledge is by abstracting common features from repeated events. *Scripts* are generalized representations of the sequential structure of events that show how an event typically unfolds (like dining at a restaurant), including roles, props, locations, and actions (Hudson, Fivush, & Kuebli, 1992). For example, one of us (GFWT) saw a four-year-old at a wedding reception, walking with her head hung low, deeply upset at having to attend a "grown-up" event. Upon seeing the wedding cake, however, her expression turned to pure joy as she shouted, "It's a party!" In a moment, the simple cue of the cake activated her *party script* and redefined her expectations.

When scripts are still being formed, script-inconsistent information is not well remembered, because the difference between normal script variations and violations is unclear (Farrar & Goodman, 1990). Script-consistent information is predictable and is thus more likely to be remembered, but reliance can lead to memory distortions (Sutherland, Pipe, Schick, Murray, & Gobbo, 2003). For example, Erskine, Markham, and Howie (2002) found that omissions in the sequence of a familiar script (going to McDonald's) were incorrectly remembered by five- and six-year-olds, and the effect increased as time passed. Hudson and Nelson (1983) found young children to be especially likely to remember out-of-sequence information (e.g., eating a birthday cake *before* blowing out the candles) as having occurred in the correct order. In contrast, older children with well-developed scripts often remember script-*inconsistent* information better. This is especially true when script disruptions or violations have emotional consequences, like dropping a carton of eggs in the supermarket (Hudson, 1988).

Schemata. As a child's knowledge grows, it becomes increasingly organized into coherent, theory-like structures (Carey, 1985). *Schemata* serve to organize information hierarchically, enabling inferences that go beyond what is observed (Martin & Halverson, 1987). For example, children begin to form schematic gender representations when they have acquired sufficient information about their own gender and cultural gender roles (Cherney, 2005).

Organization influences memory. In general, schema-inconsistent information is either ignored or distorted at encoding. Distortions are especially likely during times of cognitive challenge, for example, when the information to be remembered is ambiguous, when the original memory trace is weak, or when recall follows a long delay. In a meta-analysis of 40 studies that assessed gender schemata, Signorella, Bigler, and Liben (1997) found that children remembered schema-consistent information better than inconsistent information. Moreover, children tended to misremember inconsistent information in schema-consistent ways (e.g., remembering a female physician as having been a nurse). These effects are consistent across gender, racial, and age-related schemata (Bigler & Liben, 1993; Davidson, Cameron, & Jergovic, 1995).

Meta-memory. Although children can develop expertise in many areas, they typically possess an incomplete or even faulty understanding of how their own memory systems work. In a review of the basic findings, Vasta, Haith, and Miller (1995) note that meta-memory improves with age. By the time children begin school they know that short lists are easier to remember than long ones, that we forget more with the passage of time, and that recognizing something is easier than recalling it. But they still have much to learn about the strengths and weaknesses of their own memory systems. For example, children do not always use memory strategies spontaneously, and when they do, their strategies are not always efficient.

Strategies. With increasing age, a greater proportion of children become aware of the difference that strategies can make in remembering. Naturally, their intentional use of memory strategies becomes more frequent. But, even though preschool children use rudimentary strategies (Wellman, Ritter, & Flavell, 1975), children younger than age 5 or 6 generally suffer from a *mediation deficiency,* or inability to use memory strategies even when asked or instructed to do so. From a cognitive perspective, most children this age do not have the logical reasoning skills to implement many memory strategies. As their performance on theory-of-mind tasks suggests, these children are just beginning to show adult-like insight into the workings of the mind (Wellman, Cross, & Watson, 2001).

Children begin to demonstrate spontaneous strategy use by elementary school (Miller, Haynes, DeMarie-Dreblow, & Woody-Ramsey, 1986). At age 6 or 7, they discover for themselves that repeating information in WM stalls its decay. At first, their use of rehearsal is imperfect; for example, eight-year-olds tend to repeat each word in a list singly (Ornstein, Naus, & Stone, 1977; Ornstein, Naus, & Liberty, 1975). Not until age 10 or so do children use the more effective cumulative rehearsal strategy, rehearsing multiple elements of a set (Kunzinger, 1985; Ornstein et al., 1975). As the quality of the rehearsal increases, memory performance does too (Ornstein, Baker-Ward, & Naus, 1988; Ornstein & Naus, 1978).

In contrast to toddlers and preschoolers, children between ages 5 and 8 demonstrate a *production deficiency,* or failure to initiate memory strategies spontaneously, even though they are capable of using them. For example, young school-aged children are capable of using organizational strategies (Bjorklund & Bjorklund, 1985), but do not do so spontaneously until later elementary school or early middle school (and not reliably even then; Brainerd, Reyna, Harnishfeger, & Howe, 1993).

Some strategies, like categorization, depend explicitly on the richness of one's semantic network, and they are increasingly utilized as knowledge matures because they become easier to implement (Chi & Koeske, 1983; Schneider et al., 1989). Because the amount of effort a strategy requires partly governs whether it will be used, young adolescents use them more than young elementary school children (Guttentag, 1984; Imbo, Duverne, & Lemaire, 2007; Imbo & Vandierendonck, 2007; Lehmann & Hasselhorn, 2007). Strategic organization and elaboration are both facilitated by rich network of knowledge (Bjorklund & Bjorklund, 1985; Bjorklund & Douglas, 1997).

The Accumulation of Personal Experience

It is clear that infants form memories from their first days of life, yet they appear to carry very little explicit knowledge of the things that happen to them into later childhood. Rubin (2000) provided substantial evidence that memories of very early childhood can be divided into three rough time periods. Adults remember almost nothing of events before their third birthday, and have only faint and partial memories for events before age 6 or 7. From ages 3 to 6 or so, children demonstrate vague and temporally unanchored recollections of events that increase in quality through the preschool years. Beginning at about age 7 or so, memories are similar to those of adolescence and adulthood. One kind of memory, in particular, appears to arise relatively late. *Autobiographical memory* (AM) is episodic, relating to specific past events characterized by self-involvement (Nelson, 1993).

Some authors have argued that early autobiographical memories are indeed stored, but they are inaccessible as a consequence of the incompatibility between prelinguistic encoding and linguistic retrieval. They languish as orphaned memories that did not fit any well-understood scripts or schemas. For example, after burning popcorn set off a fire alarm in a preschool, causing an evacuation, Pillemer, Picariello, and Pruett (1994) had the foresight to record the children's memories of this highly salient event. When the interviews were conducted again seven years later, the event was more likely to be recalled in a coherent way by the children who had understood the event when it occurred. Those with poor initial comprehension of the event were unlikely to have more than fleeting images of it. This real-life example illustrates how AM, like semantic memory, depends crucially on accumulated general knowledge.

Reliability

Given the relevance of developmental changes in cognitive processing, knowledge, and experience, it is natural to question the reliability of young children's memories. Developmental studies have demonstrated that young children forget more than older children and adults, and they forget more quickly (for a review see Schneider, 2002). Even when they learn to a relative criterion, controlling for the greater retention capacity of older children and adults, young children recall a smaller proportion of what they learned (Brainerd & Reyna, 1995). Beyond simple errors of *omission*, children are also prone to more complicated errors of *commission*, such as so-called false memories. As a result, young children may be more prone than adults to remember things that never really happened, but only under very specific circumstances.

Source Monitoring

As explained in Chapter 9, children (as well as adults) are prone to making certain kinds of memory errors when they encounter incorrect information about past events. In the extreme, a child may falsely recall details that were "planted" during questioning or reminiscing about past events (which is particularly worrisome in clinical and legal settings). Some researchers have attributed this *misinformation effect* to the overwriting of old details by new ones, so that the original details are no longer represented in memory at all (e.g., Loftus, 2005). Another explanation, however, is that the original information and the misinformation are both stored in memory, and errors reflect confusion between these two *sources*. In this view, a so-called false memory is not really false at all; the memory may be true, but it is misinterpreted by way of *source misattribution*. The *source monitoring framework* (SMF; Johnson & Mitchell, 2002; Lindsay, 2008) is a theory about why people remember things without necessarily knowing how they acquired those memories in the first place.

It should be emphasized that young children are quite capable of identifying the origins of their memories when the characteristics of the alternative sources are dissimilar (Lindsay, 2008), but they do have some difficulty under specific developmentally and clinically significant conditions. Foley, Johnson, and Raye (1983) found that younger children were not as good as the older ones at remembering which words they either said aloud or imagined saying. The ability to identify the external (perceived) or internal (reflective) origin of remembered events is a special case of source monitoring, called *reality monitoring* (Johnson & Raye, 1981). Apparently, children have some difficulty with reality monitoring, at least when they try to determine whether an action was really performed or just imagined (Foley & Johnson, 1985; Lindsay, 1991). Lindsay (2008) proposed that an important developmental factor in children's source monitoring is the use of strategic meta-memory-based processes. For this reason, the development of source monitoring abilities is closely tied to the accumulation of knowledge and experience, which can make up for insufficient source cues. Another important factor is the availability of specific kinds of information in a memory that identify its source. Finally, if a child is not yet able to perform a certain cognitive operation, no record of that cognitive operation will be available in memory. Thus, any source monitoring judgment that depends on it will be particularly difficult.

Clinical Implications

Although we have stressed that children have complex and remarkably functional memory systems, there is an abundance of evidence demonstrating that they are less proficient than adults at remembering past experiences and are less likely to use strategies that might help. A wide range of experimental and applied studies support the perspective that children's memory is more reliable than people generally believe, but limited by their repertoire of cognitive processes and the extent of their accumulated knowledge and experience.

For the clinician or educator working with children, an understanding of normative developmental changes in memory provides a necessary backdrop for understanding children's recollections of their own experiences as well as their capacities to learn and remember new skills. For instance, to what extent can a clinician rely on a five-year-old's account of a recent family argument to be complete and accurate? If an eight-year-old is instructed in a set of problem-solving steps, can he later recall these steps or, perhaps even more importantly, enact these steps when emotionally aroused? Consistent with a developmental psychopathology perspective (Cicchetti, 2006), we believe that an understanding of normative developmental changes in memory, and its related cognitive processes, has important implications for both assessment and intervention with children.

Implications for Assessment

One clear implication of the developmental psychopathology perspective is that the clinician must avoid pathologizing normative developmental limitations in memory while recognizing that some memory failures and disruptions are in fact cause for developmental or clinical concern. For example, distortions in a four-year-old's recollection of an important family event are more likely to reflect developmentally normative encoding errors, or even the family's subsequent reconstruction of this event ("remember when we went on the picnic at the lake …"), rather than a pathological process.

Other memory disruptions may be similarly normative, but still offer a clinician insight into a disordered developmental process. For example, in working with a severely depressed adolescent girl, one of us (SEM) repeatedly encountered the teenager's remarkable proneness to recall information consistent with her highly ingrained script for social relationships, characterized by painful and rejecting interactions, and to appear entirely unable to recollect events that hinted at her capacity for more competent social and emotional functioning. While the connection between this adolescent's script for social interactions and her subsequent recollection of such interactions is in no way developmentally unusual, the content and processes by which these connections unfolded provided important insight into the nature of her presenting psychopathology. Moreover, an understanding of normative memory processes offered avenues for intervention. For example, by facilitating the adolescent's attention to and encoding of script-inconsistent information within her social interactions, she was eventually better able to retain and recollect the more positive and esteem-enhancing facets of her social encounters and relationships.

Regardless of one's mental health or developmental status, sleep serves as an integral step in the process of memory consolidation. Different phases of the sleep cycle have been shown to be important in different facets of memory, and sleep deprivation has clear links to memory deficits. In clinical populations, children's emotional distress and behavioral disruption are often accompanied by sleep disturbance (Rabian & Bottjer, 2008). Although most clinicians are developing an increasing appreciation for the negative impact of sleep deprivation on children's behavioral functioning (not to mention family stress and frustration), they may be less inclined to consider the effect on children's memory or learning. With respect to memory development, sleep loss has been associated with poor concentration (Epstein, Chillage, & Lavie, 1998) and with impairments in both working memory (Steenari et al., 2003) and long-term memory (Backhaus, Hoeckesfeld, Born, Hohagen, & Junghanns, 2008). In concrete terms, Sadeh, Gruber, and Raviv (2003) found that a one-hour difference in the amount of sleep children get has the same influence (in terms of effect size) as two grade levels on measures of attention and WM. For these reasons, a child whose clinical picture is complicated by sleep disruption may be particularly vulnerable to errors of encoding, storage, and retrieval, in both WM and LTM.

EXAMPLE

A psychologist working in the schools is contacted by a teacher for concerns regarding a five-year-old boy in her kindergarten class. The teacher reports that the child is highly irritable, has difficulty staying on task, and is verbally disruptive. Based upon these behaviors, the teacher would like to have the child evaluated for ADHD, but she notes that the parents are highly resistant to this. Upon meeting with the parents, the psychologist learns that the mother has been co-sleeping with the child for approximately six months, following the child's bout with a physical illness. The parents admit that this has significantly interfered with the quality of the child's sleep, which averages seven hours per night. With the help of the psychologist, a behavioral sleep plan is implemented in which the child returns to sleeping in his own room for 10 hours per night. Following this intervention, the teacher reports dramatic improvements in the child's classroom behavior.

Implications for Intervention

A child's subjective understanding of experienced events and the autobiographical narrative connecting them depends crucially on memory. Moreover, a child's memories are likely to be the material of psychotherapeutic interactions, at least with children who have developed the conversational skills necessary for describing and reflecting on their personal experiences. In general, the memory development literature supports a clinical approach in which children's memories are interpreted not as records of events, but rather as clues to how the child experienced those events in the first place and how the child is thinking about them now. Importantly, this is not to say that the clinician should categorically reject children's recollections of past events as factually inaccurate (a perspective that would have concerning implications in a situation, for example, where a child discloses a traumatic or potentially abusive experience). Rather, the clinician should recognize that children's memories reflect a complicated interplay between actual experience and their past and current cognitive processing of these events.

This perspective on memories as clues to both actual experiences and past and current thought processes can offer clinicians points of entry into their therapeutic interactions with children. For example, in working with socially unskilled and peer-rejected children (a group for whom social-cognitive processing deficits have been well documented in the literature; e.g., Crick & Dodge, 1994), the clinician must recognize that a child's recollection of a past social experience is affected by several factors: the experience itself, his or her attention to and encoding of social cues at the time of the experience, his or her subsequent cognitive processing of the experience, and in some cases the social reconstruction of a narrative that further shapes the ultimate personal significance of the event. If one goal of treatment is to help the child achieve a more accurate and realistic understanding of his or her social relationships and interactions, any one of these steps in the memory process may be a viable target for intervention. For instance, by having a child generate a narrative about an experience with a peer at school, a clinician can then ask the child questions about how that experience was similar to or different from past experiences. As has been previously discussed, here the concern is less about the accuracy of the child's memory and more about how the child processes the information. However, if you, as the clinician, happen to know details about the event that contradict the child's report, you can gently probe the child to reconstruct the event in a different way, thereby reshaping his or her current memory and overall memory schema.

Moreover, if an additional goal of treatment is to assist the child in developing strategies to more effectively cope with challenging peer interactions, the clinician must also consider the extent to which the child's memory skills are sufficiently developed to allow them to master such strategies and to subsequently recall them within real social interactions. While older children can be assisted in using organization and elaboration techniques to facilitate their retention of new skills or concepts, younger children are more likely to utilize rehearsal and practice, and to require more contextual cues to prompt their later recall. For example, consistent with this developmental perspective, many existing school-based programs that target early problem-solving and social skills utilize instruction and repeated practice opportunities, along with visual cues and other prompts to facilitate children's recall of specific skills and strategies within the classroom (e.g., Domitrovich, Cortes, & Greenberg, 2007).

Other cognitive-developmental principles can also be brought to bear in devising interventions that focus or otherwise rely on children's memory.

First, the *encoding specificity principle* holds for children as well as adults. When the context of learning is reinstated, recall performance improves (e.g., Priestley, Roberts, & Pipe, 1999). Therefore, when a child is expected to store something in memory, it will help to anticipate the setting in which that information will need to be recalled, and to establish a similar setting for learning. Second, the *generation effect* is also powerful for children. They are more likely to remember examples and explanations that they create on their own than those given by others (Snodgrass & Kinjo, 1998; Tenenbaum, Alfieri, Brooks, & Dunne, 2008). Further, to the extent that a child's knowledge of category memberships allows, categorization and clustering can be taught in children in late elementary school (e.g., Ornstein et al., 1977). Finally, instructing children to pay attention can help reduce the kinds of memory errors that occur at the time of encoding, but only when they are developmentally capable of monitoring and shifting their attentional resources.

Finally, a developmental perspective also has implications for therapeutic interactions with children's caregivers and families. In our clinical experience, lapses and distortions in children's memories can be a source of confusion and frustration to adults. Parents are often puzzled by apparent failures in children's episodic memory ("Why doesn't he remember anything about that nice vacation that we took last year?") as well as procedural memory ("Why can't he ever remember to hang up his jacket?"), at times leading to attributions of mal-intent on the part of the child ("He just doesn't care/is lazy/is lying"). The child clinician or educator is in a unique position to place parents' concerns and frustrations with their children's memory within developmental context.

EXAMPLE

David (age 6) was referred to a child therapist for adjustment problems coinciding with his family's move to a new house. During the parent intake, David's mother complained that she and David have been having frequent arguments about his memories of the old house. For instance, he claims that his bedroom was a different color (he says that it was blue, but his mother claims that it was white), that he had different (better) toys there, and that he never had to eat broccoli. His mother noted that these disagreements often end with David in tears and that he will remain somber for several hours following these interactions.

In the example above, David's mother is overly focused on the accuracy of David's memories for his old house, while missing the significance of the memories—David is sad about the move and misses his old home. By helping David's mother to understand the developmental limitations of children's memory, the clinician can help David's mother to attend to the meaning of the memory rather than the veracity of David's statements.

Parents can also be coached in the use of specific strategies that can facilitate their children's ability to recall information and instructions, for example, helping the child to effectively organize new information or to exploit their existing knowledge in order to retain new information. After all, household chores are easier to remember if you imagine which droid from *Star Wars* would be best suited to them, and monitoring one's own behavior is easier if you think about what kind of animal also acts that way (like an angry lion or a scared kitten).

Conclusions

Memories do not just store information over short or long intervals. They are shaped by the cognitive processes that were active when that information was originally encoded and by those that are active when (if ever) that information is retrieved. As a result, memory development is closely tied to overall cognitive development in two complementary ways. A child's increasingly efficient and sophisticated repertoire of cognitive processes leaves more detailed and organized traces in long-term memory. This richer base of knowledge and experience, in turn, drives even more sophisticated cognitive processes, like strategies, and the process of development continues.

Despite some age differences, a child's memory is not as unreliable or dysfunctional as common intuitions make it out to be. It is worth repeating that intuitions about memory development tend to overemphasize both the unreliability of children's memory and the reliability of adults' memory (Johnson & Foley, 1984). Children do remember things differently than adults, and often with less detail, coherence, and accuracy, but these differences do not reflect a global memory deficit. Rather, they reflect specific conditions under which children's memories are shaped by the way they process information, and by the knowledge and experience they have accumulated so far.

References

Atkinson, R. C., & Shiffrin, R. M. (1968). Human memory: A proposed system and its control processes. *The psychology of learning and motivation. II.* Oxford: Academic Press.

Backhaus, J., Hoeckesfeld, R., Born, J., Hohagen, F., & Junghanns, K. (2008). Immediate as well as delayed post learning sleep but not wakefulness enhances declarative memory consolidation in children. *Neurobiology of Learning and Memory, 89,* 76–80.

Berndt, T. J. (1997). *Child development* (2nd ed.). Madison, WI: Brown & Benchmark Publishers.

Bigler, R. S., & Liben, L. S. (1993). A cognitive-developmental approach to racial stereotyping and reconstructive memory in Euro-American children. *Child Development, 64,* 1507–1518.

Bjorklund, D. F., & Bjorklund, B. R. (1985). Organization versus item effects of an elaborated knowledge base on children's memory. *Developmental Psychology, 21,* 1120–1131.

Bjorklund, D. F., & Douglas, R. N. (1997). The development of memory strategies. In N. Cowan (Ed.), *The development of memory in childhood* (pp. 201–246). Hove, England: Psychology Press.

Brainerd, C. J., & Reyna, V. F. (1995). Learning rate, learning opportunities, and the development of forgetting. *Developmental Psychology, 31,* 251–262.

Brainerd, C. J., Reyna, V. F., Harnishfeger, K. K., & Howe, M. L. (1993). Is retrievability grouping good for recall? *Journal of Experimental Psychology: General, 122,* 249–268.

Carey, S. (1985). *Conceptual change in childhood.* Cambridge, MA: Bradford Books, MIT Press.

Case, R. (1985). *Intellectual development: Birth to adulthood.* New York: Academic Press.

Cherney, I. D. (2005). Children's and adults' recall of sex-stereotyped toy pictures: Effects of presentation and memory task. *Infant and Child Development, 14,* 11–27.

Chi, M. T. H. (1978). Knowledge structures and memory development. In R. S. Siegler (Ed.), *Children's thinking: What develops?* (pp. 73–96). Hillsdale, NJ: Lawrence Erlbaum Associates.

Chi, M. T., & Koeske, R. D. (1983). Network representation of a child's dinosaur knowledge. *Developmental Psychology, 19,* 29–39.

Cicchetti, D. (2006). Development and psychopathology. In D. Cicchetti & D. J. Cohen (Eds.), *Developmental psychopathology: Theory and method* (Vol. 1, 2nd ed., pp. 1–23). Hoboken, NJ: John Wiley & Sons.

Crick, N. R., & Dodge, K. A. (1994). A review and reformulation of social information-processing mechanisms in children's social adjustment. *Psychological Bulletin, 115,* 74–101.

Davidson, D., Cameron, P., & Jergovic, D. (1995). The effect of children's stereotypes on their memory for elderly individuals. *Merrill-Palmer Quarterly, 41,* 70–90.

DeCasper, A. J., & Spence, M. J. (1986). Prenatal maternal speech influences newborns' perception of speech sounds. *Infant Behavior & Development, 9,* 133–150.

Domitrovich, C. E., Cortes, R. C., & Greenberg, M. T. (2007). Improving young children's social and emotional competence: A randomized trial of the preschool "PATHS" curriculum. *Journal of Primary Prevention, 28,* 67–91.

Epstein, R., Chillag, N., & Lavie, P. (1998). Starting times of school: Effects on daytime functioning of fifth-grade children in Israel. *Sleep: Journal of Sleep Research & Sleep Medicine, 21,* 250–256.

Erskine, A., Markham, R., and Howie, P. (2002) Children's script based inferences: Implications for eyewitness testimony. *Cognitive Development, 16,* 871–887.

Farrar, M. J., & Goodman, G. S. (1990). Developmental differences in the relation between scripts and episodic memory: Do they exist? In R. Fivush & J. A. Hudson (Eds.), *Knowing and remembering in young children* (pp. 30–64). New York: Cambridge University Press.

Foley, M. A., & Johnson, M. K. (1985). Confusions between memories for performed and imagined actions: A developmental comparison. *Child Development, 56,* 1145–1155.

Foley, M. A., Johnson, M. K., & Raye, C. L. (1983). Age-related changes in confusion between memories for thoughts and memories for speech. *Child Development, 54,* 51–60.

Gaultney, J. F., Bjorklund, D. F., & Schneider, W. (1992). The role of children's expertise in a strategic memory task. *Contemporary Educational Psychology, 17,* 244–257.

Guttentag, R. E. (1984). The mental effort requirement of cumulative rehearsal: A developmental study. *Journal of Experimental Child Psychology, 37*, 92–106.

Hudson, J. A. (1988). Children's memory for atypical actions in script-based stories: Evidence for a disruption effect. *Journal of Experimental Child Psychology, 46*, 159–173.

Hudson, J. A., Fivush, R., & Kuebli, J. (1992). Scripts and episodes: The development of event memory. *Applied Cognitive Psychology, 6*, 483–505.

Hudson, J., & Nelson, K. (1983). Effects of script structure on children's story recall. *Developmental Psychology, 19*, 625–635.

Imbo, I., Duverne, S., & Lemaire, P. (2007). Working memory, strategy execution, and strategy selection in mental arithmetic. *The Quarterly Journal of Experimental Psychology, 60*, 1246–1264.

Imbo, I., & Vandierendonck, A. (2007). The role of phonological and executive working memory resources in simple arithmetic strategies. *European Journal of Cognitive Psychology, 19*, 910–933.

Johnson, M. K., & Foley, M. A. (1984). Differentiating fact from fantasy: The reliability of children's memory. *Journal of Social Issues, 40*, 33–50.

Johnson, M. K., & Mitchell, K. J. (2002). Source monitoring. In *Macmillan psychology reference series: Learning and memory* (Vol. 2, 2nd ed., pp. 628–631). New York: Macmillan Reference USA.

Johnson, M. K., & Raye, C. L. (1981). Reality monitoring. *Psychological Review, 88*, 67–85.

Kunzinger, E. L. (1985). A short-term longitudinal study of memorial development during early grade school. *Developmental Psychology, 21*, 642–646.

Lehmann, M., & Hasselhorn, M. (2007). Variable memory strategy use in children's adaptive intratask learning behavior: Developmental changes and working memory influences in free recall. *Child Development, 78*, 1068–1082.

Lindsay, D. S. (1991). CHARMed, but not convinced: Comment on Metcalfe (1990). *Journal of Experimental Psychology: General, 120*, 101–105.

Lindsay, D. S. (2008). Source monitoring. In H. L. Roediger III (Ed.), *Cognitive psychology of memory: Learning and memory: A comprehensive reference* (J. Byrne, Ed., Vol. 2, pp. 325–348). Oxford: Elsevier.

Loftus, E. F. (2005). Planting misinformation in the human mind: A 30-year investigation of the malleability of memory. *Learning & Memory, 12*, 361–366.

Martin, C. L., & Halverson, C. F. (1987). The roles of cognition in sex role acquisition. In D. B. Carter (Ed.), *Current conceptions of sex roles and sex typing: Theory and research* (pp. 123–137). New York: Praeger Publishers.

Miller, P. H., Haynes, V. F., DeMarie-Dreblow, D., & Woody-Ramsey, J. (1986). Children's strategies for gathering information in three tasks. *Child Development, 57*, 1429–1439.

Nelson, K. (1993). Explaining the emergence of autobiographical memory in early childhood. In A. F. Collins, S. E. Gathercole, M. A. Conway, & P. E. Morris (Eds.), *Theories of memory* (pp. 355–385). Hillsdale, NJ: Lawrence Erlbaum Associates.

Ornstein, P. A., Baker-Ward, L., & Naus, M. J. (1988). The development of mnemonic skill. In F. E. Weinert & M. Perlmutter (Eds.), *Memory development: Universal changes and individual differences* (pp. 31–50). Hillsdale, NJ: Lawrence Erlbaum Associates.

Ornstein, P. A., & Naus, M. J. (1978). Rehearsal processes in children's memory. In P. A. Ornstein (Ed.), *Memory development in children* (pp. 69–99). Hillsdale, NJ: Erlbaum.

Ornstein, P. A., Naus, M. J., & Liberty, C. (1975). Rehearsal and organizational processes in children's memory. *Child Development, 46*, 818–830.

Ornstein, P. A., Naus, M. J., & Stone, B. P. (1977). Rehearsal training and developmental differences in memory. *Developmental Psychology, 13*, 15–24.

Pillemer, D. B., Picariello, M. L., & Pruett, J. C. (1994). Very long-term memories of a salient preschool event. *Applied Cognitive Psychology, 8*, 95–106.

Priestley, G., Roberts, S., & Pipe, M. E. (1999). Returning to the scene: Reminders and context reinstatement enhance children's recall. *Developmental Psychology, 35*, 1006–1019.

Rabian, B., & Bottjer, S. J. (2008). Sleep problems. In A. R. Eisen (Ed.), *Treating childhood behavioral and emotional problems: A step-by-step evidence-based approach* (pp. 365–410). New York: Guilford Press.

Rubin, D. C. (2000). The distribution of early childhood memories. *Memory, 8*, 265–269.

Sadeh, A., Gruber, R., & Raviv, A. (2003). The effects of sleep restriction and extension on school-age children: What a difference an hour makes. *Child Development, 74*, 444–455.

Schneider, W. (2002). Memory development in childhood. In U. Goswami (Ed.), *Blackwell handbook of childhood cognitive development* (pp. 236–256). Oxford: Blackwell Publishers.

Schneider, W., Körkel, J., & Weinert, F. E. (1989). Domain-specific knowledge and memory performance: A comparison of high- and low-aptitude children. *Journal of Educational Psychology, 81*, 306–312.

Signorella, M. L., Bigler, R. S., & Liben, L. S. (1997). A meta-analysis of children's memories for own-sex and other-sex information. *Journal of Applied Developmental Psychology, 18*, 429–445.

Snodgrass, J. G., & Kinjo, H. (1998). On the generality of the perceptual closure effect. *Journal of Experimental Psychology: Learning, Memory, and Cognition, 24*, 645–658.

Steenari, M., Vuontela, V., Paavonen, E. J., Carlson, S., Fjällberg, M., & Aronen, E. T. (2003). Working memory and sleep in 6- to 13-year-old schoolchildren. *Journal of the American Academy of Child & Adolescent Psychiatry, 42*, 85–92.

Sutherland, R., Pipe, M., Schick, K., Murray, J., & Gobbo, C. (2003). Knowing in advance: The impact of prior event information on memory and event knowledge. *Journal of Experimental Child Psychology, 84*, 244–263.

Tenenbaum, H. R., Alfieri, L., Brooks, P. J., & Dunne, G. (2008). The effects of explanatory conversations on children's emotion understanding. *British Journal of Developmental Psychology, 26*, 249–263.

Towse, J. N., Hitch, G. J., & Horton, N. (2007). Working memory as the interface between processing and retention: A developmental perspective. *Advances in Child Development and Behavior, 35*, 219–251.

Vasta, R., Haith, M., and Miller, S. (1995). *Child psychology: The modern science.* New York: Wiley.

Wellman, H. M., Cross, D., & Watson, J. (2001). Meta-analysis of theory-of-mind development: The truth about false belief. *Child Development, 72*, 655–684.

Wellman, H. M., Ritter, K., & Flavell, J. H. (1975). Deliberate memory behavior in the delayed reactions of very young children. *Developmental Psychology, 11*, 780–787.

8
Remembering

ELISABETH HOLLISTER SANDBERG and BECKY L. SPRITZ

The authors of Chapter 7 described developmental changes in short-term memory capacity, working memory, and meta-cognitive strategies for moving information into long-term memory. Their intent was to provide you with an appreciation of the limits of memory capacity and memory-based processing in young children, as well as an understanding of developmental changes in memory processes. In the present chapter, we approach memory from the opposite direction—the spontaneous or cued recall by children of past events. Tales of events in which you, the clinician, played no role, but upon which you will build an understanding of the child that will critically inform your decisions. Recommendations for effectively eliciting such information from children are described in Chapter 9. We focus here on the *content* of children's autobiographical reports and the suppositions you can make about it.

Through spontaneous revelations, and in response to questions from you, children will tell you what they remember about things, people, places, and events. If what a child "remembers" strikes you as diagnostically, therapeutically, or historically relevant, you will need to consider the account with respect to the following issues:

1. How old was the child at the time of the event (and how was this determined), and how old is the child? Accuracy of memory changes developmentally.
2. Where did the memory come from? Source attribution—knowing where information came from—is a notoriously weak skill.
3. Was the reported memory formed solely by the teller? It may have been contributed to by multiple informants.
4. Is the memory really for a single, unique event? Memories for similar events fuse over time—schemas are built.
5. How might a particular memory have been revised? Schematic suppositions provide automatic enhancement of memories. Likewise, the process of retelling, particularly to an interactive audience, changes the nature of memories.

Without providing an exhaustive account of the pitfalls of memory, we will endeavor to highlight some of the most common and often overlooked intrusions and interferences that shape the process of remembering.

Using Memory

Recognizing What You've Seen Before

Recognition memory develops in infancy (c.f. Goswami, 2008). Babies only a few weeks old clearly demonstrate that they recognize faces, objects, smells, and sounds to which they have been previously exposed (e.g., Bushnell, McCutcheon, Sinclair, & Tweedlie, 1984). As the child moves into the toddler and preschool years, recognition becomes a very interesting and nuanced feature of the memory system. To know, or believe, that one has seen (or heard, tasted, smelled, etc.) something before is a critical element in behavioral decision making. Familiarity provides the basic building blocks of learning: "I know what that is [a space heater]. I've touched one before. It was painful. Perhaps I should not touch this one." Familiarity is employed by others (e.g., you) as a simple access point into a child's stored memory: "Have you seen this person before [show photograph]? Do you know who this is?"

Although recognizing whether something is familiar is one of the simplest and most direct taps into memory, recognition is not a straightforward process—especially for children. It has been well documented in the empirical literature that the features children rely upon for recognition are not the same as those used by adults. Hair color, hats, glasses, distinctive wardrobe elements, all referred to as superfluous paraphernalia, feature heavily in children's recognition decisions until at least age 10 (Freire & Lee, 2001). Put that same flowered hat on another lady's head and they will tell you that they remember seeing that lady before, whereas the original hat wearer is not tagged as familiar. Adults, though we know that certain physical features are transient, can also get caught up in the "salient detail" confound when memory is taxed in an incidental or unexpected way: "Don't you remember her from the party? … Oh, was she the one wearing that skimpy red dress?"

A particularly interesting feature of memory for familiar things by children concerns their love of repetition (e.g., reruns). A story or movie may be entirely memorized through repeated exposure, and yet young children lack full awareness for the constancy of the content. Like adults, older children find comfort and gratification in the predictable elicitation and resolution of emotional arousal that is associated with repeated viewing. Reruns allow the viewer to "relive the past and know the future" (Weispfenning, 2003, p. 165). Yet, there are times when "knowing the future," the basic tenet of familiarity, seems to be lost on young children—"I think I know what might happen next" is different from "I remember what happens next." So, when a young child evinces her hope that the outcome of the Sea Witch's fury might be different the 30th time through *The Little Mermaid*, she is demonstrating her lack of understanding of the irreversibility or permanence of past events. This is especially evident in the early preschool years, seems to persist through first or second grade, and is fully left behind by age 10. This developmental feature in children's thinking has clinical implications. For example, most young children believe that death is reversible. This makes it very difficult to explain the death of a family member, friend, or pet to young children. They may continue to wonder and inquire about when the loved one will return. Moreover, the child may display a delayed response or reexperience the loss after further cognitive maturation. Interestingly, young children's belief in the changeability of previous events is a very accurate representation of the cultural evolution of oral stories. This process is also highly relevant to one of the most important aspects of human memory to a clinical practitioner, children's narratives. For a greater discussion of the role of children's narratives in relation to interviewing young children, see Chapter 4.

Recalling the Past

Each time a story is recounted, it changes at least a little bit. A host of cognitive factors contribute to making our memories imperfect representations of past realities. These factors, with emphases on their relations to children's memories, are described in turn below.

Contributions of Schematic/Scripted Knowledge to Memory for Events.   There are two sets of details in most memories—those elements that are unique to that particular episode and those that are shared across multiple instances of similar events. It is natural for us to develop schemas or scripts for recurring events (Pipe, Lamb, Orbach, & Esplin, 2004). We take details from multiple instances of an event and combine them into a single schematic memory. The common elements of categorical experiences—going to birthday parties, what happens at the dentist, grocery shopping with Mom—are what permit us to create generalized and generalizable descriptions of life's events. We create schemas, representational understandings of the world; and scripts, wherein events unfold in predictable, sequenced ways (see Chapter 7 for more detail about schemas and scripts).

In the absence of schemas and scripts, we would have cognitive chaos. Schemas increase the efficiency of our memories by combining many detailed events into a single cognitive representation. Schemas also impact remembering in two different ways. In one sense, they provide support for the *encoding* of information in our memories. The effect of schemas on what is remembered is inconsistent. There is evidence that schema-irrelevant details—things that don't "fit"—decay more in memory (Tuckey & Brewer, 2003), and also that the uniqueness of elements that don't fit might enhance future recall (Cordon, Pipe, Sayfan, Melinder, & Goodman, 2004; Wagenaar, 1986). We are, apparently, at times attuned to the elements of sameness, and at others to the elements of difference.

When information and events are contextualized within an overarching structure, schemas also facilitate the subsequent *retrieval* of information from our memories. Schemas are used to fill in gaps in the actual memory of an occurrence and are used to interpret ambiguous information. The impossible unpredictability of this yields an important caveat for the clinician: Any detail reported in a particular recounted memory may not be unique to that event, may not have happened during that particular event, or may be inaccurately constructed out of other schematic knowledge.

EXAMPLE: SCHEMATIC KNOWLEDGE "SUPPORTING" RECALL

My (EHS) daughter, Liliana, recounts the following tale: "Remember when I was five years old? And I was wearing high heels and I fell down the back stairs? I fell head first and landed on my head! I had a really bad headache for a really long time!"

I was there, I witnessed the event. She *was* wearing high heels (those sparkly pink plastic mules that come with the ubiquitous dress-up kit.) She *did* fall down the back stairs. She *did* hit her head, but only the back of her head as she slid feet first down the stairs on her back. So why does she have a memory of falling "head first"? Here, I believe, her personal schemas come into play. By far, the vast majority of her falling experiences have involved landing on her hands and knees, or squarely on her behind. To hit one's head, therefore, one probably must have fallen *on* one's head, which can only (in her understanding of falling) be accomplished by having one's head hit the ground first.

Now, about the headache. I have no doubt that it hurt, and that some of that hurt was in fact in her head (literally). However, I have to take exception to the "long time" part. I'm sure her father and I assessed her for dizziness and head pain in the hours following the event, and we would have taken note of and action on any persistent symptoms. But do I actually remember doing this? I must have. That is what parents do after traumas to the heads of children. Herein come to play my schemas, perhaps augmenting, incorrectly, my memory of a specific event.

On top of all of this, what does a five-year-old mean by "a really long time"? An adult complaining of headache that has lasted a long time is probably talking about a time frame of more than a day, and can tell you about duration with more precision if queried. A long time for a small child certainly could be days and days, but it could also be 10 minutes, and it is unlikely that the child can be more precise. Nonetheless, I suspect the story as she tells it would seem probable enough to a doctor to elicit concern about serious head injury.

By the way, I'm not entirely sure she was five years old when this happened. Without having any concrete evidence to support my assertion, I would have said she was four years old if I were telling the story.

As schemas and scripts are built up through experience, distinctions among the contributing incidents may be blurred. Children as young as age 5 have been found to distort the details of a remembered event in order to make that event more consistent with stereotypical (schematic) expectations. Even after intervals as short as one week, schema-consistent memory distortions are confidently embraced by young children (Martin & Halverson, 1983). "It was my birthday party so we opened presents," when in fact that did not happen during the party itself. They are even more confident about their schema-consistent distorted memories than they are about accurately recalled memories that deviate from stereotypical expectations: "We had cookies instead of cake." The ability to pinpoint which unique components of repeated events occurred at particular times is an essential component of accurate episodic reporting. Research on memory for time and content details across recurrent events has shown that details migrate across episodes. Misplacement of details across experiences is higher for younger children (four-years-olds vs. eight-year-olds), but associating unique details with specific occurrences degrades for everyone with the passage of time (Powell & Thomson, 1997).

Compounding this rather disordered understanding of what might be "remembered best"—unique details or consistent themes—is the developmentally drifting definition of salience. That which is especially noteworthy, important, meaningful, or traumatic will change over time (Linton, 1982). For an emotionally charged event to remain charged in memory over long periods of time requires that each subsequent reprocessing of the event reaffirm its salience in spite of the new knowledge contexts for recall. Developmental changes in salience calibration may impact later memory for previously salient events and may also color the narratives of future retellings.

EXAMPLES: CHANGES IN SALIENCE OVER TIME

My (EHS) daughter, Liliana, scored well at her first belt testing in Tae Kwon Do. She had been a white belt for a *long* time (i.e., longer than her brother) and the belt-testing event environment, though at the studio she always attends, was markedly different from class. There were lots of other children there, chairs had been set up around the mats, and the usual routines of class were absent. For now, this is a highly salient memory for her. It may become less or more so if she moves through higher levels of Tae Kwon Do mastery. It may be "my first belt promotion"—vividly recalled—or it may become one of many belt promotions that blend together over time. If she discontinues her study of Tae Kwon Do, the event may cease to hold any focal importance (e.g., the start of something, or a turning point). If she remembers it at all later in life, it may be with little associated affect. Flip this around, however, and you can appreciate the turning point factor. If she had failed her eagerly anticipated first belt test and thus quit the sport, she might always remember that failure as a salient, determining moment.

My nephew James used to retell a memory of waking up from a nap on the couch and finding himself alone in the house when he was three or four years old (his mother was out in the yard weeding flower beds, but he didn't know that). He wasn't frightened, but instead marveled at his newfound freedom and independence. He remembered being thrilled with going to the pantry and getting cookies for himself, and then eating those cookies on the couch—two things ordinarily restricted. James is now 12, and the salience of this memory has faded for him. Now that he has several years of independent foraging and feeding under his belt, the affective weight of the memory has all but evaporated. He does still claim to remember waking up alone, but the component of childish awe has been outgrown. When the contextual definitions of salience change developmentally, remembered events are reprocessed through a different lens.

Where Did the Memory Come From? Most people have a fierce sense of ownership when it comes to their autobiographical memories. We become very distressed when someone presents us with an alternate account of a "well-remembered" event (you think you remember the toast at your wedding vividly, but your sister describes it entirely differently). Worse, we sometimes find ourselves presented with hard evidence such as photos or videos that are inconsistent with the way we remember things having happened. Your autobiography is supposed to be the record of things that happened to you. Two intriguing branches of research reveal that the *auto* part of *autobiography* is really quite loosely defined. Both external sources of information and internal adjustments are unconsciously incorporated into autobiographical memory.

Source attribution and source monitoring refer to the ability, respectively, to accurately identify the origins of remembered information, and then to keep track of that information over time. Parents often experience frustration when children cannot report the source of their information (Parent: "Where did you learn *that* word?!"), and for good reason doubt the reliability of children's source attribution (Child: "From Cameron, or maybe David, or Mark"). If a child makes an assertion of fact that you doubt, questioning the child about the source may not be fruitful.

There is evidence that the process of remembering alters source attribution. Experimental studies with adults reveal that the more often one recalls indirectly formed memories without specifically citing the source, the more likely one is to eventually become confused about the original source (Henkel, 2004). For children, this means that the already challenging task of identifying whether information came from their parents, teachers, peers, or other sources of information (television, books, the Internet, etc.) may become increasingly difficult and distorted over time.

EXAMPLES: SOURCE ATTRIBUTION

A child tells you, "Mrs. Teacher says that if I don't stay in my seat she will take my lunch away." This strikes you, hopefully, as odd. Consider two logical explanations:

1. Mrs. Teacher actually threatened to withhold post-lunch recess time and the child misunderstood.
2. Busy-body Jenny told the child that Mrs. Teacher would take his lunch away if he didn't say in his seat.

The burden will be on you to evaluate the probable factual background—asking your client is unlikely to yield accurate results because his source attribution skills are not fully developed. Overriding a child's conviction about the accuracy of the threat cannot necessarily be accomplished by discrediting the source!

A parent is outraged over "bullying" in the classroom. His first grader came home and reported that Simon "pushed her" out of line. There may have been pushing. It may have been malicious. Or, perhaps, there was more benign contact that was subsequently interpreted by the teacher— "Simon, stop pushing Emma out of line!" Will Emma remember that she didn't think she had been pushed until the teacher told her she had? Probably not. Perhaps Emma initiated the pushing but the teacher only noticed Simon's retaliation. Will Emma accurately report the context of Simon's crime? Not necessarily. Further investigation will surely yield multiple accounts of the same event, each of which is subject to the vagaries of remembering.

The quality of an information source, though initially taken under consideration even by children three- to five-years old, also tends to be lost over time (Pipe et al., 2004). Thus, the probability of being misled by low-credibility sources increases as time passes. This is true for both adults and children.

EXAMPLE: LOW-CREDIBILITY SOURCES

Young children, especially those in school, receive all sorts of incorrect information from unreliable sources. Say a child knows that "Amanda tells lies all the time!" and thus initially discounts Amanda's assertion that Jacob was stealing things out of children's lunchboxes. As time passes, the child may well have a distinct memory for Jacob being a lunchbox bandit. This information may be passed on to others—teachers, parents, peers—with no caveat that it was obtained from a questionable source. Jacob's reputation may be unjustly tarnished, or the child may find himself or herself regarded as the liar!

Source monitoring is not just awareness of who told you something, but also whether something actually happened to you or was something you heard about. Whether you experienced an event, saw a picture of an event, or were just told about an event is a detail that can be lost with repeated recall. Children have been shown to confuse their direct experiences with information obtained from these other sources (Poole & Lindsay, 2001; Roberts & Blades, 2000). For children up to at least eight years old, having heard about someone doing something can be translated into remembering having done that something. There are significant improvements in source monitoring between the ages of 3 and 8. Although children throughout this range will report direct experience of fictitious events introduced by another source, under direct query seven- and eight-year-olds can often identify self or other as the sources of information they are repeating, whereas three- and four-year-olds cannot reliably make distinctions. Once the information is in, it's in and it's theirs.

In addition to the memory limitations associated with managing information from external sources, our memories are also influenced by internal cognitive processes. Imagining something can actually place it in memory! This phenomenon, "imagination inflation" (Garry, Manning, Loftus, & Sherman, 1996), carries with it the implicit possibility that thinking, fantasizing, or even dreaming about something may introduce that something into your autobiographical memory. The potential implications of imagination inflation are striking, particularly with regard to memories for childhood experiences. It appears that providing a rich suggestion of particular

the event. By logical extension, closely age-matched siblings might also suffer the same disputes. There can be not only argument over the details of an event—each sibling remembering it in a different way—but also over ownership of the memory.

EXAMPLE: DISPUTED FACTS IN SHARED MEMORIES

At a recent family gathering, my (BLS) younger brother and I began to reminisce about the time when he created a life-size spider web out of his chewing gum. The event occurred when he was somewhere around five years of age; I was nine.

Me: Do you remember the time when you made your grape Bubble Yum into a human spider web?

Him: Of course I do. That was during my superhero phase. Spider Man was my favorite. I'll never forget the way the gum stuck to the vinyl upholstery of Mom's car.

Me: What are you talking about? It was in your room. Mom was in the kitchen; I was watching television. You had been in your room playing quietly for an exceptionally long time. Mom went in to check on you. Suddenly, I heard her shrieking. I ran in to see what was happening. The gum crossed between your four bedposts, doubled back across your dresser, and was anchored in multiple places on each of the four walls. You don't remember this at all, do you?

Him: Of course I do. It was a work of art.... I could have sworn it happened in her car.

What is illustrated by this example is that even though my brother was the protagonist in this childhood event, this event was *my* memory. He was clearly put out by the fact that his memory of the event occurring may or may not have been from any actual memory of his own.

Social Effects on the Interpretation of Autobiographical Events.   As discussed in the previous section, what you remember and how you remember it is as much affected by the others around you as it is by your own representational knowledge base. This is especially true for children. Social referencing plays a role in the interpretation and encoding of events. Even one-year-old infants look to the older, more experienced people around them for help in interpreting experiences (Hertenstein & Campos, 2004; Sorce, Emde, Campos, & Klinnert, 1985). The reactions of others affect what is encoded as a salient event, and how it is processed. A child is running through a room and falls down. The child is physically startled and immediately looks to her mother to help her interpret the stimulation. The mother's reaction to the event will in large part determine whether the child will laugh (it was a funny, unexpected "oops") or cry (you must have hurt yourself!). Similarly, young children will attend to and focus on the sights, sounds, people, and events that capture the attention of the adults around them. If the adults on a scene are making a tremendous fuss over the arrival of someone at a party, this is likely to be remembered by a child witness, even if the child has no idea what the fuss is about.

In addition to the social effects on what gets into memory in the first place, the social group plays a huge role in the retrieval of information. Parents in the United States routinely engage in memory elicitation exercises with their offspring (Hyman, Husband, & Billings, 1995; Ornstein, Haden, & Hedrick, 2004). It is part of an overall trend in parenting that has been referred to as "concerted cultivation" (Lareau, 2003). Beginning early in development, parents teach children the types of cognitive and social skills they believe will help them to succeed at school. Thus, within everyday parent-child interactions, parents engage in dialogues with their children designed to "improve" children's memories. General queries are followed with directive questions, cues, and elaboration that enable a child to provide a coherent, ordered narrative of a recent event.

EXAMPLE: MATERNAL ELABORATION OF STRUCTURE IN MEMORY

One day a few weeks ago I (BLS) went to the zoo with my two children: Sam (age 6) and Alison (age 3½). That night, over dinner, I prompted them through our experiences that day:

Mom:	What did we see at the zoo today? Do you remember what we saw first? It was an animal from Africa that lives on a grassy plain.
Kids:	A zebra!
Mom:	Right! What did we see next?
Alison:	Then we saw the penguins.
Sam:	No, no, no! Penguins do not live in Africa.
Mom:	Right, the penguins came much later. After the seals.
Alison:	But we couldn't see the seals! They were hiding under the water.
Mom:	Right. But, let's back up. What came after the zebra?
Sam:	The giraffes, the elephants, and then the seals.
Mom:	Good job! Do you remember now, Alie?

Alison:	Yes! And then the penguins. I liked the penguin named Ruby because she had a pink bracelet on her foot.
Mom:	You did? Which was your favorite, Sam?
Sam:	Fanny was my favorite because she had the rainbow bracelet and I like rainbows.
Alison:	So, Ruby was my favorite and Fanny was Sammy's.

Providing this scaffold for recall almost certainly leads to the subsequent reprocessing of the event along the lines of the cueing. A child will remember the parts that he is prompted to retell by his parent. The parent may assist in the filling in of gaps, or the correction of misinformation, and this information, without attribution, may become a part of the child's memory. The memory of the zoo will not be, "my mom/dad said that we saw …"; it will be "I saw…"

Understanding an event also promotes memory for that event (Pillemer, Picariello, & Pruett, 1994; Pillemer, Winograd, & Neisser, 1992). If stimuli aren't meaningful, they don't stick in memory. In a classic study of preschoolers' memories for an unusual event, in which an emergency school evacuation resulted from a burned popcorn-induced fire alarm, Pillemer et al. (1994) compared memories for the event proximally (two weeks postevent) and distally (seven years postevent). Compared with 3½-year-olds, older preschoolers, age 4½, provided more sophisticated proximal narratives about the event that indicated understanding of temporal sequencing and causal relationships in the event. Ultimately, in early adolescence, only children from the older preschool group demonstrated long-term memory for the event. Events are remembered best when they have a cohesive contextual structure. Practically speaking, then, children will probably have very little accurate recall for events beyond their conceptual grasp, and one should probably question the source of an unusually cogent and mature memory (Ornstein, 1996).

EXAMPLE: UNDERSTANDING DRIVES ENCODING

Last fall, my (BLS) children and I attended my aunt and uncle's 50th wedding anniversary party. Because they have never attended a wedding reception, let alone this type of event, they searched to find schemas for understanding what was happening. The actual sequence of events was that we had dinner, followed by several toasts and speeches, and then the culmination of the ceremony was when my aunt and uncle led their original wedding party in a dance. From my children's perspective several days later, we ate, and then my aunt and uncle "got married." When asked why they thought my aunt and uncle were married at the event, they explained: "Because they danced. Like the Prince and Cinderella." The other details of the event were lost to them. Only with the scheme of dancing and marriage were they able to create some understanding and memory for the event. Since that time, I have naturally tried to correct their misperceptions about dancing being connected with marriage, and through this process, I have likewise altered their memory for this event.

My (EHS) children were sitting at the dinner table one evening as per the usual routine. I was sitting with them, and their father was facing us from the opposite side of the kitchen island where he was chopping vegetables with a large chef's knife. Also as per the usual routine, both kids were loudly protesting the injustice of being asked to eat both a source of protein *and* a vegetable. On this particular occasion, however, having had quite enough of the dissent, my husband said, "Alright you two," pointing in their direction with the knife in his hand, "I don't want to hear one more word about what you don't like!"

Months later, Liliana (6) said to Aiden (9), "Do you remember that time dad chased us with a knife because we wouldn't eat our dinner?" "Yes!" replied Aiden. I was initially aghast, but then realized that there probably is no other way for a child to encode the event of a parent brandishing a huge knife in the air while commanding you to eat your dinner. Now I find this memory foible amusing—but really hope they never repeat it at school!

Clinical Implications

A child tells you an autobiographical story. Our natural inclination is to assume the veridicality of memory unless we are smacked in the face with a reason not to, such as in the following example:

EXAMPLE: THE CREDULITY FILTER

In contrast to the superficially plausible, but incorrect memory of the high heels-stairs incident described in an earlier example, Liliana has a memory of another head injury (yes, Liliana's noggin has had a rough time of it at our house.)

Lili: When I was six … (*yes, she was, it was right before first grade picture day*) … a big blue glass pitcher fell on my head and cracked it right open! It broke on my head

and then fell on the floor. I got blood on my shirt, and
on Paula's shirt, and on the bathmat. Dad came home
and glued my forehead.

This is all true and verifiable thus far. But if you ask her, as so many
have done, how a glass pitcher came to be falling on her head, she will
tell you that her older brother's imaginary friend did it. Contrary to the
conclusion the reader might be leaping to, her brother was not responsible for this. Liliana was alone in the room at the time. The glass pitcher
resided atop a small, low cabinet in which puzzles are stored. The only
plausible explanation for the descent of the pitcher involves the tipping
of the cabinet—meaning she probably grabbed a shelf or a door to pull
herself up. She must have been aware, at the time, that she was directly
responsible for the subsequent head and pitcher breakage. She did not
want to admit this and claimed that she "didn't know" how the pitcher
fell. Her brother helpfully added that maybe Zucco (his imaginary
friend) did it. She embraced this face-saving explanation firmly, and it
became a part of her retelling of the event. Until, that is, the day I sat her
down and told her that imaginary friends are strictly imaginary and not
capable of acts of violence against others. This prompted a few moments
of deep consideration on her part. She then suggested that perhaps the
pitcher fell off the cabinet because there was an earthquake (we live in
Massachusetts). I don't believe that she is engaging in deliberate deceit
about her own role in the bloody disaster, but that her role is not a part
of her long-term autobiographical memory. I will wait a few years before
dispelling her earthquake theory.

The point is that the high heels-stairs story might make it into a
record, a history, a report. The pitcher story is instantly a less credible
one due to the obvious confabulation. In point of fact, both memories
are equally distorted—but one in a way that does not get caught in the
adult credulity filter.

Practitioners working with families have probably encountered parents
distressed (and in some cases mortified) by the inaccuracies of their child's
storytelling, particularly when they believe that it may reflect poorly on their
relationship with their child or their parenting ability. Teachers and other
educators regularly experience this at parent-teacher conferences, at which
time parents feel compelled to "right" any "wrongs" they believe have been
conveyed by their children. This is also a common occurrence in family therapy, where the accuracy of the details of storytelling can become a point of
contention and, consequently, the focus of a therapy session. As a practitioner,

it is important to remind oneself (and sometimes the family members as well) that the child's version of the event provides important information about his or her perceptions of that event regardless of the strict accuracy of the details. As a clinician, it will be up to you to decide whether any "misperceptions" of events should become a goal of the therapeutic intervention.

All professionals working with children should be especially cognizant of the fact that talking with children about their memories may change their memories. In some cases, the real truth of the memory doesn't matter. As a professional, it is important to ask yourself what about the story is important to you. It may not be the facts that are critical, but rather the child's perceptions of or beliefs about those facts. For example, many professionals working with children are highly attuned to children's stories of interactions with their parents or other family members. Indeed, a child's description of family events can provide an important source of information regarding the quality of family relationships. However, in many cases, the accuracy of the details of a particular story is unimportant because we are most interested in the child's overall schema regarding the relationship. These relationship schemas, referred to by attachment researchers as "internal working models," are compilations of collected memories of the quality of interactions with an individual (Belsky & Fearon, 2002; Bowlby, 1980). Thus, when our professional goals involve gaining an understanding of the child's overall perceptions of relationships, the specifics of the story matter only in so far as they reflect information that is concordant or discordant with the child's relationship schema.

In other cases, however, obtaining accurate details of a childhood story is not only desirable but also necessary, and carries with it grave clinical and legal implications, such as in instances of children's reports of physical or sexual abuse (see Chapter 9). As noted earlier in the chapter, there are numerous ways in which children's memories for specific events may be tainted. This has important implications for therapeutic approaches with young children. Many professionals facilitate young children's reenactments of situations or events (e.g., the first day of school, an argument between their parents) through the use of pretend play (Gil, 1991). Although a thorough review of play therapy and its efficacy is beyond the scope of this chapter, this strategy is believed to facilitate children's understanding of events and to allow them to reprocess and more effectively cope with their emotions (Gil, 1991). Yet, research on children's memory suggests that children's memory errors are compounded by the use of dolls, pictures, and other toys and props, which increase the likelihood that young children will confabulate about their experiences (Ornstein, 1996). This suggests that the process of play therapy may in fact alter the nature of children's memories. From a therapeutic perspective, changing a child's memory for negative or emotionally distressing events could be very therapeutic, and in fact, may be the goal of therapy. However, there may be cases in which this approach has the opposite effect; that is, the child reconstructs a memory that is more traumatic or emotionally distressing than the original event. Such potential negative effects of therapy are rarely discussed in the literature with children, although there has been considerable debate regarding this process in the formation of adults' repressed memories (Loftus, Garry, & Hayne, 2008; Loftus, 1996).

In sum, there are caveats associated with memories. Keeping sources and information linked in memory over time is difficult. Memory for a "single" event may in fact be a larger conglomeration of schematic knowledge. A single memory may also be the tying together of multiple sources of information that include information not directly experienced. The real-life experiences of children are frequently accompanied by or followed by elaborative adult discourse, overheard conversations, or even specific memory coaching. A memory, even an inaccurate one, becomes a part of one's autobiography—in turn shaping other memories and informing new experiences.

We are not suggesting that clinicians need to assume that all reported memories are inaccurate, but that they can't be used to blindly develop an accurate historical record. Autobiographical memories cannot necessarily tell you what a child has directly experienced, but they can tell you about what a child believes his or her personal history to be. Remember (pardon the pun) that a child's autobiographical memory is a rich tapestry of reality, perceptions of that reality, inputs of others, imagination, and contextualized reprocessing. Autobiographical memory will not tell you what, precisely, happened to whom and when, but it will tell you what the truth is for that particular child.

References

Belsky, J., & Fearon, R. M. P. (2002). Infant-mother attachment security, contextual risk, and early development: A moderational analysis. *Developmental Psychopathology, 14,* 293–310.

Bowlby, J. (1980). *Attachment and loss: Loss* (Vol. 3). New York: Basic Books.

Braun, K. A., Ellis, R., & Loftus, E. F. (2002). Make my memory: How advertising can change our memories of the past. *Psychology & Marketing, 19,* 1–23.

Bushnell, I. W., McCutcheon, E., Sinclair, J., & Tweedlie, M. E. (1984). Infants' delayed recognition memory for colour and form. *British Journal of Developmental Psychology, 2,* 11–17.

Cordon, I. M., Pipe, M. E., Sayfan, L., Melinder, A., & Goodman, G. S. (2004). Memory for traumatic experiences in early childhood. *Developmental Review, 24,* 101–132.

Freire, A., & Lee, K. (2001). Face recognition in 4- to 7-year-olds: Processing of configural, featural, and paraphernalia information. *Journal of Experimental Child Psychology, 80,* 347–371.

Garry, M., Manning, C. G., Loftus, E. F., & Sherman, S. J. (1996). Imagination inflation: Imagining a childhood event inflates confidence that it occurred. *Psychonomic Bulletin & Review, 3,* 208–214.

Gil, E. (1991). *The healing power of play.* New York: Guilford Press.

Goswami, U. (2008). *Cognitive development: The learning brain.* New York: Psychology Press.

Henkel, L. A. (2004). Erroneous memories arising from repeated attempts to remember. *Journal of Memory and Language, 50,* 26–46.

Hertenstein, M. J., & Campos, J. J. (2004). The retention effects of an adult's emotional displays on infant behavior. *Child Development, 75,* 595–613.

Hyman, I. E., Husband, T. H., & Billings, F. J. (1995). False memories of childhood experiences. *Applied Cognitive Psychology, 9,* 181–197.

Lareau, A. (2003). *Unequal childhoods: Class, race, and family life.* Berkeley: University of California Press.

Linton, M. (1982). Transformations of memory in everyday life. In U. Neisser (Ed.), *Memory observed: Remembering in natural contexts* (pp. 77–91). San Francisco: W. H. Freeman.

Loftus, E. F. (1996). The myth of repressed memories and the realities of science. *Clinical Psychology Science and Practice, 3,* 356–362.

Loftus, E. F., Garry, M., & Hayne, H. (2008). Repressed and recovered memory. In E. Borgida & S. T. Fiske (Eds.), *Beyond common sense: Psychological science in the courtroom* (pp. 177–194). Malden, MA: Blackwell Publishing.

Martin, C. L., & Halverson, C. F. (1983). The effects of sex-typing schemas on young children's memory. *Child Development, 54,* 563–574.

Ornstein, P. A. (1996). To interview a child: Implications of research on children's memory. *Monographs of the Society for Research on Child Development, 61,* 215–222.

Ornstein, P. A., Haden, C. A., & Hedrick, A. M. (2004). Learning to remember: Social-communicative exchanges and the development of children's memory skills. *Developmental Review, 24,* 374–395.

Pillemer, D. B., Picariello, M. L., & Pruett, J. C. (1994). Very long-term memories of a salient preschool event. *Applied Cognitive Psychology, 8,* 95–106.

Pillemer, D. B., Winograd, E., & Neisser, U. (1992). Preschool children's memories of personal circumstances: The fire alarm study. In E. Winograd & U. Neisser (Eds.), *Affect and accuracy in recall: Studies of "flashbulb" memories* (pp. 121–137). New York: Cambridge University Press.

Pipe, M. E., Lamb, M. E., Orbach, Y., & Esplin, P. W. (2004). Recent research on children's testimony about experienced and witnessed events. *Developmental Review, 24,* 440–468.

Poole, D. A., & Lindsay, D. S. (2001). Children's eyewitness reports after exposure to misinformation from parents. *Journal of Experimental Psychology: Applied, 7,* 27–50.

Powell, M. B., & Thomson, D. M. (1997). Contrasting memory for temporal-source and memory for content in children's discrimination of repeated events. *Applied Cognitive Psychology, 11,* 339–360.

Roberts, K. P., & Blades, M. (2000). Discriminating between memories of television and real life. In K. P. Roberts & M. Blades (Eds.), *Children's source monitoring* (pp. 147–169). Mahwah, NJ: Lawrence Erlbaum Associates Publishers.

Roediger, H. L., Meade, M. L., & Bergman, E. T. (2001). Social contagion of memory. *Psychonomic Bulletin & Review, 8,* 365–371.

Sheen, M., Kemp, S., & Rubin, D. (2001). Twins dispute memory ownership: A new false memory phenomenon. *Memory & Cognition, 29,* 779–788.

Sorce, J. F., Emde, R. N., Campos, J. J., & Klinnert, M. D. (1985). Maternal emotional signaling: Its effect on the visual cliff behavior of 1-year-olds. *Developmental Psychology, 21,* 195–200.

Tuckey, M. R., & Brewer, N. (2003). The influence of schemas, stimulus ambiguity, and interview schedule on eyewitness memory over time. *Journal of Experimental Psychology: Applied, 9,* 101–118.

Wagenaar, W. A. (1986). My memory: A study of autobiographical memory over six years. *Cognitive Psychology, 18,* 225–252.

Weispfenning, J. (2003). Cultural functions of reruns: Time, memory, and television. *Journal of Communication, 53,* 165–176.

9

Talking With Children About Past Events
Children's Memory and Suggestibility

AMY HYMAN GREGORY, ROLANDO N. CAROL,
and NADJA SCHREIBER COMPO

Although much of this chapter will have a legal/forensic perspective, the issues discussed have important implications for all clinicians, practitioners, and educators who are working with children in a variety of settings. Namely, to understand the harmful effects that suggestibility can have on children's recollections of personal experiences is important for anyone interacting with children. For example, what would you do if you suspected that a child might be the victim of abuse or a bullying situation? How do you verify a child's report about a domestic violence situation or make decisions regarding the child's best interests when a child is trapped in the midst of a bitter parental divorce? Having the best interest of the child at heart, most professionals would strive to obtain as much information as possible from the child, resulting in the child being asked many questions. However, the way a child is questioned about a negative experience may influence his or her memory for what happened. Therefore, a primary goal of this chapter is to build upon what we know about children's memory (Chapters 7 and 8) to help readers understand the most effective and least damaging procedures to use when talking to children about past experiences. Investigating children's nonabuse experiences (e.g., witnessing a bad car accident, negative interactions with a teacher) should be approached with the same care and precautions that one might use when concerned about an abuse situation. The variables and techniques described in the following sections evolved from forensic interviews surrounding suspected child abuse but should be applied to *any* situation in which children talk about negative events.

Very little research had been conducted on children's memory and suggestibility since early 20th-century European researchers such as Binet, Varendock, and Stern conducted a series of experiments showing that children can be highly suggestible (c.f. Ceci & Bruck, 1993). For example, Binet varied the types of questions children were asked and found that children produced inaccurate statements in response to misleading questions and also expressed high confidence in all their responses (regardless of memory accuracy). This early finding was important because it revealed that children can give false answers when asked misleading questions, while still being confident in these false answers. Although there were reports about children's encounters with the legal system in the following decades, several highly publicized daycare abuse cases in the 1980s spawned a wave of new studies on children's suggestibility and how children should be interviewed to maximize recall quantity and quality (Ceci & Bruck, 1993, 1995). These studies are directly applicable not only to forensic psychologists and law enforcement personnel, but also to the information gathering needs of clinicians and educators in general.

History of the Study of Children's Suggestibility

During the 1980s and 1990s, several daycare abuse cases in the United States and Europe brought attention to the reliability of children's past recollections. In the United States, cases such as the McMartin preschool case in Manhattan Beach, California, and the Kelly Michaels case in Maplewood, New Jersey, included dozens of preschoolers who accused their teacher(s) of sexual abuse. Some of the allegations included bizarre stories (e.g., children being taken away in helicopters), and many included sexual coercion (e.g., children being forced to play "naked games") (Nathan, 1988; Nathan & Snedecker, 1995). Subsequently, during the 1990s, several European daycare abuse cases emerged, such as the Nottingham case in the UK, the Oude Pekela case in the Netherlands, and the Montessori case in Germany, baring a striking resemblance to the onset and content of allegations from the earlier U.S. cases (Steller, 1997, 1998; Volbert, 1999). More importantly, in all of these cases the investigations centered on assertions made by the children as part of the fact-finding process. Were children telling the truth in these cases? How reliable are children's reports about their memories in general? It is the multifaceted answer to the latter question that is the content of this chapter.

Biased Interview Techniques

Psychologists who more closely examined the daycare abuse cases noticed patterns of interviewing styles used with the children (e.g., Bruck & Ceci, 1995; Goodman, Quin, Bottoms, & Shaver, 1994). Some of the characteristics of these interviews included investigators repeating questions even if the child had already provided an answer, sharing with children information that other classmates had (supposedly) provided, making negative comments about the alleged perpetrator, promising children rewards if they provided specific information, criticizing children for "wrong" answers, and asking children to confabulate about the events in question. Further criticisms included that some interviews with children lasted longer than an hour, with little to no rapport building and with several interviewers present who were sometimes in a clear position of authority (e.g., police officers). Interviewers also ignored children's repeated requests to end the interview or see their parents.

In a quantitative analysis that compared interviewing techniques in the McMartin preschool case and the Kelly Michaels case with interviewing techniques in "normal" Child Protective Service (CPS) investigations, Schreiber and colleagues (2006) organized several of the criticized techniques into categories and compared them between cases. The authors' sample of CPS interviews consisted of audiotaped forensic/investigative interviews that trained personnel, mostly social workers, conducted with children who were suspected victims of sexual abuse. Results confirmed the anecdotal evidence of commentators in the 1980s and 1990s that the interviews in the McMartin preschool and the Kelly Michaels case were characterized by highly suggestive techniques. Daycare abuse case interviewers used significantly more biased interviewing techniques than interviewers in ordinary CPS interviews. They also used a significantly higher proportion of yes/no questions and a significantly smaller proportion of specific questions than CPS interviewers (see also Schreiber, 2000). It is important to note that even CPS interviewers used several of these biased techniques and relied predominantly on yes/no questions when interviewing the children. This finding suggests that there is also room for improvement in the interviewing techniques routinely applied to abuse cases in clinical practice.

In the past 20 years many studies have examined empirically the impact of these techniques on children's statements. Initially, much of the research focused on the techniques and question types found in the daycare abuse cases, namely, negative or potentially detrimental techniques. More recently, research has also focused on positive techniques, or techniques that will help elicit accurate testimony. These techniques are consistent with more general strategies for interviewing, and thus are discussed in greater detail in Chapter 4. Below, we provide a review of early research on negative techniques.

Reinforcement

Reinforcement as an interviewing technique includes both positive reinforcement and punishment, both of which can have a strong influence on children's behavior (e.g., Ettinger, Crooks, & Stein, 1994). Positive reinforcement in an interview context occurs when the interviewer praises a child for a response consistent with the interviewer's expectations. The more children are positively reinforced, the more they are likely to repeat or answer in line with the reinforced response. Punishment in an interview context occurs when the interviewer criticizes a child for a response that is inconsistent with interviewer expectations. The more often children are punished, the less likely they are to repeat the response (or type of response). In the context of children's interviews, recent research has suggested that reinforcement can have a strong influence on the accuracy of children's accounts (Garven, Wood, & Malpass, 2000).

In one particular study, children between five and seven years of age were visited in their classrooms by a young man, Paco Perez (Garven et al.,

2000). When questioned about his visit a week later, children were interviewed using both mundane leading questions ("Did Paco break a toy while he was visiting?") and fantastic leading questions similar to the McMartin case ("Did Paco take you somewhere on a helicopter?"). Half the children were also reinforced for their answers—with praise when giving answers that were accusatory toward Paco, and with mild negative feedback for nonaccusatory responses. Results indicated that reinforced children were more likely to make false accusations against Paco than nonreinforced children (35% vs. 12%). This difference was even more pronounced for fantastic questions, with children who were misled with fantastic questions much more likely to make false allegations than children who were interviewed with mundane questions (52% vs. 5%). Interestingly, even a week later, when children were interviewed again without any reinforcement, those children who had been reinforced earlier still reported more false accusations than the initially nonreinforced children. These findings indicate that the accuracy of children's reports about past experiences is highly influenced by interviewer reinforcement, and that the effects of interviewer reinforcement last over time. The implication of this research is therefore very clear: Professionals should avoid using punishment or positive reinforcement when talking to children about experiences.

Repeated Questioning

Several studies have indicated that repeated questioning during an interview can negatively impact children's accuracy when reporting experiences (Cassel, Roebers, & Bjorklund, 1996; Memon & Vartoukian, 1996; Poole & White, 1991, 1993). Repeating a question to a child implies that the child's previous answer was insufficient and, as such, is a form of negative feedback (Garven, Wood, Malpass, & Shaw, 1998; Siegal, Waters, & Dinwiddy, 1988). Repeating questions is especially common in response to a child's "I don't know" answer. Interviewers often ask a question again after a child's "I don't know" response without intending to negatively impact the child's memory; they may merely be trying to determine whether or not the child understood the question. Or, through the use of reinforcement and punishment, described above, interviewers may simply subtly communicate that a child's response is insufficient. It is important nonetheless for interviewers to recognize that "I don't know" can be a perfectly legitimate answer and hence should not be probed further. If the child changes his or her answer due to a further probe, it becomes impossible to disentangle whether the change of answer is due to the repeated question or due to an actual memory. As such, if a child has already reported that he or she does not know the answer to a question, it is best to make a note of this and move on instead of asking the child the same question again.

EXAMPLE: REPEATED QUESTIONING

Interviewer: If someone in school touched you, do you think you would like it?

Child: No.

Interviewer: Why not?

Child: I don't know

Interviewer: Hmm?

Child: I don't know.

Interviewer: Really? Do you think it would feel good or bad?

In the above example, the clinician's response ("Really? Do you think it would feel good or bad?") implies that the child's "I don't know" response is not acceptable, and in essence is the same as repeating the question. In follow-up questions, this may lead the child to make up a story, simply as a result of the interviewing strategy.

It is important to note that, despite these problems, there are circumstances in which rewording or repeating open-ended questions can lead to an increase in information *if* it provides a nonsuggestive memory probe. The negative impact of question repetition seems to depend on the question type, with more specific, close-ended questions more likely to encourage children to report inaccurate (or fictional) information than open-ended questions.

EXAMPLE 1: INTERVIEWING WITH CLOSED-ENDED QUESTIONS

Interviewer: Do you know why you are here?

Child: My parents have been fighting nonstop. They're getting divorced.

Interviewer: Have they been fighting for a long time?

Child: I don't know. I guess so.

Interviewer: How long have they been fighting for?

Child: It feels like forever.

Interviewer: How long?

Child: I'm not sure.

Interviewer: Well, how long do you think?

Child: I'm not sure. I guess six months or so.

EXAMPLE 2: INTERVIEWING WITH OPEN-ENDED QUESTIONS

Interviewer: What brings you here today?

Child:	My parents have been fighting nonstop. They're getting divorced.
Interviewer:	Tell me more about that.
Child:	My Mom is always saying mean things about my Dad. I don't understand why she married him in the first place if she hates him so much. I can't stand it when they fight.
Interviewer:	Tell me more about that.
Child:	It makes me wonder why they had me in the first place. I hate feeling this way. I feel trapped, like I have nowhere else to go. I try staying at friends' houses when I can because I don't want to be around them. I never know when the fighting is going to start.

Co-Witness Information

Since Asch's famous experiment in 1955, psychologists have recognized the power of social influences on people's behavior (Cialdini, 2001; Pratkanis, 2007). Recent research has replicated the strong effect of social influence in the context of children's interviews: Providing co-witness information (information about what another child supposedly said or did) during a conversation with a child can induce children to say and do things consistent with what the other children have said or done. This can further influence children's responses to other questions and decrease the accuracy of children's reporting (Garven et al., 1998, 2000; Leichtman & Ceci, 1995).

EXAMPLE: CO-WITNESS INFORMATION

Interviewer:	You are the third child that I am helping today. I would like to find out what happened the other day in school. Do you remember what happened?
Child:	No.
Interviewer:	No? You weren't there?
Child:	I don't remember.
Interviewer:	I already talked to Susan and Mia today and they told me what happened.
Child:	Already?
Interviewer:	You know Mia and Susan? We also talked to the other teachers about what happened.

Introducing peers into a conversation to convince a child to talk about a certain event is problematic for the same reason repeating a question is. Namely, if a child discloses information after "peer pressure," then it will be difficult to disentangle later whether the child's answer is based on an accurate memory for the event or whether the child is providing information simply to be "compliant." Additionally, if interviewed again at a later point in time, information that the child originally provided falsely in order to be compliant may have been incorporated into their memory for the event. This in turn may render a source attribution difficult. As is discussed in Chapters 7 and 8, information that is "added" to a memory can become a part of that memory.

Inviting Speculation

Inviting speculation refers to a cluster of interviewing techniques involving a hypothetical component. Specifically, an interviewer asks a child to change the reality level of the conversation by asking the child to elaborate on something that did not happen or could have happened, for example, asking a child, "What might it feel like to be bullied? What could happen to you?" These strategies have also been referred to as *confabulation*. Two studies to date have examined the use of a particular technique involving asking children to speculate about a witnessed live event (a clown show) in the form of a question: "What else could he or she have done?" These studies have found that children who were invited to speculate are more likely to later falsely remember their speculations as true than children who were not invited to speculate (Schreiber, Wentura, & Bilsky, 2001; Schreiber & Parker, 2004)! Other studies have confirmed that having children confabulate can increase later memory errors (e.g., Ackil & Zaragoza, 1998) or that asking children to think about events that did not happen can increase false memories (Ceci, Huffman, Smith, & Loftus, 1994). (In fact, hypothetical confabulation is not something young children have cognitive mastery of—see Chapter 10.) Practitioners should therefore avoid using these techniques if the veracity of the child's statement is of importance. A speculated answer could be problematic on two levels: at the time of speculation it is unclear whether the child is referring to an actual true statement or is making up the answer. At a later time these speculations may further be falsely remembered as having actually happened (see Schreiber & Parker, 2004).

Introducing Information

Many studies have demonstrated that children's reports about their experiences can be altered and can become less accurate if interviewers introduce new information or ask misleading questions (e.g., Ceci, Ross, & Toglia, 1987; for a review see Ceci & Bruck, 1995; Poole & Lamb, 1998). For example, if an interviewer asks "Did he give you a present?" when the child had not previously mentioned any gifts, this could later increase the chances that the child later falsely remembers seeing a present.

There are several other investigative techniques that were not included in Schreiber et al.'s (2006) categorization but have received research attention. For example, *stereotype inducement* has been pointed out as potentially detrimental to children's accuracy. Interviewers induce a negative stereotype if they make a negative comment about a party involved in the child's experience or suggest/imply that the person is "bad."

EXAMPLE: STEREOTYPE INDUCEMENT

Interviewer: This is my friend Rich. Rich is a police officer. He's not going to hurt you. He's the guy who arrested Kelly.

Child: Oh.

Interviewer: Pretty neat, huh?

Child: Yeah.

Interviewer: How do you feel about that? Good?

Interviewer: How do you feel about that, you like the fact that she's in jail?

Child: Yeah.

Interviewer: How come? You didn't like her too much?

(Example taken from Schreiber, 2000)

Leichtman and Ceci (1995) tested the impact of this technique on children's recollections. Two groups of children witnessed a person named Sam Stone paying a two-minute visit to their classroom. Half of the children had previously been told that Sam Stone was clumsy and that he was known for breaking things. The other half did not receive such negative stereotype inducement. After the uneventful visit, during which Sam Stone did not break anything, those children who had previously been exposed to the negative stereotype were more likely to later falsely claim that Sam Stone had broken something than those children who had not been exposed to the negative stereotype. This study suggests that negative stereotyping could have consequences for how children reconstruct their memory for events (and people) across a variety of circumstances. For example, children whose parents are engaged in contentious custody battles often have relatives, siblings, and lawyers present them with negative information about one of their parents. Although it may be more difficult to induce a negative stereotype about someone (very) familiar rather than a stranger, this research suggests that, in those circumstances, children may be more likely to remember false information about that parent. Thus, across many different, practical situations, it is of paramount importance for professionals to avoid the use of negative stereotypes when talking with children.

Question Types

Finally, much research on (child) interviewing has addressed which types of questions are best used in investigative interview settings (for a review see Ceci & Bruck, 1995; Eisen, Quas, & Goodman, 2002; Poole & Lamb, 1998). There is consensus in the literature that children are most likely to be accurate if interviewed using open-ended questions. One of the reasons why many investigators resort to closed (e.g., "When did he give you the present?") or yes/no (e.g., "Did he give you a present?") questions is because children, especially young ones, tend to report very little when asked open-ended questions and may not be as precise as the interviewer would like. However, when using closed questions instead, especially yes/no or multiple choice questions (e.g., "Did he take you to Chuck E. Cheese or to the movies?"), interviewers run the risk of introducing information, confirming preconceived notions and response bias (children may be more likely to guess and choose the latter or convenient option; Ceci & Bruck, 1995). Under certain circumstances, the use of yes/no questions can be considered a subtle form of suggestive questioning, for example, if the interviewer repeats questions to signal that the child's previous answer was unacceptable (Ceci & Bruck, 1995).

System Variables Versus Estimator Variables

When discussing children's suggestibility and interviewing, it is important to distinguish conceptually between variables that are under the interviewer's control (system variables) and those whose influence can only be estimated (estimator variables). This distinction was first introduced by Wells (1978). So far, all of the techniques mentioned in this chapter involve *system variables*; that is, all negative interviewing techniques discussed above are variables that are under the direct control of interviewers. *Estimator variables,* on the other hand, are not under the control of interviewers but rather were part of the original event circumstances. As described below, in cases of abuse, trauma, or other highly negative experiences, estimator variables refer to the characteristics of and the nature of the experience. Due to this lack of control, their influence on children's recollections can only be estimated. Despite the fact that estimator variables cannot be controlled, they should not be ignored.

Length of Exposure

One estimator variable that influences children's memory is length of exposure. Whereas some experiences last for mere seconds, others can last for hours, or occur repeatedly, and over long periods of time. The longer a child is exposed to an event, the stronger the memory trace will be for subsequent recall. The weaker the memory, the more vulnerable the child is to interviewer suggestion and the more difficult it is to obtain detailed and accurate information from the child.

Proximity

Another relevant estimator variable is the child's proximity to the situation. Children may not only be directly involved in negative incidents, but they may also be witnesses to events (e.g., observing the abuse of their mother at the hands of their father). The same event can be viewed by many different observers from many different viewpoints. In general, the closer in proximity children are to a witnessed event, the more likely they are to encode the central details of the incident. Closer proximity allows for more encoding of incident details and produces stronger, more vivid memory traces that may be easier for the child to recall when questioned later.

Familiarity

A child's familiarity with the event surroundings is another estimator variable that can be a fairly reliable predictor of recollection accuracy. Many negative childhood experiences occur at familiar locations, such as home or school. If a child was injured in her family's dining room, the details recalled by that child are more likely to be accurate than if she was assaulted in a large, unfamiliar shopping mall. A child's familiarity with an experience (people, place, and type of event) also increases the likelihood that the child will remember specific details as part of her memory. This means that the more familiar children are with a given situation, the less malleable their memories will be, even if interviewers use suggestive techniques. It should be pointed out, however, that children who are very familiar with a repeated event may have difficulties pinpointing details of *specific* instances, as they may have developed a gist or script of what typically happened while unable to remember every single episode distinctively.

Recall Delay

Recall delay is the interval between experiencing an event and recalling it, and can be either a system or estimator variable. Although interviewers have some control over how promptly questioning begins, recall delay is also determined by when the child is referred for an assessment (or comes forward about what happened). Recall delay is strongly related to the quantity, precision, and accuracy of details reported. In general, as time passes, memory decays (see Chapters 7 and 8) and children's reports about their memories become less precise and possibly less accurate (especially if they have been exposed to many interviews and postevent information in the interim). To prevent a decrease in both accuracy and precision, children should ideally be interviewed about the circumstances surrounding an event as soon as possible after the event occurs.

Number of Interviews

Another variable that can be both a system and an estimator variable is the number of formal or informal interviews that have occurred. Albeit ideal, it is rarely the case that children are interviewed only once. On the contrary, children are typically questioned about an incident multiple times by parents, teachers, doctors, clinicians, and so on. By the time children are asked to testify in court, they have typically been interviewed many times, with many of the interviews undocumented and sometimes conducted by untrained or ill-trained individuals. With each interview, the risk of misinformation, leading questions, or suggestive interviewing techniques increases, rendering the final statement less likely to be based on the original event. In cases where matters of fact must be established as accurately as possible, children should ideally be interviewed first, and only once, by someone who has been trained thoroughly on how to elicit as much accurate information as possible without using suggestive interviewing techniques.

Memory for Emotional Events

Another estimator variable, for which the impact on children's memory is less clear, is children's emotional experiences associated with an event. For example, a child involved in a highly traumatic car accident will recall this incident differently than a child observing the accident. A major problem with assessing emotions related to memory for negative events is the difficulty in identifying and distinguishing between different emotions, such as stress, anxiety, arousal, or negative emotionality (Deffenbacher, Bornstein, Penrod, & McGorty, 2004). Furthermore, the vast research on memory and emotion has mostly been conducted on adults and suggests a complex relationship between type and intensity of emotion, and different recall measures (Reisberg & Heuer, 2007). While some findings suggest that stress or anxiety at the time of encoding enhances memory (Burke, Heuer, & Reisberg, 1992; Christianson & Loftus, 1991; Christianson, Loftus, Hoffman, & Loftus, 1991), others indicate that emotional arousal at encoding can be detrimental to the retention of information (Clifford & Hollin, 1981; Loftus & Burns, 1982). This discrepancy in findings is also partly due to the difficulty in quantifying emotion, that is, determining how much of a particular emotion constitutes low, medium, and high levels of arousal. There is no standard method for identifying type and intensity of emotion; oftentimes emotions are assessed by simply asking children what they were feeling at the time. A child's ability to understand and to report about their internal states also changes over the course of development (see Chapter 3). Estimating the accuracy of a child's recollections on emotional states at the time of the event cannot be used as evidence of the veracity of a child's memories. In fact, some studies have demonstrated that children are more likely to incorrectly remember highly stressful memories compared to less stressful memories (e.g., Merritt, Ornstein, & Spicker, 1994). Taken together, the relationship between emotion and memory is a complex one. Thus, it is important to keep in mind that children can misremember and can be misled about past experiences, even if those memories are very salient, emotional ones.

Developmental Trends in Suggestibility

To date, research on children's memory and suggestibility has mostly focused on kindergartners, preschoolers, and sometimes elementary school-aged children. The overall finding is that suggestive questioning typically has more detrimental effects to the accuracy of recall by younger than older children (e.g., Ceci & Friedman, 2000; Lyon & Saywitz, 2006; Ornstein & Haden, 2001). For example, older children seem to be less likely to assent to interviewer suggestions or report postevent misinformation than younger children. However, several studies (e.g., Poole & Lindsay, 2001; Schreiber & Parker, 2004) have shown no or reverse age effects for certain suggestive techniques. For example, if the suggestive technique involves speculation, an ability that is more advanced in older children, older children may be more at risk or at least at a similar risk for later memory errors than younger children.

Some other research has also suggested that under certain circumstances younger children produce fewer false memories than older children (Brainerd, Holliday, & Reyna, 2004; Metzger et al., 2008). This specific increase in false memories with age has been explained in relation to children's increased ability to recall the gist of a situation, as opposed to relying on specific, verbatim information as a part of remembering (see Chapters 7 and 8). These developmental changes further underscore the fact that certain negative interviewing techniques, such as asking children for script- or schema-consistent (confabulated) information, may be particularly risky with older children.

Talking With Children About Negative Experiences

Because the goals of investigative and clinical interviews differ, the way the interview is conducted and the questions that the interviewer may ask will also differ. Clinical interviewers will want to obtain information about the child's feelings, symptoms, coping strategies, and physical and psychological well-being and will be less concerned with the details and logical coherence of the allegation. Conversely, investigative interviewers will want to obtain a lot of information and, above all, accurate information regarding the details of the abuse. They will further need very specific information about what happened to the child so they can determine the proper charges to file. Despite the fact that the goals of investigative and clinical interviews differ, it is still important that children are interviewed using established good practice interviewing techniques. Using recommended interviewing techniques and refraining from using possibly detrimental interviewing techniques when talking to children about incidents may preserve overall witness accuracy.

What to Do

As a result of research surrounding the daycare abuse cases of the 1980s and 1990s, several child witness interviewing guidelines and books have been published (Home Office, 2007; Poole & Lamb, 1998; Sternberg, Lamb, Esplin, Orbach, & Hershkowitz, 2002). All recommend the same common components when interviewing children about abuse, including the use of rapport building, establishing ground rules for the interview, practicing free narratives, introducing the topic of abuse, using open-ended questions while avoiding specific and closed-ended questions, and closing the interview in an appropriate manner. Regardless of whether an investigative or clinical interview is being conducted, it is best to use investigative techniques that have received empirical support when interviewing child witnesses to avoid contaminating the interview and the child's memory. However, depending on the state and jurisdiction where the clinician practices, the clinician may be mandated by law to report any information regarding the physical or sexual abuse of a child to appropriate authorities. Once law enforcement has been notified regarding the abuse either via a therapist or via a parent/teacher/friend or others, the child will likely undergo an investigative interview in which the goal shifts to determining whether criminal charges can be filed against the accused and acquiring evidence that can potentially be used in court.

Although it is hardly an interviewer's intent to use biased interviewing techniques, the objectives of a clinical interview may call for interviewing techniques that are not in line with best practices of investigative interviewing. On a practical level, if there is a chance that a child may still be involved in legal proceedings, any interviewing technique used, whether it be either a clinical or a forensic interview, should adhere to national guidelines. However, if the case has already been closed, or if there are no legal issues, there is less reason to solely adhere to best practice interviewing in clinical interviews. Therefore, it is imperative that interviewers keep the nature of the case in mind.

As has been previously noted, one of the most important factors in relation to interviewing children is to keep the number of formal and informal interviews with the child at a minimum. In practice, this means that the interviewer should interview a child as quickly as possible after an initial allegation and should only interview the child a second time about the same allegation if it is absolutely necessary to obtain additional information that was not previously attained. Individuals in the child's environment should be encouraged to minimize the number of interviews with the child and, if possible, to document any interviews that do take place. Specifically, for forensic interviews, interviewers should videotape the interview and keep the recording in a secure place. One of the most valuable pieces of evidence in the case will be the recording of the child witness interview. Clinicians, on the other hand, can maintain the same record keeping they would use in an ordinary interview with a child.

What Not to Do

Established guidelines for interviewing children are all critical of the use of potentially contaminating techniques such as suggestive questions, repeated questions, yes/no questions, reinforcement, social influence, co-witness information, inviting speculation, and stereotype inducement, and recommend that interviewers avoid using these techniques (Home Office, 2007; Sternberg et al., 2002). Exposure of the child to any of these potentially harmful interviewing techniques may decrease the overall quantity and quality of the child's account and may even contaminate the child's memory beyond repair. Finally, to avoid interviewer bias, it would be helpful if interviewers knew as little as possible about the case. With this goal in mind, interviewers may wish to ask a colleague or another professional who knows nothing about the case to interview the child. We acknowledge that this might be challenging in the real world, as investigative interviewers' objective is often to validate certain allegations that have unique legal implications. However, research suggests that a preconceived notion about the alleged event may be inadvertently translated into the interview and may present itself as suggestive questions (Davis & Bottoms, 2002).

When you know, via other reliable sources, that a child was involved in a negative event, it is important to remember that most children will disclose their experience the first time they are prompted about it (London, Bruck, Ceci, & Shuman, 2005; Sternberg et al., 2002). However, if the child does not mention anything about the event in question after he or she has been asked for the first time, Sternberg and colleagues recommend that the child be asked a second time. If the child still does not provide information after the second prompt, then the use of a more specific question may be necessary (e.g., I heard something may have happened to you at school). Specific questions should always be followed up with an open-ended question (e.g., Tell me everything about that). The interviewer should never ask a question that indicates the details of the allegation to the child. Correspondingly, interviewers should always avoid asking suggestive or leading questions. In an analysis of child witness interviews conducted in the United States, the UK, and Israel, Sternberg and colleagues found that when children were reluctant to disclose abuse, interviewers almost always resorted to the use of suggestive or leading questions. Yet, as has been mentioned throughout the chapter, research suggests that the risks of asking suggestive questions clearly outweigh the potential benefits (London et al., 2005; Poole & Lamb, 1998; Sternberg et al., 2002).

Conclusion

In the real world, there are many practical issues related to talking with children about their life experiences. These issues stem from developmental limitations in children's memory and the way that it is influenced by biased interviewing techniques. Before conducting an interview with a child, the purpose of the interview (clinical vs. investigative) should be established. Clinical practitioners and other professionals must strike a delicate balance between gathering information using recommended interviewing techniques, maintaining the therapeutic relationship, and addressing and treating children's clinical symptoms. In contrast, to be deemed valid, forensic interviewing must adhere to stringent guidelines regarding the use of the same techniques. The multitude of issues related to children's memory and interviewing highlight the importance of considering children's suggestibility within the larger context of children's cognitive development.

References

Ackil, J. K., & Zaragoza, M. S. (1998). Memorial consequences of forced confabulation: Age differences in susceptibility to false memories. *Developmental Psychology, 34*, 1358–1372.

Asch, S. E. (1955). Opinions and social pressure. *Scientific American, 19*, 31–35.

Brainerd, C. J., Holliday, R. E., & Reyna, V. F. (2004). Behavioral measurement of remembering phenomenologies: So simple a child can do it. *Child Development, 75*, 505–522.

Bruck, M., & Ceci, S. J. (1995). Amicus brief for the case of state of New Jersey v. Michaels presented by commitee of concerned social scientists. *Psychology, Public Policy, and Law. Special Theme: Suggestibility of Child Witnesses: The Social Science Amicus Brief in State of New Jersey v. Margaret Kelly Michaels, 1*, 272–322.

Burke, A., Heuer, F., & Reisberg, D. (1992). Remembering emotional events. *Memory & Cognition, 20*, 277–290.

Cassel, W. S., Roebers, C. E. M., & Bjorklund, D. F. (1996). Developmental patterns of eyewitness responses to repeated and increasingly suggestive questions. *Journal of Experimental Child Psychology, 61*, 116–133.

Ceci, S. J., & Bruck, M. (1993). The suggestibility of the child witness: A historical review and synthesis. *Psychological Bulletin, 113*, 403–439.

Ceci, S. J., & Bruck, M. (1995). *Jeopardy in the courtroom: A scientific analysis of children's testimony.* Washington, DC: American Psychological Association.

Ceci, S. J., & Friedman, R. D. (2000). The suggestibility of children: Scientific research and legal implications. *Cornell Law Review, 86*, 33–108.

Ceci, S. J., Huffman, M. L. C., Smith, E., & Loftus, E. F. (1994). Repeatedly thinking about a non-event: Source misattributions among preschoolers. *Consciousness and Cognition, 3*, 388–407.

Ceci, S. J., Ross, D., & Toglia, M. (1987). Age differences in suggestibility: Psychological implications. *Journal of Experimental Psychology: General, 117*, 38–49.

Christianson, S., & Loftus, E. F. (1991). Remembering emotional events: The fate of detailed information. *Cognition & Emotion, 5*, 81–108.

Christianson, S., Loftus, E. F., Hoffman, H., & Loftus, G. R. (1991). Eye fixations and memory for emotional events. *Journal of Experimental Psychology: Learning, Memory, and Cognition, 17*, 693–701.

Cialdini, R. B. (2001). *Influence.* Boston: Allyn & Bacon.

Clifford, B. R., & Hollin, C. R. (1981). Effects of the type of incident and the number of perpetrators on eyewitness memory. *Journal of Applied Psychology, 66*, 364–370.

Davis, S., & Bottoms, B. (2002). Effects of social support on children's eyewitness reports: A test of the underlying mechanism. *Law and Human Behavior, 26*, 185–215.

Deffenbacher, K. A., Bornstein, B. H., Penrod, S. D., & McGorty, E. K. (2004). A meta-analytic review of the effects of high stress on eyewitness memory. *Law and Human Behavior, 28,* 687–706.

Eisen, M. L., Quas, J. A., & Goodman, G. S. (2002). *Memory and suggestibility in the forensic interview.* Mahwah, NJ: Lawrence Erlbaum Associates.

Ettinger, R. H., Crooks, R. L., & Stein, J. (1994). *Psychology: Science, behavior and life.* Fort Worth, TX: Harcourt Brace.

Garven, S., Wood, J. M., & Malpass, R. S. (2000). Allegations of wrongdoing: The effects of reinforcement on children's mundane and fantastic claims. *Journal of Applied Psychology, 85,* 38–49.

Garven, S., Wood, J. M., Malpass, R. S., & Shaw, J. S. (1998). More than suggestion: The effect of interviewing techniques from the McMartin preschool case. *Journal of Experimental Psychology, 83,* 347–359.

Goodman, G., Quin, J., Bottoms, B., & Shaver, P. (1994). *Characteristics of allegations of ritualistic child abuse.* Final report to National Center on Child Abuse and Neglect, Washington, DC.

Home Office. (2007). *Achieving best evidence in criminal proceedings: Guidance on interviewing victims and witnesses and using special measures.* London: Author.

Leichtman, M. D., & Ceci, S. J. (1995). The effects of stereotypes and suggestions on preschoolers' reports. *Developmental Psychology, 31,* 568–578.

Loftus, E. F., & Burns, T. E. (1982). Mental shock can produce retrograde amnesia. *Memory & Cognition, 10,* 318–323.

London, K., Bruck, M., Ceci, S. J., & Shuman, D. W. (2005). Disclosure of child sexual abuse: What does the research tell us about the ways that children tell? *Psychology, Public Policy, & Law, 11,* 194–226.

Lyon, T. D., & Saywitz, K. J. (2006). From post-mortem to preventive medicine: Next steps for research on child witnesses. *Journal of Social Issues, 62,* 833–861.

Memon, A., & Vartoukian, A. (1996). The effects of repeated questioning on young children's eyewitness testimony. *British Journal of Psychology, 87,* 403–415.

Merritt, K. A., Ornstein, P. A., & Spicker, B. (1994). Children's memory for a salient medical procedure: Implications for testimony. *Pediatrics, 94,* 17–23.

Metzger, R. L., Warren, A. R., Shelton, J. T., Price, J., Reed, A. W., & Williams, D. (2008). Do children "DRM" like adults? False memory production in children. *Developmental Psychology, 44,* 169–181.

Nathan, D. (1988, August 2). *Village Voice,* pp. 31–39.

Nathan, D., & Snedecker, M. (1995). *Satan's silence: Ritual abuse and the making of a modern American witch hunt.* New York: Basic Books.

Ornstein, P. A., & Haden, C. A. (2001). Memory development or the development of memory? *Current Directions in Psychological Science, 10,* 202–205.

Poole, D., & Lamb, M. E. (1998). *Investigative interviews of children: A guide for helping professionals.* Washington, DC: American Psychological Association.

Poole, D. A., & Lindsay, D. S. (2001). Children's eyewitness reports after exposure to misinformation from parents. *Journal of Experimental Psychology: Applied, 7,* 27–50.

Poole, D., & White, L. (1991). Effects of question repetition on the eyewitness testimony of children and adults. *Developmental Psychology, 27,* 975–986.

Poole, D., & White, L. (1993). Two years later: Effects of question repetition and retention interval on the eyewitness testimony of children and adults. *Developmental Psychology, 29,* 844–853.

Pratkanis, A. R. (2007). Social influence analysis: An index of tactics. In A. R. Pratkanis (Ed.), *The science of social influence: Advances and future progress* (pp. 17–82). Philadelphia: Psychology Press.

Reisberg, D., & Heuer, F. (2007). The influence of emotion on memory in forensic settings. In M. P. Toglia, D. J. Read, D. F. Ross, & R. C. L. Lindsay (Eds.), *The handbook of eyewitness psychology: Memory for events* (Vol. I, pp. 81–116). Mahwah, NJ: Lawrence Erlbaum Associates Publishers.

Schreiber, N. (2000). Interviewing techniques in sexual abuse cases—A comparison of a day-care abuse case with normal abuse cases. *Swiss Journal of Psychology, 59,* 196–206.

Schreiber, N., Bellah, L. D., Martinez, Y., McLaurin, K. A., Strok, R., Garven, S., et al. (2006). Suggestive interviewing in the McMartin preschool and Kelly Michaels daycare abuse cases: A case study. *Social Influence, 1,* 16–47.

Schreiber, N., & Parker, J. F. (2004). Inviting child witnesses to speculate: Effects of age and interaction on children's recall. *Journal of Experimental Child Psychology, 89,* 31–52.

Schreiber, N., Wentura, D., & Bilsky, W. (2001). "What else could he have done?" Creating false answers in child witnesses by "inviting speculation." *Journal of Applied Psychology, 86,* 525–532.

Siegal, M., Waters, L., & Dinwiddy, L. (1988). Misleading children: Casual attributions for inconsistency under repeated questioning. *Journal of Experimental Child Psychology, 45,* 438–456.

Steller, M. (1997). Kinderschutz durch Forensische Aussagepsychologie [Child protection through forensic statement psychology]. *Monatsschrift für Kriminologie, 80,* 274–282.

Steller, M. (1998). Aussagepsychologie vor Gericht—Methodik und Probleme von Glaubwürdigkeitsgutachten mit Hinweisen auf die Wormser Missbrauchsprozesse [Statement psychology at trial—Methodology and problems of credibility assessments in reference to the abuse trials in Worms]. *Recht und Psychiatrie, 16,* 11–18.

Sternberg, K. J., Lamb, M. E., Esplin, P. W., Orbach, Y., & Hershkowitz, I. (2002). Using a structured interview protocol to improve the quality of investigative interviews. In M. L. Eisen, J. A. Quas, & G. S. Goodman (Eds.), *Memory and suggestibility in the forensic interview* (pp. 409–436). Mahwah, NJ: Lawrence Erlbaum Associates Publishers.

Volbert, R. (1999). Determinanten der Aussagesuggestibilität bei Kindern [Indicators of statement suggestibility in children]. *Zeitschrift für experimentelle und klinische Hypnose, 15,* 55–78.

Wells, G. L. (1978). Applied eyewitness-testimony research—System variables and estimator variables. *Journal of Personality and Social Psychology, 36,* 1546–1557.

IV
Developing Reason and Executive Control

Take what you know about the world and use it to build more knowledge. Reasoning is the ultimate form of cognitive bootstrapping. Generalizing, hypothesizing, deducing, and evaluating—the hallmarks of sophisticated thought—are skills that develop very gradually, and in very knowledge-based-driven ways, over childhood. Because of this, "reasoning" with children sometimes feels as futile as bashing one's head into a brick wall (over and over and over). As Sandberg and McCullough describe in Chapter 10, small logical victories (it is snowing, so I must wear boots) at early ages give the illusion of more abstract competence and don't foretell that regression in reasoning comes with the burden of worldly knowledge (and that precedes moving to the higher plane of abstract thought).

Moving beyond the brass tacks of inductive, deductive, and systematic thinking, reasoning can be examined with respect to the content-specific domains of any field. White-Ajmani and O'Connell describe for us the development of children's moral reasoning in Chapter 11, an area of particular relevance for clinicians and educators. They provide useful guidelines for interpreting children's decisions about good/bad, right/wrong, and do/don't.

Finally, Holler and Greene (Chapter 12) sketch the picture of the child as gatekeeper and tender of his cognitive kingdom. Effective rulers possess the capacity for organization, planning, control, and flexibility over cognitive processes such as attention and memory. By grounding this discussion in developmental theory, emphasis is placed on the process of learning how to become an effective ruler, a process that begins in childhood and continues well into adulthood.

10

The Development of Reasoning Skills

ELISABETH HOLLISTER SANDBERG and
MARY BETH McCULLOUGH

Reasoning, the subject of this chapter, is perhaps one of the most obviously complex and sophisticated cognitive activities in which people engage. Even simple reasoning tasks require the active manipulation of stored information, and many reasoning tasks take us well into the domain of metacognition (thinking about thinking). Although developmental trajectories can be articulated for content-specific types of reasoning (e.g., quantitative reasoning, reasoning about object constancy, moral reasoning), we concern ourselves in this chapter with the description and analysis of three broad classes of domain-general forms of reasoning: inductive reasoning, deductive reasoning, and scientific reasoning.

Briefly defined, inductive reasoning is the process of moving from the specific to the general—taking data from individual observations and experiences and using those data to form more global, generalized rules about the world. Conversely, deduction is the process of moving from the general to the specific—taking established general premises and applying rules of logic to draw valid conclusions that would apply to new specific instances. Scientific reasoning is arguably a step up from induction and deduction in that it is the most complex and explicit of the forms of reasoning. Scientific reasoning should not be confused with knowledge about science; it is a method, not a content area. One could think of it as systematic reasoning. It involves formulating and testing hypotheses, gathering and evaluating evidence, and drawing conclusions that represent links between hypotheses and evidence. Inductive and deductive reasoning are both essential components of scientific reasoning.

The cognitive skills required for all three of these reasoning processes show considerable developmental variability across childhood and into adolescence. For reasons not entirely clear (faulty reasoning perhaps?), we adults make a lot of erroneous assumptions about the sophistication of children's reasoning skills. As scholars of human behavior, our academic expectations of reasoning from children diverge from the intuitive expectations we evidence in typical day-to-day interaction with children.

In clinical and educational contexts, we routinely expect children to generalize information and skills from one situation to another, to use general rules to guide behavior, and to make connections between causally–related events. We expect these skills from even very young children, ages 3 and 4; yet the skills required to draw inferences develop gradually over childhood. The most sophisticated form of reasoning—in which you develop an idea that is testable—does not develop until adolescence. Yet who among us (yes, even the authors) hasn't been guilty of asking a five-year-old something along the lines of "What do you *think* would happen if you were allowed to eat candy at every meal?" followed by looking pointedly at the child, confident that our implicit message carried its intended weight?

Inductive, deductive, and scientific reasoning are stacked in ascending order based on the cognitive resources required to execute them. Successful application of all forms of informal and formal reasoning requires manipulating knowledge or information to gain new insights into or to draw new conclusions about new data. An important theme that arises from consideration of the cognitive skills of informal and formal reasoning is that of accumulated knowledge and experience. Reasoning by induction, or analogy, is greatly facilitated by knowledge and familiarity. The more information that a child possesses and can access, the easier it is to draw analogies. Deep understanding of the elements to be relationally mapped, or the domains from which and to which generalizations are made, facilitates extracting the necessary similarities and relationships required for transfer of information. On the other hand, reasoning by deduction, the drawing of logical inferences, is clouded by associated knowledge and experience. Although young children cannot solve truly abstract logical problems (*if P, then Q; P, so Q*), with concrete referents early logical proficiencies can be observed. Being able to generate evidence of possibility—utterly irrelevant to questions of argument validity—is easier with an extensive base of knowledge and experience. Similarly, scientific reasoning is heavily influenced by prior knowledge and beliefs. Past experience serves as the foundation for theory building, and theories drive hypotheses. Closely held beliefs about the how's and why's of life may not be evidence based, but play an enormous role in the scientific approach to questions. In sum, what you know makes it easier to be inductive, but what you know gets in the way of logic and systematic inquiry.

The Development of Inductive Reasoning

In a sense, inductive reasoning is the most pragmatic form of reasoning—the one that drives much of our day-to-day learning. We observe the consequences of the behaviors of ourselves and others, and we subsequently apply our knowledge of those behavior-consequence pairs to new situations. We find regularity in, and make generalizations from, our daily experiences and encounters through inductive/analogical reasoning. Common manifestations of inductive reasoning include understanding intentionality, reasoning about causality, construction of categories, and relational mapping skills. Under carefully controlled experimental conditions, with task demands stripped down to the bare minimum, developmental scientists have found the rudiments of inductive reasoning at surprisingly early ages (Chen, Sanchez, & Campbell, 1997; Goswami & Reese, 1996).

Categorical Reasoning

Most categorical reasoning is inductive in nature (Coley et al., 2005; Gelman, 2003). Children search for similarities between sets of objects, and use the relational similarities to generalize information from member to member or set to set. Once one has developed a category—dogs, candy, doctors—new members to the category are presumed to share certain characteristics with the existing set. Similarities between existing, specific members of the category are generalized to new members of that category. In most day-to-day learning circumstances, making generalizations of this sort is an extremely efficient and useful way to go about approaching new objects and events in the world. Even though the child does not possess an exact, explicit, formal definition of what makes a creature a *dog* (as opposed to a cat, small bear, or very large rodent), the child does have a practical definition of *dog* built up from functionally relevant features such as: furry body, four-legged, tail wagging, domesticity, potential danger, and so on. When introduced to a new animal, "this is my dog, Sparky," categorical features of *dog*-ness are extended to Sparky. The more dog features that are stored for the category of *dog*, the more that can be extended. If, for example, the child's concept of *dog* includes: likes to play fetch, licks your face, chews bones, and obeys commands, the child will assume that Sparky will do these things. If the child's concept of *dog* includes only: jumps on you and knocks you down, then that is all that can be extended to Sparky. The response to meeting Sparky is predictable when you know the categorical assumptions, but we rarely do.

Practical Implications of Inductive Categories.   Generalizations of categorical information creep into children's behaviors in clinical settings. Because the specific features that define categories for individual children are collected *ad hoc* from accumulated memories of instances and events, the nature of a category definition is unknowable to an outside party (see Sparky example, above). When knowledge structures are not collectively shared, it can be very difficult as a clinician to anticipate the types of generalizations or working assumptions that a child will make to new category instances. What is the child's working representation of dogs? Or babysitters? Or vegetables? Or games? Imagine that you ask a small child, "Do you want to play a game with me?" How are you to know that the child's shocked resistance is based on a uniquely defined concept of *game* that involves getting smacked on the head by his older brother? Because this insight is impossible, we do not predicate our interactions with children on the ambiguity of idiosyncratic generalizations (questioning all of which the child speaks is impractical—a pastime suited only to Descartes!). Instead, we make a lot of assumptions. Violations of our assumptions can be very salient.

EXAMPLE: IDIOSYNCRATIC INDUCTIVE CATEGORIES

Jill, prior to age 10, knew two children who were adopted. Both of these children also happened to be the only child in their respective families.

When she went to camp at age 10, Jill met a girl who was an only child. They started to talk about their families and who they resembled most. The other girl mentioned that she didn't look like either of her parents and Jill replied with, "Of course you don't look like your parents! You're adopted!"

Instance 1: child = adopted and only
Instance 2: child = adopted and only
New instance: child = only … and so also adopted!

Analogical Reasoning

Analogical reasoning is another key subtype of inductive reasoning. De Koning, Hamers, Sijtsma, and Vermeer (2002) translate Karl Klauer's splendid definition: Inductive reasoning is the systematic and analytic comparison of objects and discovering regularity in apparent chaos and the regularity in apparent order. The ability of children to discover regularity has been studied extensively. The conditions under which analogical transfer, the application of information learned in one domain to a new domain, is successful have been very clearly charted developmentally (Bjorklund, 2005; Goswami & Reese, 1996). We see evolution of skill that begins with low-level transfer, where children can take simple conceptual or procedural knowledge learned in one domain and apply it to a target domain that is plainly equivalent. Mid-level transfer requires the use of a bit of strategy, bridging a slightly wider gap between tasks. The highest levels of transfer require decontextualized knowledge and are highly metacognitive in nature. Principles learned in one domain are applied in another domain, sharing structural similarities with the learned domain but with few or no superficial similarities.

EXAMPLE: LEVELS OF ANALOGICAL TRANSFER

Low-level transfer: A child is taught that the bathtub is slippery when it is wet. The child is able to extend that knowledge to the other bathtub in the house.

Mid-level transfer: The child is able to generalize the slippery-surface knowledge and exercise caution around a spill on the kitchen floor.

High-level transfer: Water can reduce the coefficient of friction between two objects. By wetting a surface, you can reduce sticking (run water down the slide). You can use a different fluid to try to reduce the coefficient of friction between objects—cooking oil, for example, on Lego bricks that are "stuck" (no longer recommended by the child in question!).

The relational mapping skills required in analogical reasoning emerge in children as young as three years of age (Goswami, 1991). Being able to make analogical mappings with instruction is easier than drawing analogies spontaneously. Extensive research with adults shows that the ability to analogically map solutions across superficially dissimilar problems is seldom used spontaneously (e.g., Brown & Kane, 1988; Daehler & Chen, 1993). Often, specific cues must be given to the participant to highlight the fact that the solution to the new problem is in fact isomorphic to a previously solved problem. Given that spontaneous transfer of information across settings is limited for even educated adults in formal settings (Genter, Vosniadou, & Ortony, 1989; Gick & Holyoak, 1983), it is hardly surprising that considerable instructional effort is required within the context of classrooms to induce, so to speak, children to engage regularly in analogical transfer.

Practical Implications of Analogical Reasoning. Clinicians rely heavily on being able to query a child, "Remember how you/when you…?" and then build upon (reason about) the answer. By asking focused questions, clinicians can guide children through the reasoning that leads to certain behaviors. This could serve as an instructional tool, allowing children to tap into their metacognitive reasoning abilities. By focusing on the process (reasoning) as well as the product (behavior), children and clinicians may be able to connect reasoning and behaviors in different situations, thus engaging in analogical reasoning.

EXAMPLE: ANALOGY IN PRACTICE

Failure of analogical transfer

A:	Do you remember what happened when you screamed at Mrs. White?
C:	Yes.
A:	What?

C:	She put me in the hall.
A:	Did you like that?
C:	No.
A:	What might have been a better way to get her attention?
C:	Asking nicely.
A:	Can you try to do that next time instead of screaming?

At a future appointment:

A:	I thought we agreed that screaming was not a good way to get an adult to pay attention to you?
C:	I thought that was just for Mrs. White.

Facilitating analogical transfer

Draw out the specific domain for transfer.

A:	If screaming is not a good way to get Mrs. White's attention, it probably isn't a good way to get any teacher's attention, right?
C:	Yeah.
A:	Who are the other teachers you can ask nicely for attention?
C:	Mr. Smith, Ms. Jones, Ms. Woods.
A:	Good! When *is* it okay to scream to get an adult's attention?

The Development of Deductive Reasoning

Deductive reasoning, the process of taking general rules, formally called *premises*, and drawing valid conclusions from them, is a cognitive skill routinely used by all but mastered by few. It has long been argued that the capacity to draw valid logical inferences from supposed other truths is uniquely human (it has been a subject of scholarly inquiry for literally thousands of years). The tricky thing about logical reasoning is that the functions and rules can technically take you places where reason and reality conflict.

Although even young children are observed reasoning deductively (applying general rules about familiar things to new instances) when the objects of reason are concrete (Dias & Harris, 1988, 1990; Hawkins, Pea, Glick, & Scribner, 1984), Inhelder, Piaget, Parsons, and Milgram (1958) considered true logical reasoning as a developmental benchmark of formal operations— inaccessible before adolescence, a finding supported by more recent research

(Markovits & Vachon, 1990; Overton, Ward, Noveck, Black, & O'Brien, 1987; Ward & Overton, 1990). So which is it? Formal operational thought allows for the manipulation of referent-free symbols (e.g., if *P*, then *Q*), and for reasoning about things "never experienced." Few, if any, would argue that manipulating *P*s and *Q*s is a very abstract task, but the same mechanisms underlie reasoning tied to direct, real-world experiences, such as *if it is raining, we stay inside for recess.* Using if-then statements in deductive reasoning does not, for thinkers at the stage of Piaget's formal operations, require knowledge or understanding of the elements (the *constants* in formal logic). *P* and *Q* are simply placeholders for any number of possible referents, for any one of which the observation of *P* would imply by logical extension the existence of *Q*. Most adults, and some adolescents, are able to tackle the infinite abstraction of this. Children are not, but they can apply the same logical mechanisms to problems constructed around familiar concrete referents:

If P, then Q:	If it is raining, then we stay in the classroom for recess.
P:	It is raining now.
Therefore, Q:	So we will stay in the classroom for recess today.

Children ages 5 to 7 are generally able to process (i.e., remember and use) the two initial representational elements required for the problem above (Markovits & Barrouillet, 2002). In other words, they can represent the major premise (if *P*, then *Q*), plus one other class of information (*P*). Extra propositions will exceed the processing capacities for children of this age. For example, one could introduce another element to the problem above, and connect it with the function *or*:

If P, then Q or R:	If it is raining, then we stay in the classroom for recess *or* go to the gym.
P:	It is raining now.
Therefore, Q or R:	So we will stay in the classroom *or* go to the gym for recess today.

If you ask a 5-year-old to deduce a conclusion from those more complex premises, the results will be variable.

When we encounter statements with concrete referents, our knowledge of and experiences with those referents are activated in memory. Memory and retrieval are less efficient and less accurate for young children (Kail, 1992; Kail & Ferrer, 2007). The semantic networks of knowledge are not fast or particularly thick. Usually, we think of associated knowledge as being helpful (as it is for inductive reasoning). The more you know about something, the more you can think about that thing. Associated knowledge, however, gets in the way of deductive reasoning by allowing for the spontaneous introduction of additional propositions, alternative explanations, and disabling cases—exceptions to the rule.

A disabling case is one that allows the relationship between *P* and *Q* to be violated. Disabling conditions are very difficult for children to inhibit. When they can think of an example under which the if-then relationship between *P* and *Q* might not apply, it is difficult to retain the logical necessity of *Q* resulting from *P* in the original problem.

If P, then Q:	If it is raining, then we stay in the classroom for recess, *but* there was one time when it was raining and we went to the auditorium for school assembly instead, and then there was the time that my mom picked me up early from school so I didn't have classroom recess even though it was raining.
P:	It is raining now.
Therefore, Q:	So…?

EXAMPLE: EXCEPTIONS GET IN THE WAY OF RULES!

Me (EHS):	It is raining today so you need to wear your boots.
Lili:	(age 5) I don't like those boots!
Me:	Your feet will get wet if you don't wear them.
Lili:	They might not!
Me:	Yes they will.
Lili:	They won't if I don't walk on the ground! What if the sun comes out when we open the door?

If you are especially young, with a small knowledge base and relatively weak retrieval skills, many conditional premises will activate low levels of associated information, and so very few disabling cases or alternative explanations are readily available. This is a benefit when working out a conditional problem wherein only the immediate propositions are under consideration. The reasoning of very young children is "cleaner" than for older children because access to associated knowledge and counterexamples is more limited.

In addition to increasing interference stored from knowledge and experience, there are other predictable patterns in the development of logical thought. Consider the four types of conclusions drawn in response to the major premise of *if P, then Q* plus one other statement. Two are valid and two are not.

EXAMPLE: GOOD AND BAD CONCLUSIONS
FROM CONDITIONALS

If Mom has a chapter draft to revise, then she will stay late at the office.

Mom has a chapter draft to revise.
Therefore, she will stay late at the office.
Modus ponens, VALID!

If Mom has a chapter draft to revise, then she will stay late at the office.
Mom did not stay late at the office.
Therefore, she did not have a chapter draft to revise.
Modus tollens, VALID!

If Mom has a chapter draft to revise, then she will stay late at the office.
Mom stayed late at the office.
Therefore, she had a chapter draft to revise.
Affirmation of the consequent, INVALID!

If Mom has a chapter draft to revise, then she will stay late at the office.
Mom did not have a chapter draft to revise.
Therefore, she did not stay late at the office.
Denial of the antecedent, INVALID!

Use of these inference types varies developmentally. Third graders accurately draw valid *modus ponens* conclusions, but are also inclined to produce invalid conclusions of affirmation of the consequent. Fifth graders will make all four types of inferences. Ninth graders and adults will more frequently employ the valid forms of inference, *modus ponens* and *modus tollens*, but they do commit errors of affirmation of the consequent or denial of the antecedent (Barrouillet, Grosset, & Lecas, 2000; Barrouillet & Lecas, 1998; Janveau-Brennan & Markovits, 1999).

EXAMPLE: FAULTY INFERENCES

Aiden (age 4) appears in the kitchen, in January, wearing his most recent Halloween costume. He announces that he is ready to go trick-or-treating.

If it is Halloween (P), then we wear costumes (Q).
I am wearing a costume (Q).
Therefore, it is Halloween! (therefore P).
Affirmation of the consequent, INVALID!

Practical Implications of Errors in Logic

The logical errors made by children, often as a result of poorly understood connective functions (e.g., thinking that *if* means *if and only if,* or that an inclusive *or* is an exclusive *or*), can confound our attempts to regulate their behavior through reasoning. Logical reasoning, once mastered in adolescence, becomes seamlessly integrated into our cognitive interpretations of language and behavior. Every adult who has interfaced with children is well rehearsed at saying, "Why did you do X if you knew that Y would be the result?" Prior to adolescence, that if-then relationship may not be a useful inferential tool. The current trend in parenting is to engage children in the reasoning behind everything you say or do. This is all fine and good as an exposure paradigm, but beware—you should make no assumptions that your reasoning is being understood!

EXAMPLE: REASONING WITH THE UNREASONABLE

The parent says to a three-year-old: "You are in a timeout because you hit your brother."
The underlying logic:

If you hit your brother, you will get a time out.
You hit your brother.
Hence, you are in time out.

Understanding this implied logic requires semantic knowledge of the terms *timeout, hit, brother,* and *because.* It also requires understanding *modus ponens* conditional reasoning, as well as acceptance of the second premise (that the child did indeed "hit" his brother).
And yet we wonder why the message doesn't stick.

EXAMPLE: REASONING AGAINST THE WIND

Liliana (age 7), already in trouble for squabbling incessantly with her brother, starts a new argument. I told her, "Stop fighting with your brother immediately!" She paused for about one second and then continued her rant. I got in her face and said, "Liliana, I told you to stop fighting with your brother." She looked me straight in the eye and said, with all sincerity, "I *did*! I decided just now that he wouldn't be my brother anymore!"

We also need to consider, and perhaps actively seek, the reasoning steps that might underlie "odd" reactions of stress or resistance. Are the premises from which a child is reasoning actually the ones that *we* assume?

EXAMPLE: HIDDEN PREMISES

Even though she had already been attending preschool at the Early Learning Center for a year, Alie (age 4) was very anxiously anticipating the transition to being at ELC by herself, as her brother moved on to kindergarten. She was actually complaining that she did not want to go to school, saying she didn't like school, and so on. It took six to eight weeks before she seemed like herself again. Her mother assumed she was just missing her brother and adjusting to being without him.

As her mother was bathing her one morning she was giving her a rundown of the day's expectations (it is a school day, etc.). They started talking about the fact that ELC is her school now, and not her brother's because he is in kindergarten. And she says, "You know, Mommy, I thought that when Sammy didn't go to ELC anymore that he would stop being my brother. But, now I know that we just go to different schools, and he will always be my brother and I'm glad."

Development of Scientific (i.e., Systematic) Reasoning Skills

Scientific reasoning is a more extended, multipart, deeply reflective process that requires utilization of both inductive and deductive reasoning. True scientific reasoning is planful; an experiment is conducted with a purpose in mind and alternative outcomes are considered. The ability to reason scientifically requires distinguishing between hypotheses (one's ideas, projections, theories about how things work) and the evidence supporting or not supporting a hypothesis. About 50% of fourth and fifth graders will do these things with support in a clearly delineated scientific reasoning task (Kuhn & Phelps, 1982).

Theories and Hypotheses

Theories serve as the foundation for hypotheses. Theories are developed from existing knowledge. For children, and the everyday theory building of adults, "existing knowledge" takes the form of one's accumulated knowledge and experiences. The more you know about a variable or process, the more conviction you can have in your theories about those things.

One of the most practically useful theories is that of causal connection between elements (*A causes B*). Children as young as age 3 will use covariation of events as an indicator of causality (e.g., Inhelder et al., 1958; Koerber, Sodian, Thoermer, & Nett 2005; Schulz, Gopnik, & Glymour, 2007). Covariation is a necessary but not sufficient condition for a causal connection between two elements. A single instance of covariation may lead to a theory of causation, but it is more easily modified than a theory based on multiple instances of covariation.

EXAMPLE: THEORIES BASED ON COVARIATION

Theory 1: Single data point, modifiable
Liliana, in grade 1, says, "I can't wear these shoes. The last time I wore them I had trouble with my math test." She wore them anyway and was delighted to report later that she did not have any trouble with math that day! She conceded that perhaps the shoes had nothing to do with math even though she had been "pretty sure about that" earlier.

Theory 2: Multiple data points, more robust
From her vast experience observing crying babies (at the mall, at the park, visiting our house), Liliana, at age 3.5, has extracted common elements from her observations to generate a theory about the causes of infant crying. She is very certain that babies cry when they are wearing socks.

Covariation is a driving force behind hypotheses. Hypotheses are testable predictions about specific outcomes generated from consideration of a given set of elements and a theory. In a simple task, with few factors and perfect covariation, six-year-olds can form a hypothesis. Seven-year-olds know that the hypothesis could be used to make predictions (Ruffman, Perner, Olsen, & Doherty, 1993).

Children under the age of 10 often conduct "experiments" without specific hypotheses. By ages 12 to 14, this changes (Dunbar, Klahr, Klahr, & Kotovsky, 1989; Penner & Klahr, 1996). What is the difference between an experiment driven by hypothesis and one that is not? Let's say you are posed with the question, "What makes X happen?" A truly scientific approach requires iterative conjecture: "I think Y makes X happen; let me check that." Before age 10, the approach is more likely to be: "Let me try to make X happen!"

Why is it important to examine children's use of hypotheses in designing experiments? Conducting experiments with specific hypotheses is an efficient and highly sophisticated ability. Instead of haphazardly testing many possible variables or trying to "make X happen;" using hypotheses allows one to design a controlled study around proving or disproving explicit predictions. These carefully designed studies yield results that are easier to interpret and findings in which we can have more confidence. Children who spontaneously use hypotheses in the construction of experiments are operating at a sophisticated level of cognition and can use these abilities to reason about many kinds of problems and situations.

Gathering and Evaluating Evidence

Technically speaking, scientific reasoning revolves around attempting to disprove one's hypothesis. Confirmatory evidence, however, seems to have a special magnetic draw for children and adults alike. When adults and children attempt to solve everyday problems, they do not necessarily use rational strategies; instead, they tend to seek evidence to confirm a positive outcome and eliminate or disconfirm negative outcomes. In fact, this sometimes leads to a resistance to disconfirmatory evidence.

Tschirgi (1980) presented adults and children in grades 2, 4, and 6 with a cake-baking scenario with either a good or bad outcome (a good-tasting or a bad-tasting cake). There were three variables included in the scenario: (1) shortening type (butter or margarine), (2) sweetener type (sugar or honey), and (3) flour type (white or whole wheat). Participants were informed that margarine, honey, and whole wheat flour were used to bake the cake, but told that only one variable (e.g., honey) caused the good or bad outcome. They were subsequently asked to determine which levels of the variable to change or to keep constant to produce the conclusive test of causality. They could choose one of three options to "prove" causality: (1) Bake another cake using the same sweetener (honey) and change the levels of the other two variables; (2) bake another cake using a different level of the sweetener variable (sugar) while using the same levels of the other two variables; or (3) bake another cake using different levels of all of the variables.

The results showed that when there was a good outcome (the cake was good), all age groups wanted to maintain the positive result by holding the sweetener constant and changing the other variables, thus producing a confounded experiment. (If you want to show that sweetener is responsible for your successful cake, pointing to the result you achieve when you change the amount of flour is not going to convince anyone about your sweetener claim.) Conversely, when there was a bad outcome, all age groups chose to eliminate the negative result by changing the sweetener and holding the other two variables constant, thus producing a controlled experiment. This study suggests that both adults' and children's problem-solving strategies can be illogical, influenced by the valence of the evidence (i.e., positive, negative) instead of reasoning based on how to conclusively "prove" a relationship.

Evaluating the Evidence

Structuring your data gathering efforts to provide definitive answers to questions is difficult. Even if you have systematically collected data, interpreting and using those data present another level of challenge. Children have a great deal of difficulty evaluating evidence that disconfirms either a prior belief or a newly constructed theory (Zimmerman, 2007). Said another way, children tend to favor confirmatory evidence over disconfirmatory evidence. Even adults seek confirmatory evidence—we all like to say to ourselves, "See! I'm right!" One explanation for the popularity of confirmatory evidence may have to do with the difficulty in managing inconsistent data. When you structure your evidence gathering to seek disconfirming data, you deliberately put yourself in the position of possibly having to modify your prior beliefs (theories) with respect to anomalous data. Breaking away from "proving oneself right" requires anticipation of the possibility that beliefs and data will be inconsistent, and a plan for what to do if that occurs. This is a meta-cognitive adventure requiring a fair bit of planning in advance for unknown outcomes. Coordinating or differentiating theories and evidence, and the ability to suppress prior beliefs when drawing conclusions about new data, develops between third and ninth grade. So, if a preadolescent child, especially a child under age 8, has a belief about something, it is very difficult to get him or her to modify that belief in light of new evidence.

EXAMPLE: FAILURE TO UPDATE THEORIES

Liliana (age 7) recently suffered significant damage to personal property inflicted by her brother. He went into her room when she was absent and "modified" one of her favorite drawings. When grief finally gave way to indignation, Liliana posted a sign on her door explicitly prohibiting entry to her room by boys. A few days later, she came around asking for more tape in order to post another sign on her door because "the first one wasn't working."

Theory:	Children obey instructions (true for her in the extreme).
Hypothesis:	Instructions posted on her door should prevent breach by brother.
Evidence:	Brother came into room anyway.
Evaluation:	Evidence is attributed to equipment failure; theory is not updated.

Emma (age 4) did not want to eat the hamburger meat in a casserole prepared by her mother, instead preferring to pick out only the noodles. Her mother insisted that she eat the meat. Emma adopted a vegetarian position in response.

Mother:	Eat the meat in your casserole.

Emma:	I don't want to! I don't like it!
Mother:	Yes you do.
Emma:	No I don't! It is from a cow. I don't eat animals!
Mother:	You don't eat animals?
Emma:	No, I don't!
Mother:	You ate chicken for lunch; that is an animal.
Emma:	(*pause*) That's not an animal that we're not supposed to eat!

James (age 7)

James:	Miss Jeanine doesn't like me very much.
Mother:	Why do you say that?
James:	She always makes me stand at the back of the line.
Mother:	Maybe she wants you at the back of the line because she knows you can be trusted to make sure the kids in front of you go where they are supposed to go.
James:	No, it's because she doesn't like me.
Mother:	When I saw you come out of class last weekend you were at the front of the line!
James:	But she usually puts me at the back of the line because she doesn't like me!

Practical Implications of Scientific Reasoning. In a clinical context, scientific reasoning, with its attendant theories, hypotheses, evidence gathering, and interpretation requirements, lurks behind many seemingly simple clinical questions, questions such as:

- What do you think might make a difference?
- Why do you think she does that?
- What do you think will happen?
- How do you think that will turn out?

When children are asked to reason systematically about something, their output is marked by tendencies to:

- Be heavily influenced by prior beliefs
- Generate uninformative experiments
- Be unsystematic in recording plans, data, and outcomes
- Ignore inconsistent data
- Have a hard time disconfirming prior beliefs
- Make judgments based on insufficient or inconclusive evidence

When you ask hypothesis-oriented questions of any preadolescent child, you are virtually guaranteed an answer plagued by the aforementioned deficiencies or, at best, an honest "I don't know." You can lead a child step-by-step through the reasoning, but don't confuse this with instilling insight.

EXAMPLE: STEPPING THROUGH THE PROCESS

You are working with a family in a state of chronic low-level conflict. Recently, the mother's tolerance threshold for her eight-year-old son's inappropriate horseplay at the table was exceeded, resulting in an explosive shouting episode that troubled everyone. You are talking with the child about the incident, hoping to get him to see how his mother's "fit" was connected to his noncompliant behavior.

A: Why do you think your mother was so angry?

C: Don't know … because I got the floor all wet.

A: How did you get the floor wet?

C: I spilled all of the juice.

A: Did you spill the juice on purpose?

C: No.

A: How did it happen?

C: I don't know.

A: Did it maybe happen because you were being too silly at the table?

C: Yeah.

A: If you had not been acting silly, would the juice have spilled?

C: I don't know.

It might be tempting to read sullen resistance into the above conversation. Realize, though, that this boy is not ready to engage in abstract "what if" reasoning exercises.

Conclusion

The domains of informal and formal reasoning are some of the areas of cognitive development in which we find the most drastic variation between capacity and performance. In experimental lab-based tasks, even early preschoolers demonstrate some skills with analogical reasoning and drawing logical conclusions from if-then statements. But in the real world, the reasoning skills all of us bring to bear on problems are less perfect. Clinicians, educators, and parents must keep in mind the distinction between *can* and *do* when reasoning with children of any age. Just because a child *can* make if-then conclusions doesn't mean that the skill is universally applied or successful.

Reasoning by induction is facilitated by knowledge and improves steadily across childhood. Extending relationships is easier when you are familiar with the domains. Reasoning by deduction and application of the scientific method are, in childhood, hindered by knowledge base. Knowledge and experience provide pools of counterexamples and exceptions that interfere with drawing successful inferences. They also contribute to a system of theories and beliefs that become more robust with each confirmation. For example, the more readily you can call to mind instances of being wronged by your brother, the harder it will be for someone to convince you that he is sometimes a good guy. Naturally there must be a tipping point, or points, during development at which the abstract structure of the task can be rendered independent of the content reference of the elements (probably during Piaget's final developmental stage). When we can separate the architecture of a problem (e.g., if-then) from its referents, we can reason relatively independently of our nuisance-filled knowledge base. Decoupling concrete knowledge from a problem and approaching it with a fresh canvas is a teen and adult skill only.

EXAMPLE: REASONING WITH A CLEAN SLATE

Problem solving based on hypotheticals is a very advanced cognitive skill: "Okay, forget about X; what if you were to do Y instead?" This is clearly a formal operations level task, and yet there is probably more than one among us who has said something along the lines of the following to a child:

A: I know you are afraid to go back to gym class because you don't like it when you miss kicking the ball.

C: I hate that. Kids laugh at me.

A: Well, would it be okay to try going to gym class again on days when there isn't kickball?

Or

C: (*very upset over breakage of royal crown in the dress-up set*) I can't play princess anymore because my crown is broken!

A: You can still play princess!

C: *No ... I ... can't ...*

A: How about instead of the crown we glue some sparkles on one of your headbands and make it a tiara?

This is overreaching—plain and simple. It isn't harmful, and it might even be good foray into a zone of proximal development, but you should pause before launching into a verbal reasoning adventure with a child and consider the utility of the effort. There are times when, given the developmental stage of the child, discussions of reasoning are just a waste of time and energy. False assumptions of competence are built up when children "yes" you (they nod and agree to each step you lay out), and it is profoundly frustrating to find that your painstakingly communicated reasons don't stick.

At the risk of sounding like developmental heretics, or being struck by lightning, we are going to concede that EHS's mother was on to something in her pervasive approach to reasoning with her children. Whenever her children questioned her—"Why do I have to share my *Easy Bake Oven* with Sally?"— her uniform response was, "Why do you think?" If the child couldn't articulate a thoughtful answer to that question, the final answer was "because I said so!" When, and only when, her children evidenced ability to make reasonable conjectures about her motives was she willing to pursue further discussion. Her "show me you can talk about this before we talk about it" approach has a certain elegance.

References

Barrouillet, P., Grosset, N., & Lecas, J. (2000). Conditional reasoning by mental models: Chronometric and developmental evidence. *Cognition, 75*, 237–266.

Barrouillet, P., & Lecas, J. (1998). How can mental models theory account for content effects in conditional reasoning? A developmental perspective. *Cognition, 67*, 209–253.

Bjorklund, D. F. (2005). *Children's thinking: Cognitive development and individual differences* (4th ed.). Belmont, CA: Wadsworth/Thompson Publishing.

Brown, A. L., & Kane, M. J. (1988). Preschool children can learn to transfer: Learning to learn and learning from example. *Cognitive Psychology, 20*, 493–523.

Chen, Z., Sanchez, R. P., & Campbell, T. (1997). From beyond to within their grasp: The rudiments of analogical problem solving in 10- and 13-month-olds. *Developmental Psychology, 33*, 790–801.

Coley, J., Shafto, P., Stepanova, O., Baraff, E., Ahn, W., Goldstone, R. L., et al. (2005). Knowledge and category-based induction. In *Categorization inside and outside the laboratory: Essays in honor of Douglas L. Medin* (pp. 69–85). Washington, DC: American Psychological Association.

Daehler, M. W., & Chen, Z. (1993). Protagonist, theme, and goal object: Effects of surface features on analogical transfer. *Cognitive Development, 8*, 211–229.

de Koning, E., Hamers, J. H. M., Sijtsma, K., & Vermeer, A. (2002). Teaching inductive reasoning in primary education. *Developmental Review, 22*, 211–241.

Dias, M. G., & Harris, P. L. (1988). The effect of make-believe play on deductive reasoning. *British Journal of Developmental Psychology, 6*, 207–221.

Dias, M. G., & Harris, P. L. (1990). The influence of the imagination on reasoning by young children. *British Journal of Developmental Psychology, 8*, 305–318.

Dunbar, K., & Klahr, D. (1989). Developmental differences in scientific discovery processes. In D. Klahr & K. Kotovsky (Eds.), *Complex information processing: The impact of Herbert A. Simon* (pp. 109–143). Hillsdale, NJ: Lawrence Erlbaum Associates.

Gelman, S. A. (2003). *The essential child: Origins of essentialism in everyday thought.* New York: Oxford University Press.

Gentner, D., Vosniadou, S., & Ortony, A. (1989). The mechanisms of analogical learning. In S. Vosniadou & A. Ortony (Eds.), *Similarity and analogical reasoning* (pp. 199–241). New York: Cambridge University Press.

Gick, M. L., & Holyoak, K. J. (1983). Schema induction and analogical transfer. *Cognitive Psychology, 15,* 1–38.

Goswami, U. (1991). Analogical reasoning: What develops? A review of research and theory. *Child Development, 62,* 1–22.

Goswami, U., & Reese, H. W. (1996). Analogical reasoning and cognitive development. In H. W. Reese (Ed.), *Advances in child development and behavior* (Vol. 26, pp. 91–138). San Diego: Academic Press.

Hawkins, J., Pea, R. D., Glick, J., & Scribner, S. (1984). "Merds that laugh don't like mushrooms": Evidence for deductive reasoning by preschoolers. *Developmental Psychology, 20,* 584–594.

Inhelder, B., Piaget, J., Parsons, A., & Milgram, S. (1958). *The growth of logical thinking: From childhood to adolescence.* New York: Basic Books.

Janveau-Brennan, G., & Markovits, H. (1999). The development of reasoning with causal conditionals. *Developmental Psychology, 35,* 904–911.

Kail, R. (1992). Processing speed, speech rate, and memory. *Developmental Psychology, 28,* 899–904.

Kail, R. V., & Ferrer, E. (2007). Processing speed in childhood and adolescence: Longitudinal models for examining developmental change. *Child Development, 78,* 1760–1770.

Koerber, S., Sodian, B., Thoermer, C., & Nett, U. (2005). Scientific reasoning in young children: Preschoolers' ability to evaluate covariation evidence. *Swiss Journal of Psychology, 64,* 141–152.

Kuhn, D., & Phelps, E. (1982). The development of problem-solving strategies. *Advances in Child Development and Behavior, 17,* 1–44.

Markovits, H., & Barrouillet, P. (2002). The development of conditioned reasoning: A mental model account. *Developmental Review, 22,* 5–36.

Markovits, H., & Vachon, R. (1990). Conditional reasoning, representation, and level of abstraction. *Developmental Psychology, 26,* 942–951.

Overton, W. F., Ward, S. L., Noveck, I. A., Black, J., & O'Brien, D. P. (1987). Form and content in the development of deductive reasoning. *Developmental Psychology, 23,* 22–30.

Penner, D. E., & Klahr, D. (1996). When to trust the data: Further investigations of system error in a scientific reasoning task. *Memory & Cognition, 24,* 655–668.

Ruffman, T., Perner, J., Olson, D. R., & Doherty, M. (1993). Reflecting on scientific thinking: Children's understanding of the hypothesis-evidence relation. *Child Development, 64,* 1617–1636.

Schulz, L. E., Gopnik, A., & Glymour, C. (2007). Preschool children learn about causal structure from conditional interventions. *Developmental Science, 10,* 322–332.

Tschirgi, J. E. (1980). Sensible reasoning: A hypothesis about hypotheses. *Child Development, 51,* 1–10.

Ward, S. L., & Overton, W. F. (1990). Semantic familiarity, relevance, and the development of deductive reasoning. *Developmental Psychology, 26,* 488–493.

Zimmerman, C. (2007). The development of scientific thinking skills in elementary and middle school. *Developmental Review, 27,* 172–223.

11
Moral Reasoning

MANDI L. WHITE-AJMANI and SAMANTHA SAMBERG O'CONNELL

This chapter provides a synopsis of current theory and empirical research on the development of moral reasoning in childhood. After reading this chapter, you will be more equipped to disentangle intent from immature behavior and will be more aware of how children at different developmental stages understand others' moral behavior and intentions. We take the stance that an understanding of children's moral reasoning is a necessary tool for prescribing age-appropriate explanations that they can grasp. It is our hope that, with this knowledge, you will be able to better understand the children with whom you work and to provide appropriate consultations with parents, teachers, and administrators involved in the children's lives.

What Is Moral Reasoning, and How Does It Develop?

Moral reasoning focuses on a child's ability to make judgments and decisions about ethical issues with ever-growing sophistication. The increasing ability to reason about moral intentions and actions is distinct from a child's growing ability to *be* moral, which, in early development, may be construed as the ability to comply with adult requests. Although Aksan and Kochanska (2005) showed that compliant conduct is increasingly related to conscience as a child ages, compliance itself may be driven by factors other than the internalization of moral rules, such as attachment or fearful temperament (van der Mark, Bakermans-Kranenburg, & Van IJzendoorn, 2002; Wachs, Gurkas, & Kontos, 2004). Thus, compliance is not necessarily contingent on morality. Further, some would argue that morality doesn't necessarily involve compliance at all. Therefore, the development of moral reasoning must encompass the maturation of other processes. To begin, we will briefly examine some foundational theories.

Theories on the development of moral reasoning generally fall into one of two camps: the cognitive-developmental camp or the social learning camp. The cognitive-developmental category is best exemplified by the classic Kohlberg stage theory of moral development (Kohlberg, 1976) and its more gender-sensitive expansion by Gilligan (1977). Though these theories differ in their emphases (see Donleavy, 2008; Jorgensen, 2006, for a discussion of the Kohlberg-Gilligan conflict), both agree that moral development occurs as an individual's cognitive capacities mature. Progression to higher stages occurs when new ideas and moral conflicts highlight the limitations of a person's current moral stage. Cognitive maturation gives the person greater ability for deeper and more nuanced thought, and thus new ways of conceiving morality are born.

In contrast, social learning theorists, such as Bandura (1986), assert that moral development is dependent on one's interactions with others. An individual learns a model of behavior through others' direct teachings and through passive observation. Regardless of the mechanics of development, both camps theorize that individuals, children in particular, display similarities in moral reasoning at specified age ranges, thereby allowing us to discuss the typical developmental course of most children.

Before discussing specialized applications of moral reasoning research, it is helpful to understand the different strategies that children use to make judgments about morality. Moral development theorists have generally found that younger children (ages 3 to 7) think of morality in egocentric, consequence-driven terms where right and wrong are determined by what an authority figure says. The way acts are judged is based primarily on the punishment given to the instigator. Moreover, the intensity of this judgment is mediated by how much the punishment negatively impacts the child.

EXAMPLE: UNDERSTANDING MORALITY

When I (one of the authors) was 4, I stole a delicious pack of orange Tic Tacs from a grocery store. Upon returning to the car, I remember climbing into the back seat, opening them up, and munching them down. Interestingly, I have no memory of trying to hide the deed in question from my mother, but I do remember realizing later that I had done something bad because my mother made me walk all the way back into that boring store, find the weird man working the cash register, and tell him that I was sorry. Clearly, at that moment, I did not identify stealing as bad because it was the act of taking something that did not belong to me, but rather because I got in trouble for it.

Maturation of moral reasoning, as well as of perspective taking and false belief (see Chapters 5 and 6), leads to a greater understanding of others' needs and motivations and an internalization of society's moral code. Thus, the strategies more typically used by children eight years and older are more sophisticated. Children are better able to understand the motivations behind an action and are more likely to say that hurting someone else by accident is not immoral. Because older children are also better at perspective taking, they will understand that an intentional act that hurt someone is wrong, even if it wasn't punished. Further, children eight years and older begin to realize that rules are hierarchical and that a child who disobeys one rule may simply be following a different, more important rule (see Krcmar & Cooke, 2001, for a review of the literature related to children's developing strategies). As children's capabilities for moral reasoning develop, they are better able to discern rules of convention, those societal niceties we all must follow to be polite and to fit in with norms, from rules of morality, where infractions involve hurting someone in some way (Nucci, 2002). They also tend to view the rules of morality from a more objective viewpoint, believing their moral code to be universal and not dependent on a particular situation (Nichols & Folds-Bennett, 2003).

EXAMPLE: UNIVERSAL MORAL CODE

I distinctly remember, as a child, going to the beach with my father on an unusually warm January day. Despite the beautiful weather, we were the only ones there, and, from the looks of it, no one had been there for some time. As we were walking, we came upon a large, albeit somewhat deflated beach ball, and my father suggested that we play a game of kickball. I, however, was adamant with my response: "Daddy, we can't play with that! It's not ours!"

How Do Kids Understand Lying?

Most clinicians who work with young children have firsthand knowledge that their clients can and do lie. Children as young as three years old may have the ability to lie through verbal deception, although it becomes much more common between four and seven years (Talwar & Lee, 2002a). Talwar and Lee showed that much of the deception that occurs at this age is intended to hide a transgression the child has committed and an attempt to avoid punishment.

Though children's ability to lie was discussed more fully in Chapter 6, questions regarding children's moral understanding about lying remain. Children between ages 3 and 5 distinguish between lies and truths mainly by evaluating the factuality of the statement. Sometime between ages 6 and 10, children incorporate the intention of the speaker to deceive, as well as the belief of the speaker about the issue, noting that a statement is not a lie if the speaker thought it to be true (Talwar & Lee, 2008). Bussey (1999) further found that although four-year-olds seemed to pay attention most to the factuality of a statement when distinguishing between lies and truths, they still evaluated the severity of the lies at the same level as eight- and eleven-year-old children. Antisocial lies were rated as the worst type of lie, followed by "trick lies" (jokes) and "white lies" (prosocial lies), but all lies were evaluated negatively, even from the youngest age.

EXAMPLE: PROSOCIAL LYING

Laura, who is six years old, designed an "I love you" art project at preschool to be given to a relative of her choice. Laura's mom, knowing that her sister Beth (Laura's aunt) had been feeling particularly sensitive to a lack of bonding experiences with her niece, insisted that she give the "I love you" art project to Aunt Beth. After Aunt Beth thanked Laura for being so sweet, Laura stated matter of factly, "I wanted to give it to Uncle Dan, but Mommy told me I should give it to you!"

The benefits of prosocial lies, those white lies told in order to spare the feelings of the recipient, are understood beginning around age 3 or 4 (see Bussey, 1999). In fact, children may start to tell white lies in certain situations beginning around age 3 (Talwar & Lee, 2002b). However, Broomfield, Robinson, and Robinson (2002) found that children up to age 8 or 9 preferred telling others the truth rather than telling a prosocial lie; they suggested that younger children may not yet realize that society considers some lies to be acceptable.

EXAMPLE: DEVELOPMENT OF LYING

Four years after the "I love you" art project mishap, Laura sat in the open chair next to her aunt at dinner. When asked why she was pouting, she said, "My belly doesn't feel good." After dinner, she asked if she could talk to her uncle. "Uncle Dan, I lied when I said that my belly didn't feel good. I actually was sad because I hadn't gotten to sit next to you all day, but I knew Aunt Beth would feel bad if I said that."

Society's understanding of and preference for prosocial lies furthermore appears to be impacted by sociocultural factors. Chinese children, whose culture promotes modesty and interdependence, rated prosocial lies more positively than did Canadian children, particularly as the age of the Chinese children increased (Lee, Cameron, Xu, Fu, & Board, 1997). Chinese children were also more likely to favor lies that helped the collective but hurt the individual, whereas Canadian children exhibited the opposite preference (Fu, Xu, Cameron, Heyman, & Lee, 2007). It will be important for anyone who works with children to be aware of and sensitive to these cultural influences on moral reasoning development. This concept will be discussed further later in this chapter.

Wagland and Bussey's (2005) vignette research suggests that adults can help to mitigate children's lying behavior. They showed that children as young as five years old predicted that characters would lie more often when truth telling would be followed by negative consequences. However, when truthfulness was encouraged, children predicted more truth telling, even in the face of punishment. This may imply that if clinicians or parents highlight the value of truthfulness for children, they may be more likely to tell the truth, even after their own transgressions.

How Do Kids Understand Aggression When They See It?

This section will deal specifically with the normative aggression that children tend to see, experience, and engage in at school or in play. A discussion of the effects of a traumatic level of aggression is included in a later section of this chapter.

Children's use of aggression changes as they develop. Babies begin to use physical aggression in toddlerhood to get their needs met (Côté, Vaillancourt, Barker, Nagin, & Tremblay, 2007), and the rate of physical aggression, such as punching or biting, increases through the preschool years but then drops off between the preschool years and adolescence (Broidy et al., 2003).

Indirect or relational aggression involves harming someone by manipulating or threatening relationships and social status (Theodore-Oklota, Glick, Demir, & Orsillo, 2008). The use of tactics like tattling or gossiping increases during the elementary school years and is more likely to be used by older children than by younger children (Vaillancourt, Miller, Fagbemi, Côté, & Tremblay, 2007). Boys are typically more likely to use physical aggression than are girls, and although conventional wisdom would make it seem that girls are the masters of relational aggression, gender differences in the use of relational aggression are negligible (Card, Stucky, Sawalani, & Little, 2008). Card et al. further found that the use of physical aggression and the use of relational aggression were highly correlated but predicted different psychological outcomes for the aggressor: Physical aggression was associated with conduct problems and emotional dysregulation, while relational aggression was associated with clinical or subclinical depression and anxiety.

Many studies have investigated the thought processes that precede a child's aggressive act, but few researchers have evaluated children's moral reasoning of aggression itself. One exception is research by Murray-Close and colleagues (Murray-Close, Crick, & Galotti, 2006). They found that ten- to twelve-year-old children distinguished between types of aggression, reporting that physical aggression was more morally wrong than was relational aggression. While both boys and girls believed that physical aggression was wrong, girls were more likely than boys to identify relational aggression as morally wrong. This suggests that girls view both types of aggression, both physical and relational, as moral issues (i.e., those that hurt someone), rather than as conventional issues (i.e., those that have no victim but are required by social norms). As stated earlier, this moral/conventional issue distinction is often identified as the first step in moral reasoning development (Nucci, 2002). Murray-Close et al. suggested that adults might be able to reduce children's aggressive behavior by emphasizing that it is immoral to engage in both physical and relational aggression. Adults should also discuss the existence and consequences of relational aggression, especially with boys, who might understand the immorality of relational aggression a bit later than girls.

EXAMPLE: RELATIONAL AGGRESSION

Most of the sixth graders from East Side Elementary can be found playing or watching an intense game of four-squares during recess. Lately, the game has become quite competitive, territorial, and closely affiliated with social status. As a result of this dynamic, the teachers establish a new set of rules by which players for each game are rotated on an alphabetical basis. When Owen's name is called, the other boys announce that they aren't interested in playing four-squares and initiate a game of "monkey in the middle" (with Owen being the monkey). When confronted by their teachers about the "bullying," one of the boys replies, "But Ms. Jenkins, we never touched him!"

There is also some evidence that the aggression that children see in the media may have an effect on their moral reasoning development. Krcmar and Curtis (2003) investigated the effects of fantasy violence on moral reasoning strategies and found that children who viewed a violent end to a conflict were more likely to judge future violence as more morally acceptable. Greater exposure to fantasy violence was associated with more assertions that justified violence was morally right. The researchers also found that children with lower abilities to perspective take watched more fantasy violence and displayed less developed moral reasoning. It is important to emphasize, however, these associations do not necessarily imply that fantasy violence causes deficits in moral reasoning; it may be that children with less developed reasoning prefer violent programming.

What People in a Child's Life Influence His or Her Moral Development?

Parents and peers are both significant influences in a child's life in many respects, and it stands to reason that they may impact a child's moral development as well. Parental figures, as the first and most intimate teachers of society's norms, take a front-row seat in driving their child's development, especially in the earliest years. Research shows that a child's maturational level can be predicted in the expected direction from the parents' own moral reasoning, the child's hostile or supportive interactions in general, and the child's ego functioning (Walker & Hennig, 1999). Parents who were defensive, rigid, and insensitive were more likely to have children with less mature moral reasoning development. Parents' direct interactions with children may also be important: Warm support predicted higher levels of child sympathy and less cheating on an assigned research task, particularly among boys (Spinrad et al., 1999). Furthermore, parents' moral teachings to their children should be both developmentally appropriate and domain specific; moral development best occurs when topics discussed are of personal relevance to the child (Walker, Hennig, & Krettenauer, 2000).

The quality of a child's attachment to his or her caregiver may also influence the child's development of moral reasoning. Van IJzendoorn (1997) argued that emergent morality depends, in part, on the development of empathy and the internalization of parental instructions. He theorized that these qualities would be better developed in securely attached children, because parents of these children are more emotionally attuned to their children and better provide opportunities for exploration without fear of failure. Some research has supported these theories: Laible and Thompson (2000) showed that attachment security was one predictor of early conscience development in four-year-olds.

Peers can also play a role in fostering moral reasoning maturity in children. In the cognitive-developmental view—that favored by Kohlberg and Piaget— maturity occurs when an individual encounters a situation that challenges his or her current thinking. This *cognitive disequilibrium* is unsettling and pushes the individual toward higher levels of thinking, thereby restoring equilibrium and promoting development. Disequilibrium in the development of moral reasoning may occur when interacting with someone who is at a slightly higher level of moral thinking. Views are challenged, and equilibrium is regained by accepting new ideas and cognitive processes. Research has shown that such interactions work best when the interactions are between people who are close to each other in development (Berkowitz, Gibbs, & Broughton, 1980). Therefore, peers, who are usually similar in moral development stage, are in a unique position to facilitate the moral reasoning development of each other. In particular, Walker and colleagues (Walker et al., 2000) showed that supportive peer interactions that also utilize a Socratic style of intervention to gently probe opinions and challenge ideas were most associated with moral growth among children.

Do Different Cultures Develop Moral Reasoning in the Same Way?

Does a universal morality exist? In the literature on moral development, researchers argue that while specifics of behavior may differ drastically in terms of right or wrong, moral conceptions of harm and fairness do not change cross-culturally (Gibbs, Basinger, Grime, & Snarey, 2007). For example, in the

Hindu culture, eating chicken after the death of a loved one may be seen as one of the most immoral acts one could commit because this act is thought to prevent the loved one's soul from salvation (Nucci, 2002). While this act is neutral in the Western world, the act of harming another person is not. Therefore, when the meaning of behavior is made universal, moral theorists argue, there is little, if any, discrepancy between what is right and wrong. Cross-cultural research on moral development has found that similar ideas of morality exist by age 3 in most areas of the world (Nucci, 2002), and the cognitive-developmental theory of increasing sophistication of moral reasoning appears to fit many non-American cultures (Gibbs et al., 2007).

Nevertheless, the specifics of moral reasoning must be considered in the cultural context (see Haste & Abrahams, 2008, for a theoretical discussion). For example, in contrast to Western children, Chinese children's judgments about morality tended to weigh heavily on concepts of collectivism and tradition, such as family honor, respect for authority, and sacrificing one's own needs for the greater good (Fang et al., 2003). Further, Miller (1994) found qualitative differences when comparing moral codes of American versus Hindu Indian populations. She found that an individually oriented interpersonal moral code develops among Americans, one that stresses personal freedom and responsibility. In contrast, a duty-based interpersonal moral code develops among Hindu Indians, stressing broad social/interpersonal obligations and the importance of assessing the contextual situation. See Jensen (2008) for a proposed cultural-developmental model through which to view moral development, including the basic, universal progression through developmental stages, as well as the culture-specific factors that moderate this progression.

In cross-cultural interactions with children, it will be important to ensure that you (the clinician) and the child share an understanding of the child's motivation before moving forward. Premature action based on a Western lens of moral action or inaction could be confusing, counterproductive, and culturally insensitive. A prophylactic measure would be to ensure that you provide an environment that encourages a dialogue about diversity between children, parents, and co-workers. In order to best serve the children and families with whom we work, there is no place for being "color (race, gender, socioeconomic, sexual orientation, disability, etc.) blind" because it would be a disservice and a perpetual insult to fail to recognize how differences affect experiences and rationale for behavior. Potential costs of ignoring cross-cultural differences in moral standards include dehumanizing a family's value system, damaging rapport, and enabling learned helplessness in children who are punished for acting in a way that they understand to be "right."

In addition to awareness of racial and ethnic differences in moral reasoning, clinicians should also be aware of American subcultures, such as inner-city gangs. We will briefly discuss the subculture of gang behavior, as this issue is timely, highly disruptive, and often not well understood.

EXAMPLE: MORAL REASONING AND GANG BEHAVIOR

"But, Miss, he killed my best friend. How do you expect me to stay here at school and not hurt him? It's not right. If I stay here and do nothing, I'm nothing. I'm not loyal to my boys." (Gang member, twelve-years-old.)

When studying the subcultures of gangs, we are reminded that many innocent and unprovoked bystanders are harmed, as well as other gang-involved persons. Are gang members or children of gang members less morally developed than the greater population? And what about this idea of "snitching" being the most immoral act?

EXAMPLE: MORAL REASONING AND VIOLENCE

Youth gang member: That time, right before I got locked up, I would have shot him if the teacher wasn't coming. I would have shot anyone who was in the way.

Therapist: Would you have shot me if I were there?

Youth gang member: (*without hesitation*) Yeah … if I didn't know you.

What is implied here, in this quite frightening discourse, is that this young man does not adhere to a standard moral tenet of abstaining from committing acts of unprovoked violence to bystanders. His acts would most likely be considered immoral across culture, class, and race. In his idea of morality, however, honoring his friends' deaths takes priority.

This young man reports not shooting someone because of the direct consequences of getting caught. Is he a sociopath? Core components of pathological antisocial behavior include lack of remorse, impulsivity, and failure to conform to social norms. This young man *does* feel remorse (for *not* acting); he is *not* impulsive (he is in counseling discussing this); he *is* conforming to his learned social norm (that of his gang or "family") where snitching and not backing up a loved one are the most immoral acts a member could commit. This young man would be classified at Kohlberg's preconventional stage of moral development, where a person judges morality based on an action's consequences. As the quote above demonstrates, adolescents (and in some cases preadolescents) involved in tightly woven groups, such as gangs, tend to value interconnectedness and loyalty above issues of justice and equality (Nucci, 2002). Also, as one student below explains, there are agreed-upon limitations to even a gang member's view of morality when both groups share a common goal.

EXAMPLE: RATIONALES FOR MORAL VIOLATIONS

There is one of 'em [an opposing gang member] here, but we won't start nothing. We nod when we see each other in the halls because we know we're here to go to school. On the streets, well, it's a whole different game. (Gang member, 15 years old.)

Being aware of the rules and norms of a subculture will help you to make educated inferences about where and how these might influence the morality of a subcultured client. Perhaps a behavior that appears to be a limitation in a child's moral reasoning may actually represent an adaptive survival mechanism within one's subculture. In the same vein, misjudgments in moral reasoning must not be assumed to reflect deficits in cognitive functioning or intellect, as they include both affective and cognitive components.

Is the Development of Moral Reasoning Different for Children With Psychological Disorders?

Most of the information covered here focuses on the normal course of moral reasoning development. However, the moral development of children with psychological disorders may follow a different path. Several disorders commonly linked to children's moral development are covered below.

Autistic Spectrum

Baron-Cohen (2008) argued that autism is partially defined by what he calls "mindblindness." Broadly speaking, mindblindness is a deficit in theory of mind and particularly a deficit in empathy (some discussion of theory of mind can be found in Chapters 5 and 6). As empathy has been theorized to be a cornerstone of moral development (see van IJzendoorn, 1997), a deficit in empathy may hinder moral reasoning maturation. While children with Asperger's disorder do not experience clinically significant problems with language (as those with autism do), their qualitative impairments in social interactions, as well as a retarded development of empathy, are reflected in the way they meander through and understand moral situations.

EXAMPLE: ASPERGER'S DISORDER

Charlie, a twelve-year-old with Asperger's disorder, does not understand the difference between secrets and privacy. He was told that telling secrets is "bad because they hurt people," and he views discussing his family in therapy as telling secrets. He was suspicious of me (his therapist) when I would close the door and did not understand why I would put on the white noise machine during counseling. He reported to his mother that if I was taking precautions to keep others from hearing our sessions, then he must be telling secrets.

In Charlie's case, while he may lack certain cognitive skills, this does not mean that he lacks the capacity for moral development.

EXAMPLE: MORAL GESTURES

After a few months of counseling, and after the sound machine broke, Charlie asked me where the "swoosh swoosh machine" was. When I asked why, he said that he wanted to give it to the girl in the waiting room so that she could have some privacy.

Some have argued that empathy is required in order to understand the difference between moral and conventional rules: Acts that break moral codes have victims and produce distress on behalf of the victim (Blair, 1996). Yet Blair (1996) reported that children with autism are able to distinguish between moral violations and social-conventional violations, showing that perhaps not enough is yet known about the complexity of the deficient structures of autism. More recent research by Blair (1999a) showed that children with autism demonstrated physiological signs of empathic distress. This suggests that some structures of empathy are intact, thus allowing for some moral reasoning development.

Conduct Disorder

While we discussed aggression in an earlier part of the chapter, it is worth noting that heightened and impulsive aggression is characteristic of conduct-disordered children. How are we to distinguish natural and adaptive aggression from the more clinical and disruptive type that might present itself as antisocial personality disorder or sociopathy in adulthood? When a child with conduct disorder exhibits oppositionality or antisocial behavior, is he or she intentionally acting immorally? Or has his or her moral development been arrested in some way? There is some evidence that children with conduct disorder have lower levels of empathy than other children (Blair, 1999b); compared to other children, conduct-disordered children show less physiologic response to empathic-distress situations. As argued above, empathy may be a core feature of moral development, so this apparent deficit has implications for the development of moral reasoning. Indeed, compared to control children, children with behavioral problems were less likely to make appropriate distinctions between moral issues and conventional issues, and they were less likely to discuss moral issues with regard to a victim's welfare (Blair, Monson, & Frederickson, 2001).

EXAMPLE: GRAND THEFT AUTO

Quite a bit of press was given to the seven-year-old African American boy from Florida who was charged with grand theft auto of his grandmother's car. He said, "I did it because I was mad at my mom," and later, "It's fun to do bad things with my friends." In this case, he reported knowing what he did was wrong, but he chose to do it anyway. He displayed a lack of empathy for others when told his grandmother would have to pay for damages by replying, "Can't my mother help her?"

In the "grand theft auto" case above, it impossible to discern if the seven-year-old's behavior is due to a lack of cognitive development in general or to his lack of moral development, as they are inextricably intertwined. While children with behavioral problems may have difficulty making moral distinctions, there is increasing evidence that not all forms of behavioral problems are the same. For some children, we may be able to "teach" them moral reasoning, while for others—those en route to becoming a true sociopath—we may not. It is important to explore whether a child is biologically predisposed to violence, as is thought with antisocial personality disorder, or if there are sociocultural factors that precipitate the violence. Research suggests that those exhibiting violent behaviors as *reactions* to their life situations can be rehabilitated.

Hardy and Laszloffy (2005) theorize that there are four characteristics young people who exhibit violence share: devaluation (through abandonment, abuse, peer rejection, and stigma), disruption of community (primary or extended), dehumanized loss (death, divorce, abandonment, neglect, moving, loss of physical safety, love, and economic security), and rage. Through counteracting devaluation, restoring community, rehumanizing loss, and rechanneling rage, perhaps we can alter violent paths. While it is difficult to tell which children will go on to develop antisocial personality disorder, interventions such as those offered by Hardy and Laszloffy are promising.

Attention-Deficit Hyperactivity Disorder

As will be discussed in Chapter 12, ADHD has three core components—attentional difficulties, poor impulse control, and hyperactivity—that often result in children acting or reacting without having reasoned through the morality (or even the consequences) of it. Disentangling issues of intent versus impulsivity is crucial to understanding whether a child is acting outside of his or her moral code. It is important to consider if *planning* was involved in the act and if there was a perceived sense of *choice* involved (i.e., "I knew it was wrong, but I did it anyway" versus "My body made me"). Little research has been conducted in this area, but so far, no differences have been found in the moral reasoning of participants with ADHD and that of those without ADHD (Rose, 2006).

EXAMPLE: ATTENTION-DEFICIT HYPERACTIVITY DISORDER

Ms. Smith and ten-year-old Alex are both frustrated. Alex is a very bright boy who blurts out answers to questions throughout the school day. Ms. Smith has told him that if he cannot control his outbursts, she will give him detention. Alex has earned a detention every day this week. At home, Alex cries to his parents, "I can't help it; I know what I am supposed to do, but I don't know why I keep doing it."

Trauma Responses

Trauma has been shown to affect the cognitive and emotional development of children (Schore, 2001), and it has ramifications for moral development as well. Galvin, Stilwell, Shekhar, Kopta, and Goldfarb (1997) reported that boys who were maltreated (i.e., physically abused, sexually abused, or neglected) prior to three years old exhibited deficits in what the researchers called conscience. These children were less likely to inhibit their own antisocial behavior, to offer reparation for their behavior, or to see themselves as morally good. Early and frequent abuse may also impact the development of empathy (Cicchetti & Toth, 1995), which, as described above, may have negative implications for the development of moral reasoning. Thus, it seems that trauma that occurs early in development may disrupt or arrest normal maturation processes.

Conclusion

Behavior may be mediated by moral development, a process that appears to occur in predictable, quantifiable, and universal ways. During the earliest years, a child's idea of moral action is dependent on what is deemed by adults to be good or bad. Both cognitive development and social learning influence the maturation of children. While there are different schools of thought, all theorists agree that moral development is predictably progressive.

During the toddler years, children have the ability to tell untruths, but their intention lies in egocentric avoidance or gain, rather than in having the motivation to deceive. By the age of 7 or 8, with the development of a theory of mind, children are better able to understand the motivations of others, and they can entertain the idea that their viewpoint, needs, and wants are not universal. They also can understand and use deception as a way to consciously mislead others (for antisocial or prosocial intent). Furthermore, with development, children can discern rules of convention versus rules of morality and can place value on deception (rating antisocial lies as more immoral than prosocial).

Caregivers and peers have demonstrated impact on the development of moral reasoning, and all development and moral behavior must be viewed through a cultural lens. Warm support from caregivers predicts higher levels of sympathy and less dishonesty, and moral teaching appears to be most salient when personal relevance is demonstrated to the child. Peers can influence moral development by creating cognitive disequilibrium that forces the child to think differently about morality. Furthermore, while there appears to be a universal morality in terms of harm and fairness, actual behaviors may be judged differently cross-culturally.

The most important factor when working with children in situations of moral assessment will be to engage in detective work with regard to their understanding of the behaviors at hand. Through this we can better discern issues of morality versus issues of cognition, biology, and pathology. Once the child's behaviors are better understood, it then becomes possible to move toward interventions designed to supplement and strengthen moral development. By advocating for cognitive moral education, we can help instill the values of democracy and justice so that children may learn to live flexibly and adaptively in the world.

References

Aksan, N., & Kochanska, G. (2005). Conscience in childhood: Old questions, new answers. *Developmental Psychology, 41*, 506–516.

Bandura, A. (1986). *Social foundations of thought and action: A social cognitive theory.* Englewood Cliffs, NJ: Prentice-Hall.

Baron-Cohen, S. (2008). Theories of the autistic mind. *The Psychologist, 21*, 112–116.

Berkowitz, M. W., Gibbs, J. C., & Broughton, J. M. (1980). The relation of moral judgment stage disparity to developmental effects of peer dialogues. *Merrill-Palmer Quarterly, 26*, 341–357.

Blair, R. J. R. (1996). Brief report: Morality in the autistic child. *Journal of Autism and Developmental Disorders, 26*, 571–579.

Blair, R. J. R. (1999a). Psychophysiological responsiveness to the distress of others in children with autism. *Personality and Individual Differences, 26*, 477–485.

Blair, R. J. R. (1999b). Responsiveness to distress cues in the child with psychopathic tendencies. *Personality and Individual Differences, 27*, 135–145.

Blair, R. J. R., Monson, J., & Frederickson, N. (2001). Moral reasoning and conduct problems in children with emotional and behavioural difficulties. *Personality and Individual Differences, 31*, 799–811.

Broidy, L. M., Nagin, D. S., Tremblay, R. E., Bates, J. E., Brame, B., Dodge, K. A., et al. (2003). Developmental trajectories of childhood disruptive behaviors and adolescent delinquency: A six-site, cross-national study. *Developmental Psychology, 39*, 222–245.

Broomfield, K. A., Robinson, E. J., & Robinson, W. P. (2002). Children's understanding about white lies. *British Journal of Developmental Psychology, 20,* 47–65.

Bussey, K. (1999). Children's categorization and evaluation of different types of lies and truths. *Child Development, 70,* 1338–1347.

Card, N. A., Stucky, B. D., Sawalani, G. M., & Little, T. D. (2008). Direct and indirect aggression during childhood and adolescence: A meta-analytic review of gender differences, intercorrelations, and relations to maladjustment. *Child Development, 79,* 1185–1229.

Cicchetti, D., & Toth, S. L. (1995). A developmental psychopathology perspective on child abuse and neglect. *Journal of the American Academy of Child & Adolescent Psychiatry, 34,* 541–565.

Côté, S. M., Vaillancourt, T., Barker, E. D., Nagin, D., & Tremblay, R. E. (2007). The joint development of physical and indirect aggression: Predictors of continuity and change during childhood. *Development and Psychopathology, 19,* 37–55.

Donleavy, G. D. (2008). No man's land: Exploring the space between Gilligan and Kohlberg. *Journal of Business Ethics, 80,* 807–822.

Fang, G., Fang, F.-X., Keller, M., Edelstein, W., Kehle, T. J., & Bray, M. A. (2003). Social moral reasoning in Chinese children: A developmental study. *Psychology in the Schools, 40,* 125–138.

Fu, G., Xu, F., Cameron, C. A., Heyman, G., & Lee, K. (2007). Cross-cultural differences in children's choices, categorizations, and evaluations of truths and lies. *Developmental Psychology, 43,* 278–293.

Galvin, M. R., Stilwell, B. M., Shekhar, A., Kopta, S. M., & Goldfarb, S. M. (1997). Maltreatment, conscience functioning and dopamine beta hydroxylase in emotionally disturbed boys. *Child Abuse & Neglect, 21,* 83–92.

Gibbs, J. C., Basinger, K. S., Grime, R. L., & Snarey, J. R. (2007). Moral judgment development across cultures: Revisiting Kohlberg's universality claims. *Developmental Review, 27,* 443–500.

Gilligan, C. (1977). In a different voice: Women's conceptions of self and of morality. *Harvard Educational Review, 47,* 481–517.

Hardy, K. V., & Laszloffy, T. A. (2005). *Teens who hurt.* New York: Guilford.

Haste, H., & Abrahams, S. (2008). Morality, culture and the dialogic self: Taking cultural pluralism seriously. *Journal of Moral Education, 37,* 377–394.

Jensen, L. A. (2008). Through two lenses: A cultural-developmental approach to moral psychology. *Developmental Review, 28,* 289–315.

Jorgensen, G. (2006). Kohlberg and Gilligan: Duet or duel? *Journal of Moral Education, 35,* 179–196.

Kohlberg, L. (1976). Moral stages and moralization: The cognitive-developmental approach. In T. Lickona (Ed.), *Moral development and behavior* (pp. 31–53). New York: Holt, Rinehart & Winston.

Krcmar, M., & Cooke, M. C. (2001). Children's moral reasoning and their perceptions of television violence. *Journal of Communication, 51,* 300–316.

Krcmar, M., & Curtis, S. (2003). Mental models: Understanding the impact of fantasy violence on children's moral reasoning. *Journal of Communication, 53,* 460–478.

Laible, D. J., & Thompson, R. A. (2000). Mother-child discourse, attachment security, shared positive affect, and early conscience development. *Child Development, 71,* 1424–1440.

Lee, K., Cameron, C. A., Xu, F., Fu, G., & Board, J. (1997). Chinese and Canadian children's evaluations of lying and truth telling: Similarities and differences in the context of pro- and antisocial behaviors. *Child Development, 68,* 924–934.

Miller, J. G. (1994). Cultural diversity in the morality of caring: Individually oriented versus duty-based interpersonal moral codes. *Cross Cultural Research, 28,* 3–39.

Murray-Close, D., Crick, N. R., & Galotti, K. M. (2006). Children's moral reasoning regarding physical and relational aggression. *Social Development, 15,* 345–372.

Nichols, S., & Folds-Bennett, T. (2003). Are children moral objectivists? Children's judgments about moral and response-dependent properties. *Cognition, 90,* B23–B32.

Nucci, L. P. (2002). The development of moral reasoning. In U. Goswami (Ed.), *Blackwell handbook of childhood cognitive development* (pp. 303–325). Malden, MA: Blackwell Publishing.

Rose, M. S. (2006). A comparison of students with and without attention-deficit/hyperactivity disorder on measures of moral reasoning and executive functions. *Dissertation Abstracts International: Section B: The Sciences and Engineering, 67,* 1184.

Schore, A. N. (2001). The effects of early relational trauma on right brain development, affect regulation, and infant mental health. *Infant Mental Health Journal, 22,* 201–269.

Spinrad, T. L., Losoya, S. H., Eisenberg, N., Fabes, R. A., Shepard, S. A., Cumberland, A., et al. (1999). The relations of parental affect and encouragement to children's moral emotions and behaviour. *Journal of Moral Education, 28,* 323–337.

Talwar, V., & Lee, K. (2002a). Development of lying to conceal a transgression: Children's control of expressive behaviour during verbal deception. *International Journal of Behavioral Development, 26,* 436–444.

Talwar, V., & Lee, K. (2002b). Emergence of white-lie telling in children between 3 and 7 years of age. *Merrill-Palmer Quarterly, 48,* 160–181.

Talwar, V., & Lee, K. (2008). Social and cognitive correlates of children's lying behavior. *Child Development, 79,* 866–881.

Theodore-Oklota, C. R., Glick, D. M., Demir, M. R., & Orsillo, S. M. (2008). *The role of avoidant coping in the development of relational aggression.* Poster presented at the Annual Conference of the Association for the Advancement of Behavioral and Cognitive Therapy. Orlando, FL.

Vaillancourt, T., Miller, J. L., Fagbemi, J., Côté, S., & Tremblay, R. E. (2007). Trajectories and predictors of indirect aggression: Results from a nationally representative longitudinal study of Canadian children aged 2–10. *Aggressive Behavior, 33,* 314–326.

van der Mark, I. L., Bakermans-Kranenburg, M. J., & Van IJzendoorn, M. H. (2002). The role of parenting, attachment, and temperamental fearfulness in the prediction of compliance in toddler girls. *British Journal of Developmental Psychology, 20,* 361–378.

Van IJzendoorn, M. H. (1997). Attachment, emergent morality, and aggression: Toward a developmental socioemotional model of antisocial behaviour. *International Journal of Behavioral Development, 21,* 703–727.

Wachs, T. D., Gurkas, P., & Kontos, S. (2004). Predictors of preschool children's compliance behavior in early childhood classroom settings. *Journal of Applied Developmental Psychology, 25,* 439–457.

Wagland, P., & Bussey, K. (2005). Factors that facilitate and undermine children's beliefs about truth telling. *Law and Human Behavior, 29,* 639–655.

Walker, L. J., & Hennig, K. H. (1999). Parenting style and the development of moral reasoning. *Journal of Moral Education, 28,* 359–374.

Walker, L. J., Hennig, K. H., & Krettenauer, T. (2000). Parent and peer contexts for children's moral reasoning development. *Child Development, 71,* 1033–1048.

12

Developmental Changes in Children's Executive Functioning

KAREN A. HOLLER and SONIA M. GREENE

Behavior, including what children think, do, and feel, is clearly impacted by environmental issues like family functioning, economic status, and education. It is also true that behavior can never be fully extricated from what the brain, or neurological substrates, contributes to that behavior. In a fundamental way, behavioral control, including regulation, inhibition, focus, and problem solving, is most closely associated with the functioning of the frontal/executive system of the brain.

The executive system of the brain is involved in monitoring emotions and behavior, altering behavior based on feedback from others and the outside world, and regulating attention, anticipation, and flexibility, among other critical functions. These are the skills that children and adults depend upon to engage and react effectively in the world. In part, these brain functions are referred to as the executive system precisely because of their regulatory nature. The system is like the little executive or CEO of the brain responsible for integrating information from the rest of the system and ultimately guiding decisions for the system as a whole (Goldberg, 2002). Frontal/executive controls provide that essential pause between an impulse and an action. In a very real way, the executive system, when fully developed, is where mature judgment and reason reside.

This chapter will describe what constitutes executive control, discuss neurodevelopment and structure as it relates to executive control, provide a developmental framework for thinking about executive skills in children, and review some of the behavioral correlates of executive functions as they come "on line" throughout childhood. This chapter will also briefly review some common failures in executive control that are familiar to most professionals who work with children and young adolescents.

Description and Definition

Why Talk About Executive Control?

The executive control system is perhaps the most important cognitive system of the brain. It is responsible for making sure that other brain systems are functioning together smoothly and efficiently. A child can have a strong vocabulary, do well on an IQ test, or have terrific artistic ability, but if that child struggles to integrate information, attend to the right stimulus, or alter his behavior when old strategies stop working, then none of these other skills or strengths will result in a high level of adaptive functioning.

Whereas we may not notice when the executive system is functioning properly, loss of executive control is a hallmark of a wide range of psychiatric and behavioral disorders. When the executive system doesn't work efficiently, it can impact a child across all major areas of life, including school, home, and social interactions.

Definitions of Frontal/Executive Functioning

Below are two slightly different definitions of executive function adapted from Stuss and Benson (1986).

> *Executive control refers to several higher-level cognitive abilities that are essential for complex, goal-directed behavior and **adaptation** to a broad range of environmental changes and demands.*

The key word in this definition is *adaptation*. The highest form of intelligence is not necessarily a large fund of knowledge or the ability to do well on a test. Rather, the highest form of intelligence is arguably the ability to adapt and be flexible when responding to complex environmental demands as they occur.

> *Executive functions are essential for the control of organized, **integrated**, fixed functional systems.*

In this definition, the key word is *integration*. The frontal system is essentially in charge of integrating all incoming information (with other parts of the brain), making sense of it, and responding in an appropriate, measured, and timely manner. There is a tremendous amount of sensory and cognitive stimulation bombarding a child at any given time. The executive systems essentially functions as the filter or editor for all of this information, allowing the system as a whole to "keep up" without becoming overwhelmed.

Executive function includes, but is not limited to, the following cognitive abilities: selective and sustained attention, planning and sequencing, organizational skill, mental flexibility, maintenance of set, inhibitory control, self-regulation, self-monitoring, self-awareness and insight, intention, future-oriented behavior, and novel problem solving. Table 12.1 provides some everyday examples of both well-functioning and problematic executive processes.

Basic Neurology of Executive Systems

Frontal Lobe Divisions and Connections

While it is not necessary to go into great detail, some basic understanding of how the different frontal/executive areas of the brain contribute to behavioral

Table 12.1 Examples of Executive Processes in Children

Function	Good Executive Function Allows For:	Poor Executive Function May Present As:
Selective/Sustained Attention	The ability to direct, maintain, and shift focus. *The third grader who can initiate and follow through on a ten-sentence writing assignment that takes more than a few minutes.*	Difficulties attending to the right stimuli. *A fourth grader who struggles to focus on what the teacher is saying rather than what is happening outside the window.*
Planning	Planning ahead, anticipation, and the ability to make adjustments accordingly. *A sixth grader who studies ahead for a test.*	Poor time management. *The seventh grader who procrastinates and stays up until midnight to finish a paper the night before it is due.*
Sequencing	The ability to learn and internalize sequences of behavior. *A kindergartener who learns and follows a classroom routine with ease.*	Problems following a routine. *A bright preschooler who, nevertheless, struggles to follow classroom routines such as hanging up her coat before going to the play area.*
Organizational Skill	The ability to organize and integrate multiple sources of information. *The seventh grader who can write an essay after reviewing several sources.*	Difficulty organizing personal belongings. *A fifth grader who cannot find his completed homework in his messy backpack.*
Mental Flexibility	The ability to respond to new and different situations, emotionally and behaviorally, in an appropriate and well-regulated manner. *A preschooler who can cope with an unexpected change in plans.*	Rigidity or perseveration in thinking and behaving. *The second grader who cannot tolerate transitions or "blows up" when plans are changed.*

Table 12.1 Examples of Executive Processes in Children (Continued)

Function	Good Executive Function Allows For:	Poor Executive Function May Present As:
Novel Problem Solving	The ability to generate and test solutions to a variety of everyday problems. *A fourth grader who can come up with an alternate plan when her mother cannot take her to a playdate with a friend.*	Difficulties altering behavior based on the situation or feedback. *A sixth grader who can articulate appropriate problem-solving strategies, but cannot implement those strategies when overwhelmed in the "heat of the moment."*

presentation is important. The frontal lobes can be broken down into three basic subdivisions (Stuss & Benson, 1986, 1987):

Dorsolateral/prefrontal—This area of the frontal cortex is associated with cognition, motor regulation, temporal attention, learning, and response selection in goal-directed behavior. Impairments in the prefrontal region may lead to processing deficits, hyper- or hypoactivity, problems with focus, and deficits in goal-directed behavior.

Medial (mesial) prefrontal—This area of the frontal cortex is associated with initiation, arousal, and sustaining effort. Impairments in the mesial region often result in low arousal, poor motivation, and apathy.

Orbitofrontal—This area of the frontal cortex is associated with emotional and behavioral regulation, insight, and personality. Impairments in the orbitofrontal region may present as euphoria or mania, and gross behavioral disinhibition.

It is also important to recognize that frontal/executive functions do not occur in isolation. There is a complete and complex brain at work with rich and intricate interconnections to other parts of the nervous system. These connections run from cortical (surface) areas to other cortical areas and from cortical areas to subcortical areas deeper in the brain. These dense connections are all mediated by chemical and electrical impulses at the level of the brain cell or neuron. To a large extent, the role of the executive control system is to mitigate drives and information from other parts of the brain, and especially the subcortical *limbic* brain (Kolb & Whishaw, 2003), which is associated with intense drives and impulses (e.g., fear, rage).

Neurodevelopment of the Executive System

When a child is born, sensory systems are essentially complete. An infant can see, hear, and experience tactile sensations in a more or less fully developed manner. Motor systems come on board soon after with rolling over, sitting up, and eventually walking by about one year of age. In contrast, executive systems are not fully complete until well into the third decade of life. The development of frontal/executive control occurs throughout childhood and follows a protracted course through adolescence and into early adulthood (Welsh & Pennington, 1988). This development appears to progress via a "multistage process" that coincides with the brain's physical maturation (Passler, Isaac, & Hynd, 1985). These stages begin prenatally and provide the anchor for all subsequent development in executive control. Without this foundation, the executive system would fail to appropriately come on line later in childhood, adolescence, or adulthood. As such, it is helpful to have a basic understanding of how executive systems emerge through certain critical stages.

Critical Stages of Brain Development

Before a child is even born, the brain is developing rapidly. Most brain cells are formed between two weeks and six months gestation via a process called *proliferation*. During *migration* (six weeks and six months gestation), cells move into the various layers of the brain. During the same time frame, *aggregation* and *cytodifferentiation* are occurring, in which cell groups adhere to form the major layers of the cortex and develop into neuronal systems and structures. It should be noted that there is a vast overproduction of brain cells initially, and during the last three months of gestation, half of those cells are pruned via *programmed cell death* (Spreen, Risser, & Edgell, 1995).

There are two other critical stages, *synaptogenesis* and *myelogenesis*, which are particularly relevant to the development of the frontal/executive system. While also beginning prenatally, these processes continue in a step-like fashion throughout childhood into adolescence and are not fully complete until the third decade of life. The fact that these two stages follow such a protracted course accounts for the prolonged development of executive control (Levin et al., 1991).

Synaptogenesis

Synaptogenesis involves the formation of electrical/chemical connections between neurons that allow for communication between brain cells. This process begins in the seventh week of gestation, with the first burst of high-density interconnectivity completed between 6 and 12 months of age. This all occurs before an infant says his or her first word or takes a single independent step. Much of this process is guided by genes; however, genetics are not enough to account for the full "wiring" of the brain. Perinatal and neonatal experiences also play a critical role in guiding the initial chemical connections between neurons. This is the intersection of experience with biology, and it is the reason why childhood specialists are so adamant about early enrichment; environment clearly impacts neurobiology.

At term, a baby is born with a full complement of neurons. By age 2, a child has *twice* as many total neuronal connections produced via synaptogenesis than will ultimately be needed. At about age 2, unused synapses, or those that have not been "exercised" via environmental experience, are pruned away (Spreen, Tupper, Risser, Tuollo, & Edgell, 1984; Spreen et al., 1995). This process of pruning over time brings the system, and especially the executive control system, from *redundancy* to *efficiency* (Mahone, 2004). In the infant and young child, there are multiple possible pathways to get information from point A to point B in the brain. While this allows for many possible networks and can be protective in a sense, it also means that processing is slow, redundant, and highly inefficient. This is clear to anyone who has tried to have a conversation with a two-year-old. They are concrete, ruminative, and meandering in their management of even fairly simple concepts.

While still concrete, by the time a child is age 6 or 7, the processing of information is rapid and quite efficient. Synaptic networks have been pared down to those that work quickly and with a minimum of effort. Those connections that have been exercised and used stay in place and result in streamlined processing. Those that have not been used have been pruned away. It is the ultimate "use it or lose it" paradigm, which again is reliant not only on genetic programming but also on environmental experiences.

Research in the last 10 years or so has highlighted a second wave of synaptic growth and subsequent pruning. This secondary burst in synaptic connectivity tends to happen just before puberty, or at about age 11 in girls and about age 12 in boys. This surge may be related to hormones, although even with premature or late puberty, synaptic growth tends to happen at about these ages (Rose et al., 2004). As with the first burst of synaptic growth in infancy, in this secondary round of synaptogenesis, those connections that get used remain and are strengthened. Those that are not exercised get pruned away. This "thinning out" of gray matter (synaptic connections) tends to begin around puberty and taper off in the early 20s (Giedd, 2004). While it seems counterintuitive, the loss of these synapses ultimately contributes to a mature, well-regulated, and efficient executive control system. Gerald Edelman (1987), a Nobel prize-winning scientist, has referred to this as "neural Darwinism," with only the most used, or "fittest," synaptic connections surviving.

Myelogenesis

Myelogenesis involves development of the fatty white sheath that covers the neuron and speeds communication between neurons. The process begins in the last month of gestation and continues through the third decade of life.

Myelination corresponds to systems coming on line, beginning with sensory/ motor systems and ending with the executive control system. There are peak periods for the growth of myelin occurring roughly between ages 6 and 8, 10 and 12, and 14 and 16. There is also emerging evidence that myelination may continue up to about age 40, with myelin thickening over time "much like the rings of a tree" (Giedd, 2004). There are corresponding growths in functional behavior and maturity, most particularly in the executive system, which may account for improvements throughout childhood in problem solving, judgment, and perspective taking.

EXAMPLES

At age 7, working with symbolic information is really beginning to "click" for Tanisha. However, in a short in-class writing assignment about her favorite stuffed animal, she does not know how to spell the word *carriage*. She draws a small picture of a carriage instead in the middle of her sentence. For this creativity, she is rewarded with three gold stars by her teacher.

At age 10, Amy is struck by a TV commercial showing children who do not get enough to eat and live in extreme poverty. She is distressed by this to the point that she tells her mother that she wants to sell all her old toys and donate the money to charity.

At 12, Jose comes home, has a snack, and finishes his homework without prompting so that he will have time in the evening to watch his favorite program.

At the end of these two processes of synaptogenesis and myelogenesis the usual outcome is a well-regulated and mature executive control system with information moving quickly and efficiently between the frontal system and all other parts of the brain. When all goes well in terms of processing, it is the difference between information meandering inefficiently down the secondary back roads and taking the Autobahn.

A Developmental Framework for Thinking About Executive Control

Jean Piaget

Before CT scans, before MRI, before functional imaging gave scientists the ability to actually monitor neurodevelopmental processes such as synaptogenesis and myelogenesis, psychologists were documenting the stage-like progression of cognitive development based largely on observation. Perhaps the best known of these theorists is Jean Piaget. When reviewing his theories of

Sensorimotor			Preoperational				Concrete Operations					Formal Operations
Birth	1	2	3	4	5	6	7	8	9	10	11	12	12+

Figure 12.1 Piaget's stages of development. Reprinted with permission from Leidtke, Amy.

development, it is fairly easy to draw parallels with the development of the executive control system. Piaget broke down childhood into stages based on skill acquisition (see Figure 12.1; Hetherington & Parke, 1999; Piaget, 1962, 1972; Yakovlev & Lecours, 1967).

The *sensorimotor* stage begins at birth and goes through the first 18 to 24 months of life. During this period, a child engages with the world primarily via inborn reflexes. The child's task is to learn to manage and understand environmental stimuli, initially through senses and reflexes alone. Toward the end of this period, there is a gradual transition to rudimentary thinking (Hetherington & Parke, 1999) or a shift from *reflexive* to *reflective*. There is a parallel move away from a focus on sensory stimuli toward understanding objects in the world around. The awareness of spatial relationships is growing and is honed through improved motor skills, such as reaching, grasping, and eventually walking. As a child moves through this stage, *object constancy*, the understanding that an object continues to exist even when out of view, develops, which likely accounts for the emergence of separation anxiety in a previously complacent 18-month-old. This shift also demonstrates a real leap in understanding of and engagement with the world.

During the sensorimotor phase, the right hemisphere and the limbic (impulse-driven) brain dominate. While conceptual thinking makes its first appearance toward the end of this stage, there is no real reasoning or abstraction. Attention span is very short, and distractibility is the order of the day. A child's approach to the world is stimulus bound and concrete. There is only a rudimentary ability to anticipate or plan ahead. Emotions and behavior are poorly regulated, changeable, and close to the surface. There is little to no ability to delay gratification. The frontal lobes are morphologically intact; however, the processes that eventually lead to executive efficiency have only just begun, and are focused primarily on pruning away unused synapses based on environmental experiences and on myelinating the sensory/motor systems.

From about age 2 until age 6 or 7, children are in the *preoperational* stage (Hetherington & Parke, 1999; Piaget, 1962, 1972). During this period, developing language skills and symbolism in general dominate the cognitive landscape. The left hemisphere, which is most often associated with language, is the focus of developing skills. There are also growing connections between the right and left hemispheres of the brain, allowing for a general increase in integration of information between brain systems (see below). The sensory/ motor systems, while not complete, are highly developed at this stage, and the focus begins to move away from the concrete toward the development of introspection and abstract thought.

EXAMPLE

At age 6, Ben has no trouble copying what he sees with a fair amount of accuracy. He can take a complex visual stimulus and translate this into a good motor output working in both the left and right side of space with ease.

Whereas executive skills are certainly emerging, integration is still limited during this phase. A child in the preoperational stage will be able to attend to a part of a process or project, but will not consistently be able to extend this to integrate parts into a whole. There is a tendency to focus on successive steps rather than the larger picture.

EXAMPLE

Jill is six years old, and she loves to go to the movies. But when her parents ask her, "What was the movie about?" Jill tends to list a string of details from the movie (e.g., "It had a dog in it, and the dog wore clothes and could talk") but misses the broader story line or theme.

Logic is difficult and remains concrete. Children in this stage can be very rigid and perseverative, repeating a request over and over, or getting stuck on a wish or an idea. Multitasking is not yet in the repertoire of a preoperational child, and problems with *conservation*, the ability to understand that certain attributes of an object remain the same or have been conserved even when there have been superficial changes, abound.

At this stage, the first round of synaptic pruning has ended and the first concentrated burst of myelination has begun. While these have been focused primarily on posterior systems and to a lesser extent on frontal lobes, with the child entering school, there is considerable improvement in basic skills, such as behavioral and emotional regulation, initiation, sustaining attention, and problem solving. The limbic brain with its rages and intensity still shows itself on a regular basis in the tantrums and emotional storms of the preschooler and first grader. Nevertheless, there is a gradual improvement in modulation, which is also due, in part, to advances in children's language development

(Chapter 2) and understanding of internal states (Chapter 3). Basic conceptual thought is emerging just in time to start connecting letters to sounds, and sounds to words on a page, and children begin to engage in intense imaginative play. Learning still occurs via imitation; however, imitation can now be deferred (Hetherington & Parke, 1999). There is a new awareness of relationships, classification, and symbolism in general. Egocentrism is the rule, although there is some ability to take on the perspective or role of another.

The *concrete operations* stage lasts from about age 6 to age 10 or 11 (Hetherington & Parke, 1999; Piaget, 1962, 1972). During this stage in development, schooling becomes the major focus. Attention at school is now quite strong; children are able to sustain their concentration for long stretches of time, up to a half hour or more, for effortful tasks. Behavior is more goal directed and better organized. Problem solving is good for both concrete and conceptual information. The ability to make logical inferences is in place particularly if practiced and when provided with concrete examples.

There is the beginning understanding of hierarchal structures, and grouping and classification will become second nature by the end of this period. There is an increased mobility of thinking due to improved understanding of logic, deduction, and reversibility (see Chapter 10 on reasoning). The understanding of complex concepts, such as space and time, is emerging. Conservation is a simple matter, and perspective taking is improving rapidly. Children in this stage are able to filter out or edit relevant from irrelevant features when solving problems and categorizing objects. There is still a concrete relationship with the world; however, the egocentric posture of the preoperational child becomes increasingly diluted. Empathy is developing quickly.

During this stage, the *corpus callosum* is also developing rapidly (Levin et al., 1991; Spreen et al., 1995). This is the vast white matter tract that connects the right and left hemispheres together. As a result, the efficiency of communication is improving dramatically, also in part due to the process of myelination that is wrapping up its first concentrated burst toward the end of this stage. Conduction among the neural networks already in place becomes more rapid, making thinking a much less ponderous and slow process. Children present as more facile in their manipulation of ideas, and generally improves abstraction. Sensory/motor systems continue to become more fluid and automatic with practice, as seen by the athleticism and coordination of the typical ten-year-old. The focus of neurodevelopment, however, has moved to association areas (those areas of the brain that connect systems) and the frontal lobes (Levin et al., 1991; Spreen et al., 1995). The executive control system is beginning to come on line in a much more intensive fashion than during earlier stages. Children in this stage are able to manage or multitask multiple demands at once: going to school, playing soccer, keeping up with homework, and spending time with friends. Information is moving between surface and subcortical structures with ease. The limbic brain is losing its dominance, with the executive system rapidly becoming poised to take charge. For the moment (at least until the hormones kick in), there may be fewer temper outbursts, and general ability to modulate attention and frustration often improves.

Formal operations was the last stage postulated by Piaget (1962, 1972). This stage begins roughly at age 10 or 11 (perhaps a little earlier in girls than boys) and is the final level of cognitive achievement based on the Piagetian model. In this stage, not only are children and young adolescents well versed in logical and symbolic thought, but they begin to think about problems in a way that is not based in the concrete. Ideas can be developed and applied that violate reality or are even frankly absurd. Thinking is facile to the extent that it can be fanciful and completely separated from concrete experiences and reality.

In addition to thinking deductively, the child in the formal operations stage can assimilate and combine information readily from multiple sources. Information can be integrated and transformed at will, and different combinations of ideas can be accepted or rejected as needed. As discussed in Chapter 10, this is flexible, abstract, and fluent hypothesis testing. There is an awareness of the complexity of information, but also an emerging and true ability to cope with that complexity. Children and adolescents in this stage are freed from the concrete realities around them and are able to explore ideas and fantasies in a full and liberated manner. Humor may be one of the hallmarks of this stage, moving away from the slapstick and corporeal, and becoming subtle, more symbolic, and more about word play than pratfalls.

Piaget believed that this represented the highest form of cognitive functioning. Judgment, reasoning, and planning—all those skills that are associated with an intact and mature executive system—were all described as part of the formal operations stage. As he conceived it, this corresponded roughly with an adult-like level of executive control. Whereas not all children were assumed to reach this stage based on inborn abilities and exposure, with normal growth and a reasonable education, he believed that higher-order cognitive development was basically achieved at about age 12 or soon thereafter.

It's worth remembering that at the time Piaget described his model, there was no way to virtually evaluate subtle neurobiological processes. Information about brain size *was* available, however, and what scientists knew at that time was that at about age 12, the brain had reached roughly adult proportions (Spreen et al., 1995). All of that has changed in recent decades with modern neuroimaging studies of normal neurodevelopmental processes. We now understand that, far from complete, children at about age 12 are entering their second burst of synaptogenesis to be followed by gradual pruning over the next decade or so of life (Giedd, 2004). We also understand that at age 12, preadolescent children have another intensive round of myelination ahead of them, followed by a gradual building up of myelin that will last for the next two decades or so of life. What Piaget conceptualized as formal operations is in actuality a process that continues to develop well into adulthood.

Mel Levine

In recent years, additional models of executive skill attainment and general cognitive development have been offered by a variety of scientists and practitioners. One of the leading voices in the description of child neurodevelopment and cognition is pediatrician Mel Levine (adapted from Levine, 2002). While not postulating a new theoretical framework for executive processes, per se, Levine provides a nice structure for thinking about how development intersects with (or drives) basic executive skills such as attention, sequencing, and higher cognition. Below are summarized general neurodevelopmental and executive themes based roughly on school-related expectations as proposed by Levine (2002). The first three stages, which are summarized in Table 12.2, bear striking similarities to the Piagetian model.

Whereas Piaget's developmental theory stops at age 12 or 13, Levine and most contemporary clinicians and scientists recognize that cognitive development, particularly as regards executive control, continues well into adolescence and beyond. High school, as it turns out, is a period of extremely rapid neurogrowth. This is at least partially accounted for in Levine's (2002) description of adolescent neurodevelopmental themes as related to school-based expectations (Table 12.3).

Although the emphasis of this chapter has been on normal development of executive control in children, it would be remiss not to comment on the special qualities of the developing teenage executive system. In addition to the general guidelines set out by Levine above, there have been some interesting expansions in our understanding of executive control and the teenage brain in the last decade.

Part of the unique nature of executive control in teenagers has already been explored related to the ongoing and prolonged processes of synaptogenesis and myelogenesis. Pruning continues into mid to late adolescence, and the last burst of myelination is just beginning. At about the same time, hormones are taking center stage, with estrogen and testosterone beginning to pour into the bloodstream (Arnett, 1999; Rose et al., 2004). The adrenal glands of the kidneys release testosterone-like sex hormones that are very active, as it turns out, in brain functioning. These hormones attach to receptors everywhere, but most especially in the brain's emotional center, the limbic brain, exerting a direct influence on neurochemicals that regulate mood and excitability.

This means two things: Adolescents reach their emotional tipping points much more easily, and they also tend to actively seek out situations in which they can experience a high level of emotional intensity (Dahl & Spear, 2004). There is a hormone-brain relationship that contributes to the appetite for thrills and strong sensations. All of this would be terrific, except teenagers live in a world where there are drugs, alcohol, cars, and other dangers, and

Table 12.2 Levine's First Three Neurodevelopmental Stages

	Preschool Through First Grade (Birth to 6/7)	Grades 1 Through 3 (Ages 6/7 to 8/9)	Grades 4 Through 8 (Ages 8/9 to 13/14)
Neuromotor	• Eye-hand coordination • Hand dominance • Fine-motor programming • Growing gross-motor efficacy	• Motor memory and accuracy for symbolic information (e.g., writing) • Copying/visual-motor integration stressed • Cursive/connected writing • Comparison regarding athletic/general motor ability	• Intensification of motor competitiveness and skill • Graphomotor fluency and automatization • Gross-motor synchronization
Attention	• Modulation of activity level • Demand for concentration in group setting (e.g., story time) • Delayed gratification • Conformity to rules • Brief periods of sustained effort (with prompting and cuing)	• Greater demand for sustained concentration and filtering distraction • Reflection on tasks, planning, self-monitoring • Expectation of persistence and independent task completion (with modest cuing) • Teachers stress consistency and control	• Managing decontextualized detail and coping with less predictable information flow • Increasing social awareness leads to distractions • Need for attention in low-interest contexts (e.g., hour-long lectures) • Extended mental effort, planning, and self-regulation stressed • Independence expected (with minimal cuing and support)

Table 12.2 Levine's First Three Neurodevelopmental Stages (Continued)

	Preschool Through First Grade (Birth to 6/7)	Grades 1 Through 3 (Ages 6/7 to 8/9)	Grades 4 Through 8 (Ages 8/9 to 13/14)
Sequencing	• Basic concepts of time/seriation emerge • Some exposure to multistep directions (e.g., follow two- to three-step directions by age 6) • Beginning of ordering (e.g., numbers, alphabet)	• Phonetic segmentation and resynthesis as reading skills develop • Stress on serial order recognition and recall in spelling • Practical sequences (e.g., days of the week, months of the year) take priority	• Narrative organization in writing • Use of extended causal/temporal/procedural chains • Staging tasks in sequence • Independent prioritizing/schedule planning • Step-wise work and problem solving
Higher-order cognition	• Reliance on sensory data and perception • Developing awareness of discovery and concept • Exposure to abstract symbols (e.g., written language, numbers) • Classification skills exercised for first time	• Improved use of experiential knowledge for reading comprehension • Assimilation and confirmation of rules (e.g., spelling) • Logic and ability to brainstorm increase • Emergence of rule learning and application	• Emergence of preferred modes of thought • Stress on abstract concepts • Flexible rule application and generalization • Implementation of conscious problem-solving methods • Critical thinking required

Table 12.3 Levine's Adolescent Neurodevelopmental Themes

Neuromotor	• Adept at gross motor skills • Academics call for speed writing, note taking, keyboarding • Increased opportunities for artistic craft • Development of musical motor talents
Attention	• Ability to manage multiple degrees of saliency in information • Reading goes beyond surface comprehension to analysis of symbolic meaning and analogy • Heightened attention/memory and attention/language interactions • Affective and social distractions present challenges • Thinking is adaptable, flexible, and creative
Sequencing	• Routine demand for sequential solutions • Heightened stress on time management • Daily need for logical step-wise reasoning/production • Late adolescence brings increasing appreciation of historical perspectives (e.g., individual, family, nation, world)
Higher-order cognition	• Facile use of third-order analogies • Ability to develop multiple alternative solutions for solving problems • Ability to easily reconcile knowledge from multiple sources • Daily need to deal with abstract concepts • Hypothesis generation is required and expected • Evaluative skills become paramount, even in context of immature judgment and unpredictable behavior

those parts of the brain that "just say no" are not yet fully mature (Martin et al., 2002). The frontal systems, those parts of the brain that provide the brakes and exercise judgment, are still under construction.

Recent research by Yurgelun-Todd and her colleagues (Killgore, Oki, & Yurgelun-Todd, 2001) has begun to suggest that young preteens and teens tend to use primarily their limbic brain, the drive brain, to process emotions. As a result, this process is mediated heavily by fear and other "gut" reactions, more so than the frontal lobes and executive regulation. Young teenagers tend to see hostility and anger where an older teen or adult would see fear. As teenagers get a little older, brain activity during tasks that tap into emotions tends to shift to the frontal lobes, leading to more reasoned perceptions. There is an inescapable intersection of brain development and the paucity of emotional controls that is often evident in adolescence (Dahl & Spear, 2004).

EXAMPLE

Lynne, age 12, came home complaining that her teacher "hates" her based on a comment and a look during social studies. In a follow-up call, her mother discovers that the teacher had no intention or recollection of any such exchange and certainly no memory of a negative interaction. They conclude that Lynne must have "misread" the comment and the look.

Studies on risk taking and decision making (Steinberg et al., 2004) suggested that, although both teenagers and adults made safe decisions when working individually, teens made more risky decisions than adults when working together in groups of same-aged peers. Such results suggest there may be significant age differences in decision making and judgment that appear under conditions that are more emotionally arousing or stimulating, such as in a group. In reality, most violent crimes are committed by teenagers and young adults in packs (Volavka, 2002), and many times other risk-taking behaviors, such as alcohol or drug experimentation, are more likely to occur in group contexts than when teenagers are alone.

To an extent, this understanding is even beginning to filter into the legal system. A few years ago, the American Bar Association (ABA) released a statement to all state legislatures urging them to ban the death penalty for teenagers because "for social and biological reasons, teens have increased difficulties making mature decisions and understanding the consequences of their actions" (ABA, 2004). Parents of teens already know this. Making mistakes, including poor judgment calls and impulsive errors, is part of how the brain optimally grows. It is the intersection between biology, social context, experience, and environment. The best estimate we have for a truly mature brain in terms of executive control is around age 25 (Giedd, 2004). It is no accident that this is also about the age that car insurance gets a whole lot cheaper. It is the job of parents to stay in tune with their teen, and to provide support and love, as well as structure.

Clinical Implications

Tips for Clinicians, Practitioners, and Educators

Table 12.4 presents several strategies for understanding and fostering the normal developmental course of executive functions.

Understanding the Nature of Executive Dysfunction in Children

Whereas this chapter has focused on normal development of the executive system, it is important to have a framework for understanding when the system

Table 12.4 Tips for Clinicians, Practitioners, and Educators

1. Consider developmental discontinuity	Children's executive functions follow a protracted course of development, meaning that their ability to attend, initiate, organize, plan, problem solve, adapt, integrate, and self-monitor will come on line at varying ages. The demands placed on children to perform these functions, as well as the behavioral strategies adults use, should be adapted, accordingly, over time.
2. Provide external supports for behavioral and emotional control	Provide external structure by setting clear limits and expectations, providing feedback and consistent consequences, and teaching self-regulation strategies (e.g., counting to 10, deep breathing, progressive muscle relaxation). As the executive system matures, children will be able to gradually shift toward more internalized regulation of behavior.
3. Teach and practice higher-order skills	Reinforce higher-order thinking skills through rehearsal, coaching, and practice in the environment to support learning and automaticity (Mahone & Slomine, 2007). This may be particularly helpful in developing problem-solving strategies, social skills, and other abilities requiring mental flexibility and adaptability.
4. Aid in the development of meta-cognitive skills	The development of metacognitive skills (e.g., self-monitoring, self-evaluation, insight) occurs gradually, and is essential in promoting functional competence and independence (Marlowe, 2000). Functional life skills improve when children are taught explicitly to identify the causes of their own success and failure, and when they are provided direct feedback about their performance/behavior (Mahone & Slomine, 2007).
5. Foster cognitive efficiency at every age	Support executive systems at developmentally appropriate levels throughout childhood. For example, planning and organization skills can be reinforced in the following ways (adapted from Mahone & Slomine, 2007): <ul><li>*Preschool*: Establish routines, encourage the use of narrative language to promote organization (e.g., "When we come into the house, we take off our shoes and hang up our coats"), use photos or symbols to guide the child through multistep tasks (e.g., a picture schedule to identify steps in morning routine—getting dressed, eating breakfast, brushing teeth).</li><li>*School age*: Teach mnemonic strategies and categorization skills (e.g., group a list of items by semantic category in order to remember them better), teach strategies to identify goals, and plan steps to attain goals.</li><li>*Adolescence*: Create timelines for long-term projects; carry a written log of activities, schedules, assignments, and due dates; monitor effectiveness of organizational systems.</li></ul>

Table 12.4 Tips for Clinicians, Practitioners, and Educators (Continued)

6. Provide structure while fostering independence	Provide a balance between providing external structure and encouraging independence. That balance will shift dramatically as a child develops from preschooler to adolescent. Whereas young children do not yet have the skills to plan and organize their behavior independently, older children benefit from having external supports decreased gradually so that they take responsibility for using the executive skills they are accumulating in their "toolboxes." Opportunities for exerting independence are important teaching moments to test and refine executive skills, while still having an adult safety net. Examples of incrementally reducing external supports and encouraging independence include: • *Preschool*: Allowing a child to pick out her own outfit from among several weather-appropriate options. • *School age*: Moving away from sitting with the child to do homework to merely checking to make sure that the assignments have been completed at the end of each evening. • *Adolescence*: Encouraging a teenager to think about ways to resolve a conflict with a teacher and to independently initiate a discussion with that teacher.

is not working appropriately. The frontal/executive system ideally functions as an individual's "brakes," censor, editor, and problem solver. Without the mitigating effects of the executive system, a child's drives and impulses can get him or her into trouble behaviorally, socially, and emotionally.

In children, when behaviors occur out of the normal developmental time-line, it is important to ask: (1) What processes are disrupted? (2) When in the developmental process are they disrupted? (3) Does the disruption represent a deficit, delay, or deviance?

Deficit: A lack of a skill or behavior, not necessarily time referenced (e.g., never walks).

Delay: Behavior that is normal but should have occurred earlier (e.g., first words at age 2).

Deviance: Behavior that does not occur in normal development at any time (e.g., vocal/motor tics, self-injurious behaviors).

These questions are important in guiding identification and evaluation of executive dysfunction, as well as leading to recommendations for intervention. Such intervention likely involves an increase in external structure, a decrease in expectations for independence, and support for higher-order thinking abilities.

Attention-Deficit Hyperactivity Disorder: An Example of Executive Dysfunction

As indicated, the executive system is particularly vulnerable to insult, injury, and disruptive neurologic/psychiatric processes. As such, loss of executive control is associated with a wide range of neurodevelopmental and neuropsychiatric disorders, including attention-deficit hyperactivity disorder (ADHD), obsessive-compulsive disorder, bipolar disorder, autism spectrum disorders, and dyslexia. ADHD ranks as one of the most commonly diagnosed psychiatric disorders in childhood. It also provides one of the best examples of how executive dysfunction affects behavior. As such, a more detailed description of the nature of executive deficits in ADHD, as well as important clinical implications, warrants additional discussion.

ADHD is characterized by developmentally inappropriate levels of impulsivity, hyperactivity, or inattention that present in childhood and persist over time. Its symptoms significantly impair social, academic, or occupational functioning (American Psychiatric Association, 2000). The prevalence is estimated at 3% to 7% of school-aged children (American Psychiatric Association, 2000).

Recent theories, as well as electrophysiological, biochemical, and neuroanatomical evidence, have suggested that ADHD is predominantly an impairment of the executive system (Barkley, 1997; Ylvisaker & DeBonis, 2000). Russell Barkley (1997), a prominent ADHD researcher, developed a theory of ADHD suggesting a primary deficit in behavioral inhibition, with secondary deficits in four other executive functions indirectly related to inhibition (i.e., working memory, internalization of speech, self-regulation of affect/motivation/arousal, and reconstitution). These impairments, in turn, lead to decreased motor and behavioral control. In support of this theory, studies of neuropsychological functioning have identified multiple executive deficits in individuals with ADHD.

These recent developments in conceptualization and physiological evidence suggest a shift in thinking about ADHD away from being a problem solely of attention and activity level. Rather, it is helpful for clinicians, teachers, and parents to understand that ADHD encompasses a broader set of problems with executive control, including possible disruption in the ability to formulate, plan, carry out, self-monitor, and flexibly self-correct one's behavior. Specifically, children with ADHD may present with deficits in planning, sequencing, organizing, and managing simultaneous sources of information. In addition, ADHD children frequently have problems with mental flexibility, problem solving, decision making, and monitoring their behavior. A child with ADHD often presents as quite smart and capable when observed in structured situations (e.g., during a formal evaluation in a one-to-one therapy session), but may have immense difficulties in applying his or her knowledge, skills, and attributes in "the right way at the right time" in everyday settings, especially those that are ambiguous, unstructured, or complex (Wills, 2005).

EXAMPLE

Maleek is a smart nine-year-old who is able to do very well with his schoowork as long as he gets assistance from the aide in his classroom. With her support, including cuing and redirection, he finishes his math problems, writes in his journal, and can read as efficiently as any other child in the class. However, he struggles in music class, where he does not have access to the aide or the usual structure of the classroom. In that setting, he is loud, often disruptive, and annoys the other children because he frequently "gets in their space."

Executive difficulties associated with ADHD are not limited to a single setting or situation, but are observed at home, at school, and in social environments. Executive deficits are often the primary reason children with ADHD are referred for counseling, therapy, and special-education supports. At home, problems related to planning, organizing, and sequencing behavior often affect a child's ability to follow through on multistep directions in a timely fashion (e.g., "put on your jacket and shoes, get your backpack, and meet me at the car"), to remember to do daily chores independently, and to maintain belongings in an age-appropriate manner.

EXAMPLE

Barbara is a bright sixth grader who consistently does well on tests, but often loses grade points because she fails to hand in her homework. Often her homework has been completed but she "forgets" it, can't find it, or it is crammed into the bottom of her backpack. She loses her work in her room, which her parents refer to as "the disaster zone." She fails to write down assignments in her agenda book, and often forgets to bring books home that she needs to study for tests. Her parents are constantly bringing her back to school after hours to pick up necessary but forgotten items. This creates considerable stress for Barbara, but also for her entire family.

Problems related to behavioral regulation are common in this group of children, such as inhibiting responses, thinking flexibly, and solving problems.

This often affects family relationships in very significant ways (e.g., "getting stuck" asking a parent the same question again and again, pushing or hitting a young sibling who takes a toy without asking). Parents often report that they spend "hours" each evening with their ADHD child trying to get 30 minutes' worth of homework completed, often to the detriment of their other, less demanding, children.

At school, there are often obvious problems with staying seated, talking out of turn, and tuning out. In addition, children with ADHD frequently present with executive difficulties that affect their *efficiency* in completing work. This may include losing or forgetting their materials and homework; difficulties regulating their attention and speed of processing to complete in-class work; and deficits in prioritizing assignments, managing their time, and following through in order to meet deadlines. Executive problems associated with ADHD can also have a negative effect on specific academic skills, especially as work becomes more abstract and complex. Difficulties may include comprehending and retaining reading assignments; formulating, organizing, and integrating written material; and following lengthy, multistep procedures (e.g., math problems).

For children with ADHD, social problems frequently stem from executive weaknesses in inhibition, mental flexibility, and problem solving. Such weaknesses may lead to rough play, rigid patterns of play (e.g., only wanting to play with a certain toy, problems sharing and turn taking), and trouble resolving conflicts with peers. Whereas a child can get away with being impulsive during early elementary years, peers begin to react negatively to the child who does not understand personal space, shouts out inappropriate or odd comments, or can't keep his hands to himself as he gets a little older.

EXAMPLE

Kevin is a sweet eight-year-old who nevertheless is constantly getting into trouble on the playground because of his dysregulated behavior. He sometimes throws objects in an unsafe way and fails to attend to personal space. His rough-and-tumble play sometimes escalates to pushing or hitting. He is "annoying" to other children because of his tendency to blurt things out. He can't seem to "tune in" to the pace of their play or conversation. Although Kevin still has two or three friends, he is increasingly left out by his age-mates because of these behaviors.

It is important to note that medication for ADHD can be very effective in reducing hyperactivity and improving attention and concentration, but it does not directly address the problems with executive function discussed above. Organization, planning, and problem solving can remain quite poor even when attention has improved. Children with ADHD can learn strategies and skills to improve their executive function, but they also benefit from a higher level of structure and support from others in the environment. Some practical recommendations for working with children with ADHD are included in Table 12.5.

Table 12.5 Recommendations for Working With Children With ADHD

General Issues	School-Related Issues
• Break down directions and requests into single-step units, and repeat as necessary.	• Divide work into small units, with praise or concrete reward for perseverance and completion of each unit.
• Rules and behavioral expectations should be clearly defined and based on established principles of behavior management (e.g., positive reinforcement, response cost, consistent consequences).	• Provide scheduled breaks, as well as the opportunity to change activities (and come back to them at a later time) if the student becomes too inattentive or frustrated with tasks.
• Expectations should be presented simply, clearly, and consistently, and should be reviewed frequently.	• Homework time should be divided into short, manageable sections, either by subject or by time interval (e.g., work for 20 minutes, then take a break).
• Keep routines as predictable as possible. Provide reminders about transitions, as well as assistance, remaining flexible when unexpected changes occur.	• To aid with organization, provide guidance in using checklists, assignment calendars, and other organizational aids.
• Training in active problem solving is helpful in addressing academic and interpersonal problems. A useful approach involves guiding the child through a series of questions to identify the problem, compare it to previously solved problems, generate possible solutions and choose the most appropriate one, and evaluate the effectiveness of the approach.	• Help students create organizational frameworks for projects, including outlining the necessary tasks in the project, developing a step-by-step timeline for interim deadlines, and recording progress as each step is completed.
	• Communication between parents and teachers is helpful in tracking students' work completion. In elementary school, this may involve a communication notebook to write brief, regular notes about progress. In middle and high school, the use of weekly or quarterly progress reports may be helpful.

Conclusions

In this chapter, we hoped to convey a sense of the dynamism of neurodevelopment particularly as it relates to executive control. Throughout childhood, this is a system in constant motion. From birth to young adulthood there is a layering of skills dependent first upon sensory/motor awareness, then an emerging logic, and moving into insight and self-awareness in the late teenage years and beyond. Children start with a negligible repertoire of control skills, and essentially rely on the adults in their world to function as their executive system to keep them safe and to ensure that they are learning in a way that meets them both developmentally and in a stimulating way. Hopefully, understanding the nature of executive control, including the developmental course and appropriate expectations for each age level, can be useful to parents, clinicians, and educators in making this process run as smoothly as possible.

References

American Bar Association Juvenile Justice Committee, Washington, DC. (2004, July 19). *Juvenile death penalty amicus brief.*

American Psychiatric Association. (2000). *Diagnostic and statistical manual of mental disorders* (4th ed., text rev.). Washington, DC: Author.

Arnett, J. J. (1999). Adolescent storm and stress, reconsidered. *American Psychologist, 54,* 317–326.

Barkley, R. A. (1997). *ADHD and the nature of self-control.* New York: Guilford Press.

Dahl, R. E., & Spear, L. P. (2004). Adolescent brain development: Vulnerabilities and opportunities. *Annals of the New York Academy of Science, 1021,* 1–22.

Edelman, G. (1987). *Neural Darwinism: The theory of neuronal group selectivity.* New York: Basic Books.

Giedd, J. N. (2004). Structural magnetic resonance imaging of the adolescent brain. *Annals of the New York Academy of Science, 1021,* 77–85.

Goldberg, E. (2002). *The executive brain: Frontal lobes and the civilized mind.* New York: Oxford University Press.

Hetherington, E. M., & Parke, R. D. (1999). *Child psychology: A contemporary viewpoint* (5th ed.). New York: McGraw-Hill College.

Killgore, W. D. S., Oki, M., & Yurgelun-Todd, D. A. (2001). Sex-specific developmental changes in amygdala responses to affective faces. *Neuroreport, 12,* 427–433.

Kolb, B., & Whishaw, I. Q. (2003). *Fundamentals of human neuropsychology* (5th ed.). New York: Worth Publishers.

Levin, H. S., Culhane, K. A., Hartmann, J., Evankovich, K., Mattson, A. J., Harward, H., et al. (1991). Developmental changes in performance on tests of purported frontal lobe functioning. *Developmental Neuropsychology, 7,* 377–395.

Levine, M. (2002). *A mind at a time.* New York: Simon and Schuster Paperbacks.

Mahone, E. M. (2004, November). *Neurodevelopmental disorders in children: Developmental considerations for assessment and intervention.* Paper presented at the meeting of the National Academy of Neuropsychology, Seattle, WA.

Mahone, E. M., & Slomine, B. S. (2007). Managing dysexecutive disorders. In S. J. Hunter & J. Donders (Eds.) Pediatric neuropsychological intervention (pp. 287–313). New York: Cambridge University Press.

Marlowe, W. B. (2000). An intervention for children with disorders of executive functions. *Developmental Neuropsychology, 18,* 445–454.

Martin, C. A., Kelly, T. H., Rayens, M. K., Brogli, B. R., Brenzel, A., Smith, W. J., et al. (2002). Sensation seeking, puberty, and nicotine, alcohol and marijuana use in adolescence. *Journal of the American Academy of Child and Adolescent Psychiatry, 41,* 1495–1502.

Passler, M. A., Isaac, W., & Hynd, G. W. (1985). Neuropsychological development of behavior attributed to frontal lobe functioning in children. *Developmental Neuropsychology, 1,* 349–370.

Piaget, J. (1962). The stages of intellectual development of the child. *Bulletin of the Menninger Clinic, 26,* 120–128.

Piaget, J. (1972). *The psychology of the child.* New York: Basic Books.

Rose, A. B., Menke, D. P., Clasen, L. S., Rosenthal, M. A., Wallace, G. L., Vaituzis, A. C., et al. (2004). Effects of hormones and sex chromosomes on stress influenced regions of the developing pediatric brain. *Annals of the New York Academy of Science, 1032,* 231–233.

Spreen, O., Risser, A. H., & Edgell, D. (1995). *Developmental neuropsychology.* New York: Oxford University Press.

Spreen, O., Tupper, D., Risser, A., Tuokko, H., & Edgell, D. (1984). *Human developmental neuropsychology.* New York: Oxford University Press.

Steinberg, L., Dahl, R., Keating, D., Kupfer, D., Masten, A. S., & Pine, D. S. (2004). The study of developmental psychopathology in adolescence: Integrating affective neuroscience with the study of context. In D. Cicchetti (Ed.), *Handbook of developmental psychopathology* (pp. 710–741). New York: John Wiley.

Stuss, D. T., & Benson, D. F. (1986). *The frontal lobes.* New York: Raven Press.

Stuss, D. T., & Benson, D. F. (1987). The frontal lobes and control of cognition and memory. In E. Perecman (Ed.), *The frontal lobes revisited* (pp. 141–158). New York: The IRBN Press.

Volavka, J. (2002). *Neurobiology of violence* (2nd ed.). Washington, DC: American Psychiatric Publishing.

Welsh, M. C., & Pennington, B. F. (1988). Assessing frontal lobe functioning in children: Views from developmental psychology. *Developmental Neuropsychology, 4,* 199–230.

Wills, K. (2005, October). *News they can use: Translating test results into real-world recommendations.* Paper presented at the National Academy of Neuropsychology, 25th Annual Conference, Tampa, FL.

Yakovlev, P. I., & Lecours, A. R. (1967). The myelogenetic cycles of regional maturation of the brain. In A. Mindkowski (Ed.), *Development of the brain in early life* (pp. 3–70). Philiadelphia: F.A. David and Company.

Ylvisaker, M., & DeBonis, D. (2000). Executive function impairment in adolescence: TBI and ADHD. *Topics in Language Disorders, 20,* 29–57.

Conclusion

13

Knowing What We Know
The Developing Child and the Developing Clinician

JOSEPH C. VIOLA

I almost hesitate to use the Rorschach plates as a way of trying to coalesce what this book represents with regard to the normal cognitive development of children. However, in many ways I have found that the most salient examples of this book's applicability, at least in my own professional life as a psychologist, ring loudest and most clear when I consider those isolationist moments when it is just me and the child.

The Rorschach technique has been debated for many years, particularly as it relates to how to code and interpret responses to the inkblots and, more specifically, how to embrace the notion that one's viewing of an ambiguous stimulus (and subsequent response to a query about what one sees) can represent personality functioning, unconscious motivations, and internal conflicts. The Rorschach is not a "cognitive measure"—yet it is completely contingent upon shared cognition.

EXAMPLE: COGNITION IN ACTION

Tester:	*(handing Plate 5 to the child)* What might this be?
Child:	*(boy, age 6)* A bat, with wings, and a head, and ears.
Tester:	Good, thank you. Look some more, take your time, you may find something else.
Child:	Um, the bat has *testicles* coming out of his head, and feet, and wings.
Tester:	*(frozen)*
Child:	*(content, ready for another inkblot)*
Tester:	*(still frozen, already thinking about the range of deviant response scores that this child will undoubtedly accumulate in the next few cards, begins to worry)*

(Free association phase completed, move into the inquiry phase)

Tester:	*(Plate 5)*
	You said you saw testicles coming out of the bat's head, feet, and wings. Can you help me to see it just like you saw it?
Child:	Oh sure, you see how the whole picture looks like a bat? It's black. Can you see his head (pointing), and feet (pointing), and these big parts are the wings (pointing)?
Tester:	Uh-huh.
Child:	OK, well, on top of the head are two skinny things like arms. And those two skinny things are also on the bottom near his feet and then again on the wings. I think an octopus has a lot of them. Eight I think. Eight testicles.
Tester:	Testicles, like on an octopus?
Child:	Yeah, that's it.
Tester:	*(obsessing over whether or not to ask whether the child means* tentacles, *or will doing so improperly skew coding and interpretation—he decides to make the leap)* Do you mean tentacles?
Child:	Um, no. I mean testicles.

(And the coding fun begins)

It's no secret that there is a very mechanistic side of the Rorschach technique that requires the person administering the test to make challenging decisions. What is clear from the above example, however, is that the accuracy of your coding (and therefore your subsequent interpretations) is heavily dependent on the abilities of your clients to convey information to you about what they know, what they see, and how they experience the inkblot. Thus, regardless of how many batteries you have administered, in order to best appreciate the process-oriented findings of the Rorschach, you must first acknowledge the role that children's cognitive development plays in shaping their responses. We must wrestle with the cognitive suitability of the responses before we can progress to deeper analyses about what those responses represent internally for the child.

I reference this particular example because it is freshest in my mind, especially as I supervise graduate students learning about assessment and psychotherapy with children. Future psychologists need to know about the idiosyncratic, yet entirely normal, cognitive tendencies of the children with whom they work. I often find myself engaged in conversations with students about how best to interview a child for the first time; what to expect from a ten-year-old just starting therapy; and what we know about a child's ability to learn new tasks, develop alibis for their own behavioral indiscretions, remember school lessons, and (perhaps most pertinent to the above example) become trapped by their own language development. This book is filled with illuminating examples of how difficult it is to align children's cognitive abilities with their chronological age and emotional development. We sometimes assume that children know more than they are capable of expressing, without standing back and asking ourselves *how* to best bridge this divide. Similarly, there are times when we (adults) are resistant to acknowledging what is not there. The danger of this approach cannot be overstated when you consider the monumental responsibility we have to the families that entrust us with their children.

My goal going forward is to simply reflect on four important principles and constructs to guide us—psychologists and other professionals—in our work with children. We must continue to educate ourselves about what is considered *normal* so as to best recognize and understand what is not.

Patience—A Virtue and a Necessity

Even those of us without children of our own are familiar with the soft spots on a newborn baby's head. These spots are called fontanels and there are usually two of them: one on the very top of the head and another near the back. These anatomical depressions give new meaning to the familiar phrase "children are impressionable." Children are indeed soft and impressionable, and fontanels are a powerful reminder for us that there are physical safeguards in place to allow for normal growth to occur. They are also a powerful reminder of how fragile a child can be. There are times in a child's life when the "sponge" analogy makes sense, insofar as the child is constantly taking in information from his or her environment, but there are also times in a child's life when treating the child like a sponge—assuming he or she absorbs what you say and do—can be detrimental.

Put another way, be patient. There is nothing in this world that takes the place of experience. Children must be given adequate time and support to create their own cognitive schemas, particularly given what the authors contributing to this book have shown us about how easily children confuse their own experiences with those of others. Imposing onto a child either your own or another's cognitive schema is in some cases fruitlessly artificial, and in others it changes the entire landscape. Adults take for granted the ease with which they can generalize about other people, places, and experiences. We forget that children learn this gradually. It takes years for adults to understand the value of metacognition and self-awareness; so why are we so quick to not give children the same amount of time? A heightened awareness of self increases one's ability to understand and generalize about other people. Being mindful of this can serve as a powerful base for understanding the inner experience of a child whose abilities for thought, reflection, memory, reasoning, and language are not all on the same plane. While not the focus of this book per se, it is worth pointing out the importance of parallel developing processes that children experience, most notably the development of the self. As play, social opportunities with peers, interactions with teachers and caregivers outside of the home, and growing comfort with siblings in the home increase, the connection between children's cognitive development and the development of the self becomes more pronounced. Although adults are quick to acknowledge the patience required to allow children to "come into their own" as a social beings, they often will not show similar patience allowing children to grow into their cognitive abilities. This disparity carries significant implications.

Virtually every chapter of this book used the word *patience* at some point as a plea to clinicians to first consider what it is about a child's particular behavior that is normal, before driving for particular pathology. One very basic and straightforward way to do this is to start by granting all children you meet the cognitive capabilities of a three-year-old and then working up. Consider (or learn) how a three-year-old thinks, remembers, talks, reasons, and so on, and align this with the child before you. Collect data and adjust your expectations of the child, repeatedly, until you have established where, developmentally, the child is. By first considering what it is about a child's development that is *normal*, we give ourselves the best inroad toward considering what is not. Swimming upstream against the current of pathology is not easy, but all of us could benefit from a more robust understanding of what to expect from the children we see. It will, at the very least, better inform our internal diagnostic templates.

Voice—Hear Yours and Theirs

Children often understand more than you think and certainly more than they are capable of expressing. Misunderstandings will arise when you talk with children, and it is vital that, as clinicians, we continually monitor, adapt, and think about our "voices." Parents need to change and adapt to the different developmental levels of their children, oftentimes becoming categorically different parents from one stage to the next (e.g., life giver, life sustainer, playmate, teacher, disciplinarian, coach, friend). So too must clinicians continually update and reflect on their clinical voices. This is as relevant for those clinicians currently in training as it is during those years when, rightly or wrongly, the chaos of training others takes precedence over your own personal reflection about your professional identity.

Just as children go through pronounced stages of cognitive development during early and middle childhood, clinicians also progress through different stages of professional development. Both developmental processes are filled with moments of risk and opportunity, albeit for entirely different reasons. Children typically handle these moments with great enthusiasm, unburdened by what they do *not* know or have yet to experience. Clinicians, however, often approach these moments with trepidation, crippled by what they *do* know about themselves, their past experiences, what lies ahead, and what to expect. Both processes also represent the beginning of a lifelong effort. Just as children continue to change, adapt, and evolve cognitively into and throughout adulthood, clinicians must also meet the challenge of refining their own clinical voices over time, with the support of well-intentioned supervisors, and in response to how they have grown and changed as people. With time and diligence clinicians can, and must, meet their professional and ethical responsibilities to update, monitor, and reflect upon what they have learned and the ways in which they have changed so as to better inform their work.

Considering our own growth as clinicians through the lens of children's cognitive development can help us better understand our strengths and limitations (both directly with children and with adults who supervise and collaborate with us). With respect to finding your clinical voice, consider the ways in which we teach clinical interviewing to aspiring psychologists: didactic instruction on types of interviewing techniques, lab courses focused on application, video and audio taping for class discussion, standardized interview protocols, checklists, assessment of risk factors, and so on. Noticeably absent are discussions about what exactly a child is capable of answering when confronted with highly personal questions, and how that affects both your and the client's experience of what the interview is like. There is typically so much time spent on specific methods of inquiry that we remain blind to the incredible overlap between the cognitive development of children and the development of one's clinical voice.

This book can serve as an anchor for you as you continue wrestling with your own development as a clinician. Armed now with more knowledge about the cognitive abilities of the children with whom you work, our hope is that you are willing to reevaluate your professional voice. The relationship between children's cognitive development and clinician voice is critical for the purposes of training and continuing professional enrichment. We work in a collaborative, dynamic field, a field that often sees its best work done by those willing to be as malleable and constructive as the children with whom we work.

Context—It Is Everything

In addition to speaking of patience, many of the chapters in this book also describe the importance of context for the development of several key cognitive abilities. While issues of context were explored across many areas, memory, reasoning, and language use are some of the most salient topics.

Consider the following exchange in a family therapy session including a single mother, her older daughter (Sarah, age 14) and her younger son (Josh, age 8):

EXAMPLE: COGNITION IN CONTEXT

Therapist: Josh, can you tell me what happened in the car ride over today?

Mom: Come on, honey, try to tell Dr. J what you said to your sister that made her so angry. It's OK.

Sarah: Why do you treat him like a child? I don't even remember what he said. It's not a big deal anyway. God, he can speak for himself.

Mom: Sarah, I treat him like a child because he is a child. He needs to be encouraged when we're here.

Therapist: Josh, go ahead.

Josh: I don't remember. I just said something and she got upset.

Therapist: Do you remember what you said to her, Josh, because it sounds like your mom was very upset with you when you arrived.

Josh: Um, well, not really.

Sarah: He doesn't remember because he didn't say anything major. It was a meaningless exchange and everyone is blowing it out of proportion. It was about a stupid guy at school.

Therapist: OK, Sarah, but were you hurt by this? And Josh is this true? Did you say something about a friend of Sarah's? I don't think we're making a big deal out of this.

Josh: (*silent*)

Mom: I don't think he remembers exactly, Sarah.

Sarah: For the last time, this is insane.

Therapist: Josh, is it alright if we move on or do you have anything you want to say to your sister?

Josh: (*tearful*) Everything I say makes her mad at me.

(silence in the room)

Mom: Try to remember, Josh.

Sarah: Mom, enough. He's really upset.

Therapist: Thank you, Josh. I appreciate you sharing that with us.

Sitting in the room with this family—the context of this therapeutic inter-action—was fascinating on several levels, and strikingly similar to that of many other families entering therapy. The pressures on a single mother of raising two children are pronounced. The pressures of being a fourteen-year-old girl are significant, as are the pressures of her eight-year-old brother.

The exchange between them also highlights several important issues with respect to children's cognitive development. First, many parents have a ten-dency to hone in on details (e.g., what was said, when, where, and to whom), for reasons likely grounded in the necessity of establishing rules in the home, boundaries for punishment, and teaching concrete lessons, and so forth. Second, an eight-year-old boy may not be able to remember verbatim some-thing that he said, in anger, to his sister, making this a futile line of inquiry. Third, the therapist seems to get swept up in the detail contagion initiated by the mother (notice the therapist doing little to help the child remember con-text and focusing instead on prodding the child for pieces of detailed narra-tive). Lastly, and perhaps most importantly, the eight-year-old communicates his experience of his relationship with his sister ("Everything I say makes her made at me"), and some people in the room do not embrace its significance relative to what was actually said. For the purposes of therapy there is nothing more important in that moment than what Josh articulated so well. This fam-ily sought therapy, in part, because of how this schema is played out on a daily basis. While Josh will often fail to remember the day-to-day triggers of conflict between him and Sarah, it is clear that this particular schema will serve as a powerful foundation in shaping treatment.

This theme of context manifests itself in other ways throughout the book as well. Within the tradition of psychotherapy, particularly with adults, language serves as a medium—a context if you will—for emotional growth and develop-ment. Language is the primary way in which individuals reveal their thoughts and feelings. Language helps children develop more complex representations about their internal states. Language provides a medium for organizing knowl-edge and memories more efficiently. And language provides an entry point to navigating social interactions both within and outside of therapy.

Analysis of the context of language also brings to light important concerns surrounding how to interact with children who do not have a mastery of language yet. Like language, opportunities for play in assessment and psychotherapy can provide clinicians with a meaningful context in which to better understand the course of children's cognitive development. Play is often thought of as a means through which clinicians can establish rapport and help educate the child on the "procedure" of therapy (i.e., what to expect from week to week), while mov-ing the responsibility of leading the conversation away from the clinician. The arguments in the literature about whether play should be used *either* to create comfort *or* gather information have always seemed rather circular and counter-productive. We know that play comes easily to children, and by meeting them where they are developmentally, we can foster a safe and nurturing environment from which to strengthen a human relationship as well as create natural opportunities to observe children's cognition in action. Play provides a vehicle to gather data about children's remembering, language, and communication skills that can lay the foundation for future interventions. Observing a child engaged in play can cue the clinician in to what type of emotional discomfort the child may be experiencing that the child cannot otherwise express verbally. Through the use of play, one can observe the ways in which children deploy coping strategies when faced with challenges or moments of compromise. Efforts to better understand the progression of a child's cognitive development through play, though requiring more patience on behalf of the clinician, better inform future diagnostic considerations. Additionally, they create a culture of collaboration and trust in the therapeutic dyad.

One such case that really hammers home this particular point is that of Adam, a six-year-old boy referred for psychotherapy by his school teachers and counselors to address his father's recent deployment to Iraq. Adam's anger is palpable to all who cross his path: Teachers reference his reluctance to participate in class or raise his hand, and peers keep their distance from him on the playground. Conversations about his father's departure are met with bouts of crying or violence.

The initial intake interview was emotionally taxing for both Adam and his mother. She did most of the talking while he brooded in a chair and prompts for verbal response were met with near silence. It was agreed upon that Adam would see this therapist while in school during the course of the day. The first few sessions were spent doing a puzzle, playing Jenga or UNO, and building a house with Legos. The therapist recognized quickly that Adam struggled to take turns, compromise, or collaborate in building. Adam paid very little attention to anything the therapist was doing. He would walk into the room, grab one of those activities, open it, and expect the clinician to accept his nonverbal invitation to play. During the second and third month of therapy Adam showed more positive affect: He would refer to this therapist by name, he became more competitive and invested in his performance in the games, he would clean up the games when completed, and say "hello" and "goodbye" when appropriate. He made more eye contact, became animated when he won a game of UNO, and became a stickler for the rules in most games. These were insights into specific areas of cognition relative to his ability to take the perspective of another, and to follow, understand, and remember rules.

The fourth month saw much of the same except for three episodes when Adam referenced "something my dad said." This fourth month was also a time in which the therapist made a more concerted effort to build "talk time" into the therapy hour. Talk time was the first 15 minutes of the session, and both therapist and child were allowed to ask three questions of the other person.

In answering several questions, Adam referenced discrete times in which he and his father had conversed. It was also during this month that Adam was confronted directly about how he handles his anger. He demonstrated a keen awareness of his inability to control it, saying as much, and showing insight into how to best control it (e.g., playing sports). Talk time gave the therapist great insight into Adam's above-average language ability, strong memory, and heightened self-awareness for someone his age. It also allowed the therapist to begin hypothesizing about why his language was often impaired when compromised with feelings of anger and violence.

The winter break then interrupted the sessions for several weeks. Adam was notified of the upcoming schedule and of when therapy would begin again (the week *after* he returned to school). The week he returned to school he left art class, per usual, to attend therapy and sat alone in the room for 50 minutes, obviously having forgotten the agreed-upon schedule. The therapist, upon his return, was saddened to hear about some behavioral problems that Adam's teachers were having that first week back. At the beginning of the first session with the therapist, Adam was all business.

EXAMPLE: EMOTION IN CONTEXT

Adam:	(*loudly*) Where were you last week?
Therapist:	Oh, remember we talked about the schedule, Adam, and we agreed that this week would be our first meeting of the new year?
Adam:	(*loudly*) I sat here alone for 50 minutes. Why didn't you come?
Therapist:	I'm so sorry, Adam, I thought we were clear on the dates.
Adam:	(*silent*)
Therapist:	Adam, I wish I had been more careful in reminding you about our schedule. I'm sorry about the confusion, and I'm sorry that you sat here alone.
Adam:	(*reaching for UNO*)
Therapist:	Do you hear me, Adam? I'm sorry. I will not leave you alone like that again, OK? Thank you for telling me exactly how you feel.
Adam:	(*mumbling*) OK.

This conversation was the first time that Adam has initiated a dialogue with the therapist, albeit fueled by emotion, emotion that has historically (at least for four months) interfered with his ability to properly communicate how he feels. In so doing, this conflict highlighted several important things in relation to Adam's cognitive development:

- Cognitively, it was asking too much of Adam to remember or plan ahead for the scheduled meeting.
- Adam was able to recognize the therapist's genuine feelings of guilt and frustration with the scheduling mishap.
- Adam is capable of expressing his feelings with his words rather than through aggression.

Part of what made this so powerful and emotional is that the therapist was beginning to understand the ways in which Adam's cognitive development was quite normal, indicating that the main source of Adam's declining behavior and performance is rooted in emotional concerns about his father, rather than stemming from disordered communication skills or lack of perspective taking.

Difference—What It Means

Development is not paint-by-numbers. It is a fresco, an elaborate painting in which an underdeveloped (wet, haggard, plastered) foundation is the recipient of copious pigments, repetitive brushstrokes, and frequent manipulation. When starting a fresco, the initial process of placing pigment to plaster requires great care, attention, and hours of time spent waiting for the pigment-plaster concoction to congeal. The pigment is absorbed into the plaster, and as the pigment is allowed to dry it starts to take greater form, both structurally and aesthetically. Artists will spend years of their lives perfecting their fresco paintings. Unlike other painting media, frescos are heavily layered, with each subsequent layer taking significant amounts of time to set. Part of the allure of fresco painting is the challenge that such mandated patience can present in order to complete one. One simply has no choice but to wait for the paint to dry, and even then the work is far from over.

Like a fresco painting, the cognitive development of a child is an elaborate process involving placing layer upon layer. When you are looking at individual layers and watching the process unfold, it is often difficult to visualize what the final product or outcome will be. Each layer of cognitive development can be altered by adding color or brushstrokes, or through some other artistic manipulation. Yet, also like a fresco, the development of a child is the most spectacular when it is given time to solidify throughout the process. Children are constantly bombarded with new stimulation: adults who try to refine their behavior, peers who challenge them to look and act a certain way, and families who are so caught up in creating a masterpiece that they forget that they are not the ones who should be doing the painting. This may partially explain why we sometimes lose sight of the fact that the creation of a masterpiece is not always orderly and oftentimes transforms itself in ways that are different from what we expect.

Inconsistencies in children's cognitive processing can provide important information about their cognitive abilities and their functioning as a whole. Sometimes children's behavior appears inconsistent with respect to developmental norms and expectations (i.e., the child is *different* in relation to others). Other times, however, children behave inconsistently with respect to their own abilities (i.e., the child is *different* in relation to himself or herself). Our task, as clinicians, is to be able to recognize inconsistencies when they occur, to educate families about what we know, and to discern which components of these inconsistencies warrant closer attention.

To illustrate these points, what follows are some examples of behavioral patterns that are seemingly incongruent, but in actuality reveal important information about a child's cognitive development.

Being Different Is Sometimes Good

We know that young children are not very good liars: They are easily confused, struggle to hold contradictory thoughts and subsequent behaviors in their head, and don't readily take the perspective of another until later in childhood. Those who are good liars represent something of a developmental enigma, particularly for parents and caregivers. Lying is not a skill that parents appreciate being developed, and they routinely seek counsel to help interpret, and sometimes curb, the early deceptive behaviors of their children. That being said, the development of lying behavior and deception is associated with maturity of several key executive functions. There is a silver lining. Children who are very good at lying possess heightened cognitive strengths, inhibitory control, and working memory. In order to lie, a child must be able to hold conflicting notions in his or her mind (e.g., what they did in reality and what they said they did). Being able to do so requires some maturity in the cognitive processes involved in deliberately deceiving another: self-regulation, inhibitory control, planning, and strategy coordination.

Learning to deceive (to lie, to be sneaky) is an inevitable childhood accomplishment. And why shouldn't it be? Parents deceive their children all the time and, in many situations, actively foster this type of deceptive behavior. So why are we so quick to pathologize our young friends? At what point did lying behavior become oppositional? Certainly, in some situations it can be oppositional, but we must acknowledge that deceptive ability reflects increased cognitive sophistication. It is a normal part of children's cognitive development, but working to understand the development of these deceptive behaviors is far more nuanced than our proclivity to pathologize them, and this is a problem.

Being able to lie effectively also has ramifications for increasing social acuity. We, as adults, oftentimes see our deception as adaptive and, in many cases, protective. We feign a smile when we feel hurt inside or remain stone-faced when holding on to a full house in Texas Hold'em. Sometimes we articulate our thanks for holiday gifts that we regret receiving, or boldly proclaim an untruth just to avoid a social gathering with a friend. Given this, the tendency to judge children's behavior by different standards is unfair and confusing for them, particularly given that they are calling upon the same adaptive schemas as adults.

Differences Promote Change and Growth

Now, let's consider a different type of incongruity, one where the child's behavior is incongruent with what we have come to expect for him. This was illustrated in the delicate work in play therapy with Adam. Four months were spent, mostly in silence, strengthening a therapeutic bond with a child overwrought with feelings of abandonment. Based upon these early interactions, Adam emerged as a child with a normal but somewhat restricted range of play interests and a limited ability to talk about his internal states. The "normalcy" of the play during the early months together was undoubtedly important, but not nearly as important as his angry outburst toward the therapist in the later months. This incongruence in his behavior showcased more about his cognitive processes than anything else in therapy. Adam's outburst also illustrates an important parallel between cognitive development and clinical practice, namely, that dissonance often precedes change and growth. In the case of Adam, the angry exchange with the therapist, although unexpected, was a great catalyst for therapeutic change. Likewise, with respect to children's cognitive development, children often display incongruities in their abilities and behaviors just prior to advancing to a new stage of development. As clinicians, we often embrace things when they get a little messy because we recognize that change and growth often follow. It is important to recognize that this is also the case with children's cognitive development.

When Are Differences Causes for Concern?

How can clinicians manage, understand, and not overreact to variations in development while at the same time being on the lookout for deviations that are indeed indicative of pathology? Knowing how to discern between what is *different* (but normal) and *deviant* (abnormal) in the cognitive development of a child is perhaps our greatest challenge as professionals, especially when you consider how unexpected changes in development can cause discomfort for all parties involved. Questions will undoubtedly arise about how and why a child veers away from an expected developmental path, resulting in both cognitive and affective reactions from the child, the family, and the clinician.

When a child swims about in the continuum between abnormal and optimal, we need to recognize it for what it is and use our understanding to build collaborative discourse. When a child is in the deep end of the pool, however, where there is peril, uncertainty, and a greater need for immediate intervention, it is important for the clinician to help navigate the family through appropriate channels. Knowing exactly how to effectively discern what represents cognitive difference versus deviance in a developing child can be more easily accomplished if you:

1. Look for context. A thorough developmental history will help you detect familial, social, educational, and medical trends, as well as perturbations in those trends.
2. Use your voice. Invite rapport building into every session. Increased comfort on behalf of the child will lead to a more genuine expression of his or her true abilities.
3. Be patient. Meet the child where he or she is developmentally. Strive to understand what it is like to walk in the child's shoes.
4. Understand what difference is. Stay attuned to the literature and the ways in which our conceptualization of development continues to change. Calibrate yourself by consulting with supervisors and peers on a regular and frequent basis.

In Closing

The suggestions above are things that all good clinicians should do, not only because doing so better informs our work with children, but also, and especially, because of how pervasive our collective reliance on pathology has become. We must recognize that just as no two paintings are the same, developmental pathways are different for every child. This is an especially challenging construct to embrace for anyone who has spent time working with learning disabled, oppositional, depressed, anxious, or psychotic youth. After a while these extreme deviations from the norm actually become our norm, creating the unfortunate tendency to view every nuance as a potential indicator of psychopathology. Some argue that the prevailing ethos in the field, that of pathology, has made the road to intervention a smoother one. This is sometimes true, but children pose unique challenges to conceptualizing pathology insofar as they change so rapidly and in such pronounced ways. They are impressionable, they are moving targets, and they constantly test the limits of what they know. Part of our professional responsibility is to understand and embrace these changes for what they represent: growth. The alternative— forcing these changes into a larger construct of pathology and disability— undermines what is most natural about children's development.

Clinicians newly embarking upon their careers will likely experience children's cognitive struggles in much the same way as you experience your own. After all, virtually every step of professional development feels like a deviation: each step wider and through a more uncertain, circuitous path than the one that preceded it. For those more experienced, these deviations are cataloged, patiently deliberated upon, and built in to an already strong foundation of clinical awareness and acceptance.

People are drawn to work in this field because it is dynamic, ever changing, opportunistic, and provides the opportunity to wrestle with some of life's most enigmatic happenings. Yet, the highly predictable elements are as important as the unpredictable ones. This book has gone to great lengths to chronicle normative cognitive development for you. The hope is that with greater knowledge of what to expect from the children with whom we work will come a greater willingness to meet those children where they are developmentally. With this, we can responsibly meet the needs of the children and families we serve.

Index